T0071966

WHITETAIL TACTICS

Cutting-Edge Strategies That Work

Peter J. Fiduccia

Skyhorse Publishing

A special thank you to my good friend Ted Rose for graciously provided many of the white-tail deer images within this book.

I would also like to thank J. R. Jaskolski for proving several deer images in this book as well.

All photos provided by Fiduccia Enterprises unless otherwise noted in the photo credits.

Skyhorse Publishing books may be purchased in bulk at special discounts for sales promotion, corporate gifts, fund-raising, or educational purposes. Special editions can also be created to specifications. For details, contact the Special Sales Department, Skyhorse Publishing, 307 West 36th Street, 11th Floor, New York, NY 10018 or info@ skyhorsepublishing.com.

Skyhorse® and Skyhorse Publishing® are registered trademarks of Skyhorse Publishing, Inc.®, a Delaware corporation.

Visit our website at www.skyhorsepublishing.com.

10 9 8 7 6 5 4 3 2 1

Library of Congress Cataloging-in-Publication Data is available on file.

Cover design by Tom Lau
Cover photo credit: CanStockPhoto

Print ISBN: 978-1-5107-1902-6
Ebook ISBN: 978-1-5107-1907-1

Printed in China.

I dedicate this book to my identical twin cousins, Leo and Ralph Somma. You are my best friends and lifelong hunting companions. Deer season wouldn't be the same without us hunting together. From our wake-up call by a Felix the Cat alarm clock blasting reveille, to eating breakfast while the intercom plays "Another One Bites the Dust" by Queen, to the evening ribbing sessions, to the all-too-early sounds of snoring on the recliners—these are all traditions I look forward to sharing with you both each deer season.

I even look back fondly on the "Ultra Death Sauce" incident with laughter. Despite it being extraordinarily searing and blistering hot, we all ignored the dire warning on the label that clearly states, "*Be warned: this sauce contains ingredients 800 times hotter than a jalapeno Chile. Use sparingly. Ultra Death should not be consumed without dilution,*" and mixed it into each of our meals thinking the resulting hopping-around-on-one-foot-screaming would surely be comical. Unluckily, it was me who ended up with a tad too much Death Sauce clandestinely mixed, undiluted, into my spaghetti sauce and pasta. Through completely unintended, I even enjoyed the two-day hospital stay which followed that gag.

Foreword

There are countless professional communicators within the outdoor industry, many of whom specialize in writing about white-tailed deer. Only a handful, though, have been able to achieve the kind of respect and esteem of both readers and peers that Peter Fiduccia has acquired through his skills and knowledge on all aspects of hunting white-tailed deer.

Long before I became involved in a full-time career in outdoor television and writing, I regularly read magazine articles and books about deer-hunting strategies. Interestingly, the deer-hunting articles in these publications that I consistently found noteworthy and filled with concise information turned out to be penned by Peter Fiduccia.

Fiduccia is among the few "chosen" whitetail pros highly recognized by top outdoor editors, including Daniel E. Schmidt, Jay Cassell, Lamar Underwood, and Sid Evans. They all entrust Fiduccia's writings to supplement the pages of their publications with his highly informative articles to help take their readers' deer hunting tactics to the next level.

Fiduccia's writing style has always been straightforward. He's a no BS kind of guy who gets his points across to the readers without a lot of product propaganda or embellishment. Equally important, his skills and understanding of the white-tailed deer's biology, behavior and anatomy are impressive and second-to-none. In fact, of the countless whitetail authorities within the outdoor industry, Fiduccia's stock is like fine heavy cream, it naturally rises to the top.

His to-the-point writings make it crystal clear that Fiduccia gained his deer hunting skills the *hard* way—he *earned* them—through trial and error and inevitable unmitigated success. As a competent deer hunter, Fiduccia evolved into a superb deer hunting authority. For decades, his star as one of the nation's most prolific deer hunting communicators continues to shine as brightly as gamma-ray burst explosion.

No matter how many articles or books I have read by Peter Fiduccia, there is always one constant. I enjoy and gain knowledge from his writings each and every time. That statement continues to hold true in Fiduccia's *Whitetail Tactics: Cutting Edge Strategies That Work.*

In this book you will find plenty of solid advice written in an easy-to-read and easy-to-comprehend manner. Fiduccia addresses many topics that hunters want to know more about including: whitetail anatomy of the rut, how to interpret a deer's body language, deer glands, buck dispersal, how to make mock rubs and scrapes, and how to use "the best damn deer call ever made." In his latest work, Fiduccia shares his most guarded whitetail strategies to help readers place their tags on mature white-tailed bucks.

I can assure anyone reading this book that whether you are a seasoned veteran or a novice deer hunter you will benefit and gain valuable deer hunting skills and know-how from the pages within this volume.

After you have finished reading, I'm certain you, too, will be so impressed with Fiduccia's deer hunting expertise he will become one of your favorite deer hunting authorities as much as he is mine.

If this all sounds like I am biased, I guess I am. After all, he's not only my favorite whitetail authority, he is my husband, too.

Katharine Ann Fiduccia
Spring 2017

Contents

———

ANECDOTES

DEER FACTS

Chapter One

Anatomy of the Rut: Real-World Timing

The whitetail deer breeding season, or rut, refers to the time frame when does are most fertile and receptive to accepting the amorous intentions of male deer. Unfortunately, there is a wide array of misinformation, rumors, and long-held myths about this important subject. Two of the most commonly held erroneous viewpoints are that the rut only takes place during cold weather and only lasts for a short period of time during November. The fact is that neither of these two notions is accurate. I can assure you that since I began hunting in 1964, I have discovered that rut information handed down from old-timers generally consists of unintended distortions, half-truths, and, in some cases, unequivocal misinformation.

For instance, the whitetail's rut lasts months. At my seminars, many people are astonished when I tell them that as long as a buck has antlers attached to his head and a doe has not been successfully bred, both are willing and able to breed whether it is October, November, December, or even later.

The genesis of each phase of the rut occurs specifically in relationship to dates within the four latitude zones of the United States. If you include Canada, there are six latitude zones and if Mexico is added, there are nine. Latitudes are invisible horizontal lines that depict the angular distance in degrees, minutes, and seconds of a point north or

Photo Credit: Ted Rose

This image was taken on November 14th in Southern Indiana. November 10th to 15th are dates that consistently show up as peak days of breeding activity throughout North America within the latitudes of 37–50° north and the longitudes of 50–125° west.

south of the equator. They are also referred to as parallels. Within each of the parallels in North America, the rut takes place, whether it is cold or warm outside, with surprising regularity. Cold weather only helps generate daytime activity. In other words, when the weather turns cold, bucks are more likely to move about searching for does during the day than in warmer temperatures. The chilly weather spurs their libido and makes them more inclined to feel romantic. This phenomenon can cause the breeding cycle of whitetail deer to take place over a longer period of time than most people believe.

The internal trigger that causes deer to be aware of the onset of the rut is the preorbital gland, located in the corner of each eye. It senses cycles of waning light levels, or photoperiods, that begin in early autumn. The preorbital gland is a paired exocrine gland found in a majority of hoofed animals that is similar to the lacrimal gland found in humans. The preorbital glands are black trench-like slits of nearly bare skin extending from the medial canthus of each eye, which are lined by a combination of sebaceous and sudoriferous glands. They produce secretions that contain pheromones and other chemical compounds. All ungulates frequently deposit these secretions on overhanging branches by licking sticks, twigs, and grass as olfactory communications to other deer.

The preorbital gland serves different roles in different species. Pheromone-containing secretions from the preorbital gland might establish a buck or doe's hierarchy within its herd. As a buck or doe prepares for breeding season, they will mark vegetation within their home range with preorbital scent. Because of its critical role in scent marking, the preorbital gland is usually considered a Type A scent gland. Some biologists believe the preorbital glands might produce antimicrobial compounds to protect against skin pathogens.

The various secretions of chemicals trigger a buck's brain to recognize the start of the rut, and his testes begin to enlarge and descend, becoming more visible. With each passing day of waning light, the demeanors of deer, particularly adult bucks, go from tolerant and benign to irritable and aggressive. By the time the primary phase of the rut kicks in, a buck's testes reach their greatest size.

No matter where whitetails roam, the rut corresponds closely to the time when most female deer are fertile and, therefore, most apt to be successfully bred. If, for whatever reason, a doe is not successfully bred during the peak rut, she will come into her estrus cycle every twenty-eight to thirty-two days.

As soon as the preorbital gland detects a shortening of daylight, it triggers a release of chemical compounds that flood into a buck's brain. The buck's testes drop and he becomes more irritable and aggressive as the rut progresses.

The exception to this rule is if a doe undergoes unusually stressful situations from outside influences. In this case, the doe will skip one of her cycles.

Most adult female deer are bred between the autumnal equinox and the vernal equinox, the two nights each year where night and day are the same length that kick off the fall and spring seasons, respectively.

The intensity and length of the entire whitetail breeding cycle, three phases of the rut, differs depending on the latitude in which they live. Deer living in the northernmost latitudes (above 60–70° north) breed sooner than those living in the southernmost latitudes (25–29° south). Therefore, it becomes evident that the breeding cycle of deer is not initiated simply by cold temperatures. As I stated, it is controlled, or at the very least set in motion, by photoperiodism.

At the onset of the breeding cycle, photoperiodism stimulates another of the primary glands of the whitetail deer, the pituitary gland. It is located in the brain. This gland produces the chief hormones that control antler growth. Once again, the brain releases chemicals and they, in turn, stimulate both male and female sex glands.

Different latitude zones throughout North America experience photoperiods at different times. This affects the dates of the primary breeding cycles, causing them to vary accordingly. For instance, the northern parts of Canada and Alaska fall within latitudes of about 60–70° north. The primary breeding cycle of deer in these zones is considerably earlier than all parts of North America south of the 59° north line of latitude. From about 51–59° north, which includes the southern parts of Canada, the rut varies from what it is at 45–50° north.

In the northern sections of the United States and southern regions of Canada, the latitudes fall between about 46–52° north. This area includes the northern tip of Oregon, Washington, the Idaho panhandle, Montana, the northern portion of Wyoming, North Dakota, Northern South Dakota, Southern Minnesota, Northern Wisconsin, Northern Michigan, and the northern portions of Maine. The primary rut in these states takes place approximately the first week of November, as photoperiodism happens slightly earlier than for their southern neighbors.

The latitudes between 40–45° north are most of the Northeast, Midwest, and New England. It includes most of Oregon, Northern California, Nevada, Utah, Colorado, lower Idaho (south of the pandhandle), a majority of Wyoming, Southern South Dakota, Nebraska, Iowa, the northern tip of Missouri, the northern half of Illinois, Indiana, and Ohio, as well as a majority of Pennsylvania, New York, Northern New Jersey, Connecticut, Massachusetts, Vermont, New Hampshire, and the southern portion of Maine. Within the overall two-week or so period of the primary rut, there are about five peak days of breeding activity that occur within the general latitudes 40–45° north. The peak days of breeding activity reliably occur from November 10th to November 15th, with the 13th and 14th being particularly high activity days. These days can also be peak breeding days in the latitudes of 37–50° north and from the longitudes of 50–125° west. However, nothing about dates is written in stone. When I provide dates, they can vary by twenty-four to thirty-six hours on either end of the dates given throughout any latitude or longitude.

The zones between 35–39° north include Southern California, Southern Nevada, Utah, Colorado, Northern Arizona, New Mexico, the northern tip of Texas, Northern Oklahoma, Northern Arkansas, Kentucky, Tennessee, Southern Missouri, Indiana, the southern half of Illinois, Ohio, West Virginia, Virginia, the upper portion of North Carolina, Maryland, Delaware, the southern tip of New Jersey, and the lower portion of Pennsylvania. The primary rut takes place in these areas approximately the last week of November.

In the zones from 30–34° north, which includes the southern tip of California, Southern Arizona, New Mexico, the heart of Texas, Southern Oklahoma, Southern Arkansas, most of Louisiana, Mississippi, Alabama, Georgia, South Carolina, the northernmost tip of Florida, and northern tip of Mexico, all experience a later primary rut. The dates can vary slightly in the southernmost areas of these latitudes, but the primary breeding cycle generally takes place in late December to early January.

Photo Credit: Ted Rose

Based on the latitudes, the primary rut generally falls between November 5th and the 20th throughout most of the United States.

Zones that fall between 25–29° north include Northern Mexico, South Texas, the southernmost portion of Louisiana, and a majority of Florida. In these states, photoperiodism occurs later than anywhere north of 29° north and, therefore, the primary rut takes place from mid- to late January.

The end result is that the primary rut occurs at different times in some portions of the United States, Canada, and Mexico. However, for a big portion of the United States and Southern Canada (where most whitetail hunting takes place), the primary chase period, immediately followed by the primary peak of the rut, takes place as mentioned above—November 5th to about November 20th, give or take a few days. You can take that statement to the deer hunting bank.

While most of the time these rut dates can be relied on, there are occasional extenuating circumstances when the breeding cycle of a whitetail doe can be delayed and, in rare situations, prevent the rut. A doe's reproductive cycle can be postponed, skipped, or halted by a variety of factors including, but not limited to, poor nutrition, extremely cold temperatures, overpopulation levels within her range, scarcity of food, drought, heavy predation from wolves or coyotes, old age, poor habitat, and even heavy hunting pressure.

Some of these factors can actually improve hunting, however. For instance, if a doe skips a cycle, she may come back into heat twenty-eight to thirty-two days later. This can cause a pronounced post-rut frenzy period. I have witnessed this several times. When this happens, it usually takes place in mid-December. Bucks, frustrated by the abbreviated primary rut in November, throw caution to the wind and seek out receptive does throughout the day and night. This increased rutting activity accounts for a high level of buck sightings by hunters. A delayed heat cycle by mature does can be one of the most exciting ruts a hunter will experience.

This information is meant to provide hunters with a clearer picture of exactly how the rut is initiated and what factors contribute to its timing. By understanding what I have shared with you here and using it properly, you can increase your chances for bagging a trophy-class buck by ten fold.

Photo Credit: Ted Rose

The peak days of the primary rut are generally November 12th to 14th throughout most of the United States.

A majority of hunters try to plan their hunting vacations to coincide with the peak week or weeks of the primary rut. They often try to narrow down what days within the primary rut will have the most rut activity. While it is easier to provide solid information on when the seven- to fourteen-day period of the primary rut will take place, predicting the days with the most activity is a little more complicated. However, they, too, are accurate as long as one remembers that they can vary slightly by a couple of days on either side of the dates listed in the chart that follows.

I have spent countless hours compiling data, including videotaping deer in controlled whitetail research facilities, having discussions with biologists across the nation (and other whitetail authorities from Florida to Washington and some southern portions of the Canadian provinces), and scrutinizing a myriad of latitude and longitude maps of the United States and Canada. I have also spent years theorizing the effects perihelion and aphelion have on the rut. These terms are used to identify the closest and furthest distances any two or more planetary bodies move from one another (in this case, primarily the Earth and Sun). My research includes analyzing the moon's role in the whitetail's breeding season and I have read more articles, journals, papers, and books on the subject than I can recount. I mention this to qualify the information I have provided.

For the sake of brevity and to keep the information in the chart simple, I assumed most of you reading this will be hunting in a portion of the United States or the southern provinces of Canada, where the trigger points for the week or weeks of the primary rut occur from November 5th to November 20th, give or take a few days. A majority of these areas fall within the latitudes and longitudes of 40–50° north and 50–120° west. With that said above, however, the primary rut (which also includes the "big chase phase") falls between **November 10th to November 15th give or take a few days on either side.** This is true despite warm weather, the so-called effect of the moon phase on the dates of the rut (which according to all biologists is non-existent), and heavy hunting pressure.

This absolutely applies to those of you who primarily deer hunt in Northeast states within the latitudes of 40 to 45 degrees including New York, New Jersey, Pennsylvania, Connecticut, Rhode Island, Massachusetts, New Hampshire, Vermont, and southern Maine and within the other states falling within the same latitudes including Michigan, Wyoming, Nebraska, and Iowa, central and southern parts of Wisconsin, southern Minnesota, northern Ohio, Indiana, Illinois, South Dakota, the northern tip of Colorado, northern Utah, southern Idaho, northern Nevada, northern California, and central and south Oregon.

The chart also illustrates more general dates for the states that fall in other latitudes and longitudes within the United States. There are three major components, including the names of states and provinces, a map depicting the latitude and longitudinal degree figures for the entire United States and southern Canada, and the states and provinces highlighted that fall within the peak activity dates (November 5th to 20th, give or take a few days) of the primary rut. The information will help determine the time frame you should select for your hunting vacation to match the peak activity levels of the primary rut.

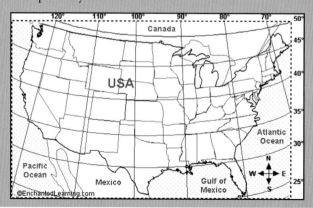

PEAK DAYS AND WEEKS OF PRIMARY RUT

STATE	PEAK DAYS DURING THE PRIMARY RUT	Latitudes 37–50° North	Longitudes 50–120° West	PEAK WEEK/S OF THE PRIMARY RUT
ALABAMA	January 18–20			January 10–25
ARKANSAS	November 17–22			November 10–25
COLORADO	November 15–20	X		November 5–20
CONNECTICUT	November 19–24	X		November 10–25
DELAWARE	November 7–12	X		November 7–21
FLORIDA	**North:** December 29-30 **Central:** January 6–13 **South:** January 22–25			**North:** December 17–31 **Central:** January 1–15 **South:** January 14–31
GEORGIA	**North and Central:** November 10–15 **South:** November15–17 December 15–17			**North and Central:** November 10–15 **South:** November 10–20 December 11–22
IDAHO	November 12–15	X	X	November 8–22

PEAK DAYS AND WEEKS OF PRIMARY RUT *(Continued)*

STATE	PEAK DAYS DURING THE PRIMARY RUT	Latitudes 37-50° North	Longitudes 50-120° West	PEAK WEEK/S OF THE PRIMARY RUT
ILLINOIS	November 10-13	X	X	November 5-20
INDIANA	November 14-16	X	X	November 7-21
IOWA	November 13-15	X	X	November 6-22
KANSAS	November 10-13	X	X	November 10-17
KENTUCKY	November 15-17	X	X	November 10-20
LOUISIANA	**Southwest:** October 15-17 **Northwest:** November 13-15 **East:** January 1-3			**Southwest:** October 10-19 **Northwest:** November 5-14 **East:** January 1-14
MAINE	November 12-15	X	X	November 3-23
MARYLAND	November 10-14	X	X	November 5-22
MASSACHUSETTS	November 12-14	X	X	November 6-20
MICHIGAN	November 9-13 UP: November 15-17	X	X	November 5-24 UP: November 10-26
MINNESOTA	November 12-14	X	X	November 5-21

PEAK DAYS AND WEEKS OF PRIMARY RUT (*Continued*)

STATE	PEAK DAYS DURING THE PRIMARY RUT	Latitudes 37–50° North	Longitudes 50–120° West	PEAK WEEK/S OF THE PRIMARY RUT
MISSISSIPPI	**North:** December 21–23 **South:** January 11–13	X	X	**North:** December 10–25 **South:** January 6–20
MISSOURI	November 10–13	X	X	November 7–21
MONTANA	November 10–14	X	X	November 5–25
NEBRASKA	November 10–13	X	X	November 4–22
NEVADA	November 17–19	X	X	November 10–24
NEW HAMPSHIRE	November 10–14	X	X	November 5–21
NEW JERSEY	November 14–16	X	X	November 5–25
NEW MEXICO	November 13–15	X		November 8–22
NEW YORK	November 11–14	X	X	November 5–25
NORTH CAROLINA	**Lower Coast:** November 22–23 **Upper Coast:** November 5–7 **Piedmont:** November17–18 **Mt.** December 5–7			**Lower Coast:** November 15–25 **Upper Coast:** November 5–22 **Piedmont:** November 14–28 Mt. December 1–14

PEAK DAYS AND WEEKS OF PRIMARY RUT (Continued)

STATE	PEAK DAYS DURING THE PRIMARY RUT	Latitudes 37–50° North	Longitudes 50–120° West	PEAK WEEK/S OF THE PRIMARY RUT
NORTH DAKOTA	November 14-17	X	X	November 5-25
OHIO	November 14-16	X	X	November 7-19
OKLAHOMA	November 13-14			November 5-20
OREGON	November 12-14	X	X	November 10-24
PENNSYLVANIA	November 12-14	X	X	November 8-22
RHODE ISLAND	November 10-13	X	X	November 5-22
SOUTH CAROLINA	November 23-25			November 14-29
SOUTH DAKOTA	November 13-15	X		November 10-25
TENNESSEE	November 18-21			November 12-27
TEXAS	**West:** December 5-7 **Hill Country:** November 15-17 **South:** December 15-17			**West:** December 1-14 **Hill Country:** November 10-24 **South:** December 10-26
VERMONT	November 11-13	X	X	November 3-19
VIRGINIA	November 15-17	X	X	November 10-22

PEAK DAYS AND WEEKS OF PRIMARY RUT (*Continued*)

STATE	PEAK DAYS DURING THE PRIMARY RUT	Latitudes 37–50° North	Longitudes 50–120° West	PEAK WEEK/S OF THE PRIMARY RUT
WASHINGTON	November 10–14	X	X	November 7–22
WEST VIRGINIA	November 13–15	X	X	November 6–21
WISCONSIN	November 12–14	X	X	November 5–23
WYOMING	November 12–15	X	X	November 4–19

Chapter Two

How to Interpret a Deer's Body Language

To become a better-informed deer hunter, hone your understanding and ability to recognize and take advantage of the different body postures deer use to communicate with one another. This is particularly important when utilizing hunting tactics, whether they are passive, such as sitting in a tree stand, or active, such as using deer calls, antler rattling, decoying, stalking, creating mock rubs or scrapes, deer drives, etc. By understanding what a deer's body language is conveying to other deer or even a predator, you will enhance your tactics to give you an edge for increased hunting success.

Before continuing, let's take a look at what body language actually is. All animals, and even insects, use body language as a mental and physical ability to express nonverbal communication through a variety of body gestures, posturing, facial expressions, and eye movements. These signals are meant to send distinct messages, which other animals interpret subconsciously and instinctively.

Scientists claim that human communication is only 10 percent verbal and the remaining 90 percent is made up of body language and paralinguistic cues. Body language provides clues to the attitude and state of mind of all animals, including humans. Deer mostly use body posturing to communicate their state of aggressiveness, dissatisfaction, stress, alarm, and sexual desire.

In the whitetail deer's world, body language is a momentous form of nonverbal communication. For male deer, it is a crucial element to specifically express what position of the social hierarchy they are currently occupying. Deer also use body posturing to display situations of attentiveness, relaxation, acceptance, recognition, pleasure, and countless other emotional states quickly and precisely. If deer had to communicate with each other only vocally, they would be unable to effectively interconnect with one another.

The different types of body posturing positions are meant to send unmistakable messages from one deer to another without actually making body contact or vocalizations. A buck can display nonaggressive body language to signal a message as simple as, "Hey, good to see you," or suggest through a different posture, "I'm warning you to back off." When they want to express a severely aggressive stance, it might say, "Back off or I'll kick your butt to within an inch of your life!"

Photo Credit: Ted Rose

This buck expresses all the elements of extreme aggression, including a curved body, arched back, raised hair, stiff-legged gait, ears laid back on his neck, tail hung down, head pointed up, and the most dangerous body sign of all—the whites of his eyes are showing. His message to all other bucks is clear, "I'm the current high-ranking male—back off or else!"

As I mentioned previously, body language is often used to send a clear-cut message of exactly which place of the pecking order each buck occupies. The higher the buck's status is on the social ladder, the more perks he is entitled to. This includes everything from getting first dibs on choice foods to breeding rights. Body language, particularly aggressive posturing used by both bucks and does, is Mother Nature's way of preventing unnecessary injuries between deer.

By mid-April, long before the rut begins, bachelor groups begin to establish their hierarchy. Most of this is done using body language to avoid injuring the soft velvet covering on the antlers. From about April to early September, this activity, plus some leg flailing behavior, determines which buck is at the top of the totem pole and which occupies the bottom. They also use a wide variety of vocalizations during the time their antlers are in velvet to communicate their status and mind-set.

Bucks begin to establish their rank or pecking order as early as April through the use of body posturing and hoof flailing.

The body language and vocalizations used during this time frame help each bachelor group form a strict pecking order that is adhered to through most of the spring and summer. Inevitably, however, this social status behavior changes as fall approaches. By learning to interpret these subtle body posturing signals, you will add a valuable dimension to your deer hunting tactics.

Have you ever wondered why soon after deer season you are able to walk past a buck that is casually feeding within view of you? Why a herd of zebra will feed within close proximity of a pride of resting lions? Or why some dogs bark aggressively at certain people and not others? An overwhelming amount of the time, it is mostly due to the signals sent by one animal's body posturing toward another.

In the instance of walking past the buck, your body language may indicate interest, but it does not exhibit an intense predatory posture as it would when you're actively hunting. In the case of the feeding zebras, they can tell by the lion's post-feeding resting posture that they are not on the hunt. A dog can interpret fearful body posture in an instant. The dog interprets the body language as a signal that it is the pack leader and, therefore, it is necessary to let you know by barking aggressively. Body language is an elaborate form of communication within the whitetail deer's environment and, as such, is something all hunters should become more in tune with.

There have been countless scientific and biological studies with findings about the captivating world of body posturing and the messages it is meant to communicate between deer. These highly visual physical signals display what is on the deer's mind. Hunters who are able to recognize and interpret body posturing exhibited by deer and other game animals vastly increase their awareness of the game they hunt, resulting in not only seeing and bagging more deer, but also increasing the odds of killing more adult bucks.

Many years ago, on a bow hunt during the primary phase of the rut, I used a grunt to call in an eight-point buck. As the buck approached my stand, I was deciding when I would pull back the string of my bow. Seconds before drawing back, I noticed the hair on the back of the buck's neck was standing straight up—a sure sign of hostility. For a split second I was confused. I didn't make an aggressive grunt and it shouldn't have caused the buck to react belligerently. Perhaps the buck, an average-sized eight-point, thought he needed to display an antagonistic attitude in response to my subtle grunt, which could have sent the vocal message that I was a younger buck than he. If that were the case, the buck wanted to be sure his body posture clearly demonstrated that he was more aggressive than the unseen younger buck. I decided to not draw back and, instead, study the buck's body more carefully.

As I watched him closely, I could see his head was pointed directly to my left. His eyes strained to look directly behind him. The hair fell flat on his neck, he tucked his tail tightly between his legs, and he slowly, but with exaggerated purposefulness, started to walk off taking sideward steps. With each placement of his hoof, he stomped it to the ground instead of placing it down normally. All at once it clicked. The buck was reacting to a more aggressive, and hopefully larger racked, buck in the woods behind him.

To keep abreast of his body language, I didn't take my eyes off the eight-pointer for a second, though I was sorely tempted to look for what I thought was a bigger antlered buck nearby. I desperately strained my eyes in hopes of seeing any peripheral movement by a second buck. Within a minute, I had my answer. In a self-assured manner, the second buck displayed intense body posturing as he walked in. I instantly knew why the first buck was concerned. The second buck was obviously the more aggressive animal, and he demonstrated a higher rank in the pecking order. Although their rack sizes were similar, the second buck had ten points, a slightly wider spread, and a larger body than the first.

As the heavier deer walked closer, he arched his back, laid his ears back flat alongside his head, and held his head low at a severe angle. His body language demonstrated he was willing to fight. The first buck sent a signal of submission by turning his rear end to the other. I don't think the heavier buck saw his gesture as I released my arrow.

Unfortunately, I didn't kill the buck. The arrow sailed harmlessly over his back. When it hit the ground, the larger buck turned and, without hesitation, disappeared. The eight-point buck seemed confused, then took the ten-point's departure as a sign of his superiority and confidently strutted around under my stand. Every time I see his mounted head on my wall, I smile. I wonder what the heck he thought happened when my arrow passed through both his lungs. My guess is that he must have thought the bigger buck ambushed him from behind.

The fact that I was able to interpret the body language of the eight-point buck allowed me the opportunity to get a shot at the ten-point. Even though I made a poor release and missed the bigger buck, I not only enjoyed seeing him, but I also learned more about body posturing from the hunt.

Photo Credit: Fiduccia Ent.

I got the opportunity to take this eight-point buck by understanding body language. His antlers netted 125⅛ inches—enough to be entered into the Pope and Young record books. (As a note, I don't enter any of my bucks into the books.)

On another hunt, I was posted in a ground blind when a doe approached. I was planning a deer management segment for our television show and was about to take the doe. Once again, as I drew the string back on my bow, I noticed the doe exhibiting body language as she flagged her tail from side to side. It wasn't a nervous twitch, but a deliberate flick of her tail. It was posturing I was familiar with, so I let the bowstring down and waited. Moments later, a good eight-point buck walked into the woodlot with his nose held to the ground. He trotted up to the doe and, as he was sticking his nose between the doe's rear legs, my arrowed passed through his rib cage.

When you see a doe purposefully flicking her tail from side to side several times in a row, you should interpret it as a straightforward and unmistakable message that she is in prime estrus. She is signaling that she is not only in the peak of her heat cycle, but also that she is receptive to a buck mounting her. Knowing what was happening, I opted to forego shooting the doe for the management piece until another day and kill the eight-point buck instead.

I took this heavy bodied buck by correctly deciphering the body language of the doe that he was with.

Deer exhibit a profusion of body language gestures. Following is a partial list of body postures that deer use most frequently, along with short descriptions. Each is meant to help you recognize the postures so you can interpret their meanings more quickly and correctly so you can adapt to them if necessary. Understanding how to identify a deer's body language will help dramatically change your whitetail hunting experiences and increase your accomplishments.

Estrus Flagging: A doe that is flagging her tail from side to side, then positioning the tail so it is purposefully held up and off to one side of her rump is in heat. She moves her tail repeatedly to help scatter her estrous pheromones into the prevailing wind. She also uses the tail movement as a visual signal to any buck who can't smell the estrus odor that she is a doe in estrus. This is one of the most crucial deer body language signals during the rut. Hunters who are unable to interpret this gesture may decide to harvest the doe because

Photo Credit: Fiduccia Ent.

Photo Credit: Ted Rose

When you see a doe with her tail held out and to the side like this doe, be prepared for a buck following her. A doe's tail held in this position indicates she is in estrus and ready to accept a buck.

they do not recognize the body language being displayed for what it is—a live decoy.

Almost assuredly, a doe flagging is either being followed by a buck or her tail flicking will soon attract one. Hunters who are aware of what doe tail flicking represents will get a quality opportunity to see and possibly kill the buck that is trailing her.

Tail Flipping: When a tail is hanging naturally and is suddenly brushed or flipped from side to side, the deer is about to move. This is one of the more important tail signals for hunters to understand and pay careful attention to. Often, a deer is seen standing still and concentrating on whatever it is doing, such as eating, watching its surroundings, or sniffing the air, a hunter may be lured into a false complacency, thinking the deer is not alarmed and will remain where it is. However, deer often stand still to gather more information before proceeding along a trail, sniffing out a food source, or picking up odors of potential danger, etc. The deer will remain where it is only as long as it does not flick its tail from one side to the other twice. When the deer flicks its tail twice, it is doing so to alert all other deer, near or far, that it is definitely about to move. If you are watching a deer that you are considering shooting and it exhibits this body posture, do not hesitate a second longer to shoot. You have about three seconds to react.

Head Faking: The terms head faking and head bobbing, as some biologists refer to it, are one in the same and both are acceptable to use. High-ranking does and younger deer most often use head faking. Bucks will also do so, but not nearly as often. On occasion, adult bucks will use the head fake to reveal a potential threat.

Wildlife photographer Ted Rose said as he prepared to take this photo, the buck saw his movement and head faked him. "A second later the buck bolted off," said Rose.

There are two stages to this particular type of body language. The first movement includes the deer elongating its neck forward to just below its shoulder after staring at something of interest. They also do this to get a better look at a potential source of worry. The deer's next movement is to dip its head down low as if it were about to eat something. Deer that can't identify a threat by sight or scent but intensely suspect something is wrong try to coax the perceived danger into giving itself away by using the head fake. The movement is meant to make the deer look as if it were unconcerned enough to relax and lower its head to eat, pretending it doesn't see or care about the danger.

It's at this point that some hunters think it is okay to move. As they change positions, they are surprised to see the deer never intended to feed at all but was preparing to instantly lift its head to catch the suspected predator moving. Countless hunters have been caught with their pants down, so to speak, after failing to properly interpret this body language.

When a deer extends its head and looks at you then puts its head down, don't move a muscle. Be assured that the deer is about to lift its head the instant it reaches the ground, if not sooner. This is a terrific behavior to fake out a potential threat, which gives the deer the all-important extra seconds it needs to escape and survive.

Ear Drop: This is one of the most common forms of whitetail body language. The deer lays its ears back along its neck with the openings visible to other deer. This communicates mild aggression.

The Walk Forward: A deer purposely walks toward another without giving ground to the deer it is approaching. This posture expresses a low level of aggression.

High Head: Many hunters have seen this type of deer body posturing. The deer stiffens its body and stands erect to appear larger to a would-be opponent. It pins its ears back, raises its head high, and tilts its nose upward to exhibit a threatening posture. Bucks use this body language when they see or smell another buck approaching. The buck using the posture is displaying an aggressive mode. His posture says, "Stay where you are if you know what is good for you." A perceptive hunter makes the immediate decision to either take the buck exhibiting the body language or carefully wait and inspect the surrounding brush before shooting, as it might conceal an even larger buck.

Head Low Threat: Biologists often refer to this posture as the hard stare. A deer will lower its head and lengthen its neck while approaching another. It will also pin its ears back. While doing this, the deer makes direct eye contact with the other deer, hence the name hard stare.

False Lunge: A deer will shoot forward toward another, often lunging its entire body close to the other deer but stopping just short of making contact. It is used as a warning to suggest that the lunging deer wants space.

A classic head shake by a high-ranking buck.

Bogus Charge: A deer will run directly at another, but pull up short of making contact. It is meant to suggest annoyance or displeasure.

Front Leg Strike: All deer use this form of body language. Bucks use it most while their antlers are in velvet. Female deer use it all year long, mostly to reprimand their fawns but also to ward off other families of does, yearlings, fawns, and sometimes even bucks. It is an aggressive behavior. A deer uses its hoof to deliver a hard blow to another deer to show anger. Often, it will strike at the other deer several times with its front feet. The hoof does not necessarily hit the other deer.

Back Raking: A buck or doe that occupies a high position within the hierarchy lifts its foreleg onto the back of a subordinate deer and drags the leg firmly along the other deer's back. This move is used by a high-ranking deer to displace a subordinate from a bed, food source, or standing too close.

Nose Poke: A high-ranking deer will poke its nose into the body of another deer. It does this to get the group to move to another area. It is also used to oust another deer from the group.

Head Shake: A deer will lower its head and the front of its body while spreading its stance. Simultaneously, the deer shakes its head from side to side repeatedly, causing its ears to flop around. This is a high-level threat posture.

Shoving: The aggressive deer uses a front shoulder to forcefully push against the rear end of another deer. Then, it presses its neck on the back of the other deer.

Flailing: Deer stand on their rear legs and strike forcefully with both forefeet at each other. Flailing continues until one deer shows submissive behavior. Does use this body language the most and it is intended to display aggression. Bucks use it mostly when their antlers have dropped or they are in early stages of velvet.

BUCK-ONLY AGGRESSIVE BEHAVIORS

Sidestepping and Circling: This is the mother of all aggressive buck behaviors. A high-ranking buck will approach another buck with an exaggerated, stiff-legged gait. He will slowly begin to circle the would-be opponent while pinning his ears as far back as possible, significantly arching his back, and forming a semicircle with his entire body. His neck hairs are raised and his head is severely tilted to one side to make his antlers appear larger and poised to use.

Photo Credit: Ted Rose

This buck is exhibiting the classic sidestepping and circling body posture, which is mostly used by high-ranking adult males.

Once when I wasn't the one hunting, I videotaped a huge 190-class buck do this in Michigan. The buck he was displaying to was equal in body and antler size but looked slightly younger. As the older buck closed the distance to within several feet, the younger buck displayed submissive behavior by turning his rump to the approaching buck and avoiding eye contact. The submissive behavior immediately relaxed the high-ranking older buck. Within seconds of seeing the younger buck acquiesce to him, the older one returned to a peaceful posture.

Nose Licking: The buck licks his nose constantly from both sides of its mouth to display anxiety and unease.

Deep Crouch: A buck will lower his head and tilt his antlers toward a potential opponent. The aggressive buck's back is usually arched and his legs tightened. The buck's hair often stands on end and it walks with a stiff-legged gait. This is performed only during the breeding season between high-ranking bucks.

Antler Threat: A buck lowers its head so its antlers point directly at another buck. If the other deer also uses an antler threat, a rush to make antler contact quickly ensues.

Antler Thrust: A high-ranking buck will quickly lower its head and aim its antlers, usually toward the rump of another deer. After making contact, the buck rapidly raises its head.

Sparring: Two bucks carefully entangle their antlers and begin to push and twist their heads back and forth. This is a nonviolent contest between bucks of all sizes to establish positions within the pecking order. After the pushing and shoving ends, the two bucks often remain companions.

Sideward Rush: The sideward rush is a common form of aggression between two belligerent adult bucks. Both bucks lunge at each other and clash antlers. One buck sideswipes the other buck, which is usually eating or tending a doe. Sometimes the contact is so forceful it knocks the buck to the ground.

Flehmen Response: Also referred to as the flehmen position, a buck will curl back its upper lip, exposing its front teeth while inhaling air, usually with his nostrils closed. He will hold the position for several seconds. It is usually performed over a urine or deer scat site that interests the buck. The flehmen response is made while the buck's neck is stretched out and its head is held high in the air. It is used to facilitate the transfer of pheromones and other scents into and over the vomeronasal organ, located in the roof of the mouth, via a duct just behind the buck's front teeth. When you see a buck doing this, you may be interested in shooting him. Make your decision to take him quickly because time is against you. Usually this indicates the buck has scented a doe in estrus and is trying to pinpoint where she is. Once he picks up the direction of the odor, the buck will usually take off quickly to locate the hot doe. If you're not ready to react, you will end up losing the opportunity to shoot the buck.

Raised Hair: Associated with the deep crouch, when a buck holds its head high and his neck hairs stand on end, it is a similar reaction to when a human gets goose bumps on the back of his or her neck. Many people have had this happen when they enter a dark room or are walking along a backwoods trail and sense something is awry. If you see a buck exhibiting this type of body language, he is at a high level of alert. Also, he is showing an aggressive posture. This is usually caused by the anticipation of an approaching buck he has not been able to identify but knows is close by scent.

As I mentioned previously, body language is often used to establish the hierarchy within a herd. For example, the most aggressive males occupying the top step of the social ladder are the leaders within their bachelor herd and, as such, they are in charge. Bucks occupying lower status positions are subordinate and will usually avoid unnecessary physical conflict with superior bucks. As the rut begins, however, all the males within the group become more aggressive and conflicts become more frequent.

This buck is on high alert and is about to foot stomp. Hoof stomping combines visual and audible posturing. The stomping noise alerts nearby deer, and also emits excess interdigital gland scent on the ground. The olfactory warns deer passing by the area later that another deer encountered likely danger here.

Hoof Stomping: In all likelihood, this is the most frequent body language used by deer and witnessed by hunters. A deer alerted to potential danger or a confirmed a threat will lift one of its front legs halfway off the ground and stomp it back down hard, creating a thumping noise. Researchers say deer stomp their hooves for a variety of reasons. In most cases, however, it is meant as a warning or to goad movement from a possible threat. A deer is also sending a visual and auditory message to deer within sight and earshot that it is encountering a problem. Most importantly, the deer is also leaving a chemical olfactory message for deer who are not close enough to receive the warning.

The chemical message is left on the ground from a gland between the deer's toes, called the interdigital gland. The excess interdigital scent is meant to warn other whitetails traveling down the trail that another deer encountered danger at this point. Hunters who see deer stomping or who alarm them into repeated stomping should consider relocating their stand. The odds of a deer coming near an area permeated with excess interdigital scent are low.

A Doe with One Ear Cupped Forward and One Ear Cupped Back: When a hunter is watching a doe walk down a trail and she stops to listen for potential danger before proceeding, he or she should pay particular attention to the direction her ears are pointing. If they are both cupped in one direction, she is probably alone. However, if one ear is forward and the other ear suddenly rotates toward her back, she is listening to what is probably either her fawns or yearlings approaching or, more importantly and especially during the rut, a buck. Try not to alarm this deer and you will increase the chances of seeing what is coming up behind her.

Flagging or Tail Waving: One of the most familiar deer body language signs is tail flagging. Deer use it as they run off to warn other deer. Does, who flag more frequently than bucks, also use it to give a visual reference to yearlings and fawns about the direction she is running. Since does flag frequently, the importance of reading this body language is evident. Should a hunter jump or perhaps have deer driven past him or her that are on the run with tails held high, he or she should be on the lookout for deer running with their tails down or tucked between their legs. Since tail waving is an action more related to does, a deer running in a group with its tail down is likely to be a buck. Focus all your attention on this animal and you will have likely picked out the only buck in the group by correctly interpreting this form of body language.

When running from danger, does flag or wave their tails more often than bucks. Most adult bucks flag only when the danger is far away.

Ears Flattened, Back Arched, and Neck Hairs Standing Up: This posture is from a buck that is nervous or extremely agitated. He is displaying every form of noncombative aggression he can muster. In most instances, he is displaying this body language to a much larger deer. By appearing aggressive and hostile, the buck hopes to fend off his rival with a bluff to avoid actual physical combat. When a hunter sees a buck displaying this body language and does not see a second buck, he or she should carefully check the surrounding area. Look in the direction the aggressive deer is watching, and chances are you will find another buck. Or, as in the example I gave previously, just sit tight and wait to see what develops as long as the first buck remains in range.

Pawing the Ground: Bucks paw the ground for several reasons, such as to search for acorns and other food, ward off other deer, and prepare or freshen scrapes. When searching for food, the body language will be relaxed. Ears are slightly forward, the tail hangs straight down between the legs, hair lies down on the back, and the muscles are relaxed. This deer

Photo Credit: Ted Rose

is content with its surroundings and unaware of the hunter. A deer pawing the ground in an aggressive manner is on full alert. It may have spotted
a hunter or be fending off another deer. A hunter must read this situation
quickly to decide whether to take the animal before it moves.

Finally, a buck pawing a round patch of earth and stomping repeatedly to scratch, sniff, and urinate is preparing a scrape. This buck's body
language will let you know if you have time to shoot or not. If he is
pawing quickly, urinating, and constantly looking in different directions,
he is probably freshening up a scrape of a more aggressive buck and will
not be at the site long. However, if he enters the scrape slowly, paws the
earth with purpose, uses an overhanging branch, doesn't bother to check
his surroundings often, and urinates infrequently, he is probably the buck
who originally made the scrape and will spend considerably more time at
the location. This will give a hunter time to make a decision whether or
not to harvest the buck.

The reason most hunters are familiar with some body language, such
as flagging or hoof stomping, is because these are common signals exhibited by deer. To learn about the more subtle forms of body language I
mentioned in this chapter and some that I didn't, spend time observing
deer during the off-season. One of the best places to observe is at a zoo
or enclosure with several penned deer. Because of their close proximity to
one another, they tend to use body language more frequently. Observing
certain forms of obvious and subtle signals of body language and watching the reactions of other deer will start to fine-tune your understanding
of this nonverbal communication.

By learning to read, correctly decipher, and react to the body language signals you receive from people and animals, you will improve your
odds of responding properly to any given situation. For hunters, reading a deer's body language is an important hunting strategy you should
plan on learning and using to your benefit, which is why I thought this
book would be incomplete without this chapter. It will increase your deer
hunting success immensely.

This buck is using assertive, nonbelligerent body language. With his tail held straight out, ears pinned back, and back arched, he is about to urinate over his tarsal glands. All this is to send a visual and olfactory warning and announcement of his high-ranking status.

Chapter Three

Deer Glands: Facts and Tactics

———

One of the most important elements for reliable deer sightings and harvests is reducing human odor to its bare minimum. Savvy hunters realize that to be more successful, they have to fool a buck's nose time and time again. In doing so, a hunter's chances to kill a buck increase dramatically.

For more than forty years, I have used a couple of natural glands removed from deer, commercially made gland scents, and a combination of both to lure deer to my stand and help me reduce my human odor. I also use the odors to fool a deer's olfactory senses into thinking what they smell is nonthreatening.

The odors from natural deer glands or commercially made glandular scents can be used successfully when stalking, posting, tracking, using deer calls, antler rattling, and more. Glandular scents are also particularly effective when hunters use them to create decoys, such as mock rubs and scrapes. In other words, no matter what deer hunting tactic you use, by properly utilizing scents you will increase your success afield.

Not all glandular scents can be duplicated by scent companies, but some of the glands can be collected from dead deer, such as from road kill where legal, wild game processing plants, and other hunter's harvested deer. It is more convenient and practical for a hunter, however, to purchase commercially made scents. They are sold in a majority of sports stores and catalogs. Don't be concerned that commercially made scents might not work as well as natural scents collected from dead deer, because they do.

Photo Credit: Buck Stop Scents

A glandular scent, such as this one, will help to enhance different types of hunting tactics. In this case, this scent can be used when creating a mock scrape.

There are many ways to effectively use deer glands to increase your deer sightings and kill ratios. The most important issue about using glandular deer scents is to be totally confident and knowledgeable enough to properly include gland scent use in your deer hunting strategies. By understanding what each deer gland is for and how you can mimic its use, you will take your deer hunting to new heights.

FOREHEAD GLANDS

The forehead glands are located between the top of the deer's eyes and the antlers. They become active in September and progressively smell more pungent throughout the rut. The potency of these glands is directly associated with the deer's age and social status. The glands produce an oily substance that makes the hair around the eyes darker. As the buck rubs a tree or overhanging branch, he deposits his forehead scent as an olfactory message to communicate his social ranking, current breeding status, and even his age. The older a buck is, the more trees and branches he will mark. Some biologists believe the odor of the pheromones left on trees and other vegetation by the forehead glands helps bring does into estrus.

Photo Credit: Ted Rose

A buck rubs his forehead glands on a branch over a scrape. The older the buck is, the more powerful the odor becomes, as these two factors are directly connected.

Using Forehead Gland Scent as a Tactic

I use commercially made forehead glandular scent. It can also be obtained from a dead buck but it is messy and a lot of work to do. The best way to do this is to take a clean rag and, using surgical gloves, rub the rag vigorously against each gland. You can also press the rag to the glands and squeeze the glands hard between your fingers so the oil gets onto the rag. Place the rag in a zip-top plastic bag and seal it immediately. Trust me when I say you are much better off using a commercially made forehead gland scent. When making a mock buck rub, massage several drops on the bare tree trunk which will help create the entire illusion to your fake rub. When making a mock scrape place several drops of forehead gland scent on an overhanging branch above a scrape. Adding forehead gland scent to my fake rubs and scrapes has been a successful tactic for me over the years. The scent encourages both bucks and does into investigating the mock rubs and scrapes.

PREORBITAL GLANDS

The preorbital or lachrymal glands are the tear ducts located in front of the deer's eyes. There are a few sebaceous and sudoriferous glands located at the lips of each preorbital gland. Some researchers think this gland does not produce a lot of odor, but others disagree. Deer often rub the preorbital glands on vegetation, overhanging branches, twigs, and trees. Many researchers, including an old friend and former business partner, Dr. Leonard Lee Rue III, feel that deer use these glands for self-marking purposes as well. Therefore, it appears that deer deposit scent from their preorbital glands purposefully on a variety of vegetation and their bodies. The preorbital gland's primary function is a tear duct. It is believed to be under muscular control. A buck may open it to emit odor or signal aggression toward another buck.

Using Preorbital Gland Scent as a Tactic

The preorbital gland is available commercially, but also can be collected the same way I described gathering the scent from the forehead gland. However, I strongly suggest you buy it commercially. I use preorbital gland scent to help complete the illusion when making mock rubs and scrapes. I have had a slightly better response from deer when I included the preorbital scent on mock rubs and scrapes. Many scent manufacturers say their preorbital scent consists of the forehead, tear duct, ear, nasal, and saliva glands. I can't confirm that, but I can say the commercially made preorbital gland scents I have

Photo Credit: Ted Rose

An adult buck rubs the innumerable chemical compounds found in the preorbital glands onto an overhanging branch. The aromas announce the buck's age, identity, rutting state, and his rank within the hierarchy to all other deer.

used have worked well for me. The pheromones they contain work well to mark rubs, scrapes, and general vegetation. Does and bucks deposit preorbital scent. However, bucks seem to have a more uncontrollable impulse to deposit preorbital scent pheromones on trees, bushes, branches, saplings, and other shrubbery, particularly along travel lanes. Communal licking branches are also a place bucks like to leave their preorbital scent on. A buck will enthusiastically rub his preorbital glands along a branch and when he is finished rubbing, he will chew the tip of the scented branch. Other bucks and does that pass by are attracted to this and deposit their preorbital scent on the branch as well. These communal licking branches and sticks are used to establish an early pecking order in the development of a temporary chain of command among bucks in the area. Bucks also like to deposit preorbital scent on all types and sizes of tree rubs. Lastly, bucks leave preorbital scent in breeding scrapes. Male deer tend to leave preorbital scent most near heavily traveled doe trails where it will do most good. Use preorbital scent on mock rubs, scrapes, on overhanging branches, licking sticks, and on other forest vegetation, particularly along well used doe runways during the rut.

NASAL GLANDS

These two almond-shaped glands are located inside the nostrils. They help the deer detect odors and some researchers feel they are also used to lubricate the deer's nose. It is believed that the nasal glands are used to leave scent on overhanging branches and rubs.

Using Nasal Gland Scent as a Tactic

While it is important to know about the nasal gland, it is not practical to use as a tactic, as gathering the scent from inside the nostrils is difficult.

VOMERONASAL ORGAN

This organ is often referred to as a buck's second nose. It is obviously not a second nose, but it does serve some of the same functions and purposes. The next time you take a buck, look on the roof of its mouth and you will see a diamond-shaped formation with a small passage leading into the palate. This is the vomeronasal organ.

The vomeronasal organ is crucial to bucks during the rut. Its primary function is to analyze doe urine. During the rut, a buck will curl his upper lip while he inhales deeply, which is known as a flehmen gesture. Urine scent passes over the organ, and a buck is immediately able to detect if it contains estrus pheromones. If it does, the buck will know if it has been left by a doe that is close by or one that passed through the area recently. This helps the buck avoid chasing after does that may not be ready to breed for twenty-four or more hours.

When the vomeronasal organ detects a high volume of pungent estrus pheromones, the buck immediately pursues that particular scent until he locates the hot doe who deposited it. According to researchers,

This buck is using his vomeronasal organ to precisely determine the doe's state of estrus.

the vomeronasal organ is capable of determining a doe's stage of estrus to within hours. Analysis of urine through the vomeronasal organ is thought to synchronize the breeding readiness between bucks and does to ensure that both sexes are in peak breeding condition.

PREPUTIAL GLAND

Photo Credit: Ted Rose

This buck is rub-urinating, or depositing urine over his tarsal glands. Directly following the urine, the buck will release fluids from his penal sheath that will also flow over the tarsal glands. The three scents combine to make a powerful olfactory statement of the buck's social rank.

This gland is located on the inside of the buck's penal sheath and is thought to serve two purposes. It is used for lubrication and might also contain sperm. However, since researchers have only recently discovered this gland, they have not yet determined its exact functions or whether it is used for communication by deer, and especially, bucks.

METATARSAL GLANDS

These glands are light tan circles of hair of about one or two
inches long located on the outside of the hind leg between
the toe and the hock, or heel,
on whitetails. Some naturalists and biologists feel the gland
is atrophying, or getting smaller
through evolution, because deer
no longer need it, and it has no
viable purpose. This is thought to
be the case because the metatarsal
glands no longer have ducts. Still,
others believe the glands emit a
pheromone deer use for communication and as an aggressive
odor to ward off other deer during the rut.

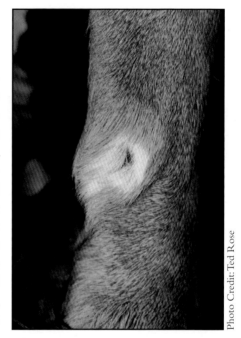

Photo Credit: Ted Rose

The metatarsals are not actually glands be-
cause they have no duct. They are not totally
understood in whitetails. Some report seeing
the hair flared when bucks fight.

Using Metatarsal Gland Scent as a Tactic

Because the glands are not totally understood, I warn hunters to be prepared for anything when using metatarsal glandular scent. I have tried
it several times. Sometimes it has helped attract deer, but other times it
has spooked them. Therefore, I suggest not using it.

SALIVARY GLANDS

These glands are located inside the mouth and produce saliva with
enzymes to aid digestion. When a buck rubs a tree, he will always lick the

rubbed trunk, thereby depositing the enzymes found in his saliva on the tree. When a buck makes a licking stick, he takes a small twig or sapling into his mouth and places it between his teeth. Then, he gently pulls his head back, which frays the end of the twig or sapling. It is thought that the buck does this to deposit scent from his salivary glands on the licking stick, as well as on overhanging branches at scrapes.

TARSAL GLAND

The tarsal gland is an external gland located on the inside of a deer's hind legs. This gland secretes fatty substances called lipids. Tan in color most of the year, this gland turns almost jet-black during the rut. Bucks continually urinate and deposit preputial scent over it, which cling to the long, thick hairs of the tarsal gland, making it darker as the season progresses.

Deer use their tarsal glands and the pheromones from them, which are mostly made up of lactones, as visual and olfactory signals. In mature deer, both bucks and does, the gland emits more pungent odors and is darker in color than in less mature deer. When excited, the hairs on the tarsal gland stand erect and can be seen for quite a distance by other deer.

Photo Credit: Ted Rose

The dark tarsal gland seen on this buck's back leg emits a strong pungent odor that indicates he has good genes and fertility. The tarsal glands also act as visual and olfactory warnings to younger bucks to keep their distance.

There is little doubt that this gland is one of the more important glands to whitetails—and hunters.

Any hunter who has harvested a buck or doe during the peak rut knows about the strong smell that is associated with this gland. However, some may not know that the tarsal gland is used in a behavior called rub-urination. Rub-urination is what a buck does as he begins to use his tarsal gland scent. He places his two rear legs together, pressing each tarsal tightly against the other. Then, he squats slightly and begins to urinate. The urine flows over both glands. Then, he squats a bit lower and excretes fluid from his preputial gland over the tarsal glands. Next, the buck rubs the tarsal glands together several times.

Using Tarsal Gland Scent as a Tactic

The optimum response period from tarsal scent is from mid-October through mid-December. Place several drops on a drag rag before walking to your stand. Once you are within thirty to fifty yards of the stand, walk a circle completely around the stand and hang the drag rag on a low branch. Then, put a few additional drops of tarsal scent on the soles of your boots and walk to your stand. The tarsal scent will permeate the area and act as an attracting scent for both bucks and does. It will also act as an agitating odor for mature bucks. Don't place tarsal scent on your clothing. You don't want a buck's attention focused directly on you. Instead, direct his attention or aggression to an area off to the side of your stand.

Another way to use tarsal scent is to place it in mock scrapes or rubs that you create. Additionally, it can be used in a natural scrape or at the base of a natural rub. I use tarsal scent in a natural scrape or rub to lure in a belligerent buck that has become agitated thinking a competitive buck is working his area. Both bucks and does will react by freshening the scrape or rub with their own tarsal scent. Mature bucks will tear up the scrape or rub significantly. If this happens, it is a sure sign you're onto a mature buck in the area.

Tarsal scent is especially effective when used with full-sized deer decoys or when using a natural deer tail as a decoy. Place a few drops on the inside of the decoy's legs to add reality to your setup. With a natural deer tail, place a few drops of tarsal scent on the ground beneath where the tail is hanging. The tail should hang about twenty-four to twenty-six inches above the ground on a branch. Lastly, you can use tarsal scent along with a doe estrus scent when hunting during the rut.

INTERDIGITAL GLANDS

The interdigital gland is a commonly used gland by whitetails. It is located between the toes of the hooves. It is a small sac that opens from a duct. When squeezed, the sac emits a yellowish substance with a potent odor that reeks of rancid cheese. The odor emitted from each deer's interdigital gland is unique to that particular animal and helps identify it to other deer.

Each time a deer puts its hoof on the ground, the gland emits a tiny amount of interdigital scent. The scent enables other deer to identify and follow a particular deer if they choose to. The odor from the interdigital gland also aids deer in identifying when a transient deer is in their range. When interdigital molecules begin to evaporate, the odor of the track changes and may be how deer and predators can judge the freshness and direction of the track.

Interdigital scent is also used to warn other deer of potential danger. When a deer stomps its hoof, it is depositing an excess amount of interdigital scent. In doing so, it alerts other deer to danger through scent, sound, and sight. A deer coming upon excess interdigital scent immediately knows there is, or was, potential danger in the area. It is alerted and will mill about nervously for several moments in an attempt to decipher the odor. It will then either walk back in the direction it came from or take a wide berth around the scent left. Deer rarely, if ever, walk directly over it.

Using Interdigital Gland Scent as a Tactic

This scent can be used in a few ways to attract, intentionally spook, or change a deer's travel route. To attract deer with this scent, it is important not to use more than a couple drops of interdigital on a drag rag or the sole of a boot before walking toward your stand. Once you are within thirty yards of the stand, walk a circle completely around it and move directly to the stand. Deer will often follow the scent with their nose held tightly to the ground.

Interdigital scent can also be used to roust deer from thick cover, such as blow downs, standing corn, laurels, etc. When a likely patch of cover is spotted, place several drops of interdigital scent on the ground. Stomp your foot several times and blow an alarm-distress snort. To create the entire illusion of a deer signaling danger, position yourself so your scent is

Photo Credit: Ted Rose

There are forty-six volatile compounds secreted by the interdigital gland. It is the second most important gland to whitetail deer. Unfortunately, many hunters are unaware of its existence because of where the gland is located. It is one of my favorite scents to use to stop, attract, or change the travel direction of deer.

blowing toward the cover. This tactic can be used without including the alarm–distress vocalization.

Interdigital scent can also be used to purposely change a deer's direction of travel toward a particular stand instead of taking another trail. It works especially well where two well–used trails intersect. Simply place several drops of interdigital scent several yards down the trail you don't want the deer to travel. Once deer smell the excess interdigital scent, they will briefly pause, become skittish, and quickly head back from where they came or turn down the trail leading to your location.

Well, there you have it, an explanation of deer glands and ways to use the odors they emit to help you either reduce your human odor or attract deer. By using each glandular scent correctly and sparingly, you will discover how much fun hunting can be as deer, particularly bucks, do a lot of strange things when they respond to gland scents. Using deer gland scents will also increase your sightings and hopefully the number of deer you bag.

Chapter Four

Buck Dispersal and Other Movement Patterns

———

The meaning of buck dispersal as it relates to whitetail deer doesn't always have one straightforward explanation. This is because buck dispersal has a dual meaning and therefore requires a two-part explanation. The first type is referred to as adult buck dispersal (ABD) and explains the various reasons adult bucks leave their home range. The second kind, which generally takes place in spring, is called young buck dispersal (YBD).

The information shared in both explanations contains a wide array of ideas and theories from an equally wide variety of sources about each type of buck dispersal movement. There are many other forms of buck movement that take place for various reasons and during specific times of the year, but these movements aren't as dramatic regarding distances covered as in the ABD and YBD movements. These other seasonal patterns are caused by an assortment of reasons and one of these less common movements, buck transition, is sometimes confused with ABD and YBD. I will explain that term and some others later in this chapter.

I am not a biologist or scientist. With that said, however, the information I share here about buck dispersal is based on studies done by

Photo Credit: Ted Rose

An adult buck, such as this one, moves from his home range for only one of three primary reasons: to locate estrus does, feed on something his home range doesn't offer, or eat ripened or more nutritious food.

professionals, articles about dispersal by animal behaviorists, and my personal observations and experiences while employing deer management practices for more than thirty years.

Knowing more about ABD and YBD will provide deer hunters with a better understanding of the two types of buck dispersals that take place. This subject is usually of prime importance to those involved with quality deer management programs or people who own or lease their hunting lands. It can also be valuable data for those who hunt on public lands, as it defines some aspects about male deer that are interesting and helpful.

Adult Buck Dispersal

For many years, I have heard varying opinions about ABD and the ramifications it causes for hunters. The most prominent viewpoint about ABD revolves around the whitetail's breeding season. It is during the peak of all four phases of the rut (including the false, big chase, primary and post rut phases) that adult resident males disperse from their home ranges and roam over long distances outside their core areas looking for receptive does. As this phenomenon occurs, hunters will notice a dramatic decline in sightings of the familiar adult bucks they have watched all summer through early fall. Sometimes these wanderings can take a buck many miles from his home range.

During the breeding season, hunters often report seeing one or more bucks they have never laid eyes on before. This is commonly reported by deer managers and hunters who own their lands and are familiar with the bucks occupying their property. Unfamiliar bucks that show up are often referred to as transient bucks and are usually mature males that, from time to time, trespass onto lands other than their home range. This type of behavior generally takes place during the breeding season when bucks are seeking does in heat. However, other elements can contribute to transient buck actions. If a buck's home range is lacking a food source that can be found on other lands, even a mile or more from its home ground, the buck may intermittently seek out these sources, including acorns, apples, etc.

The unexpected absence of resident adult bucks from a given piece of land is mostly attributed, however, to ABD—a time when all male deer undergo an instinctive urge to leave their home range and seek out does in estrus. Unfortunately, this behavior often causes hunters to believe the mature buck or bucks they have been watching have been killed by a predator, vehicle, or trespasser and are, therefore, gone for good.

Recent evidence conducted by noted biologists and scientists suggests that ABD is a temporary occurrence, not a permanent one. Research has confirmed that while a couple of the mature bucks on a given property may temporarily wander far and wide from their home range, a majority will remain within their range throughout their lives, even during the rut. I can believe this because I have found it to be true on my own land.

Exactly how far, what length of time, and for what variety of reasons an adult buck will either permanently or temporarily disperse from his home turf are yet to be precisely determined. More recent studies by noted biologists and researchers confirmed that roaming adult bucks do increase their wanderings dramatically during the rut. There is also evidence that some adult bucks travel much farther. Some have been reported to travel extreme distances of up to twenty-five to thirty miles from their home range, though these distances are not common.

They also established that a majority of adult bucks seldom travel more than a few miles from their home turf. Equally interesting is that the research documented a majority of the bucks that did wander a mile or two away, presumably to locate receptive does, returned to their home range within forty-eight hours.

Create a Well-Balanced Doe Herd

The best way to keep male deer close to home during the rut is to make sure your land is inviting enough to attract a resident population of adult female deer, yearlings, and fawns. The fact is, if hunters want to increase their buck sightings and harvest totals, they have to take all the management steps necessary to achieve a healthy doe population on their properties. To accomplish this goal, it is absolutely necessary to kill does.

Many hunters feel that more female deer translates into greater chances of having buck fawns. There is no doubt that to establish a well-balanced herd of both bucks and does and to have a normal social structure within the herd, female deer of all age classes must be taken in the right numbers. A well-managed doe herd also improves the buck-to-doe ratio and keeps the carrying capacity balanced.

Photo Credit: Ted Rose

A surefire way to limit resident bucks from dispersing and to attract transient bucks to your land is to manage the land and doe herd well enough for female deer to call it home.

When there are too many does living on a given piece of land, this can bring about breeding complications with negative side effects, particularly during the rut.

In this case, because there aren't enough adult bucks to breed all the receptive does, inferior bucks get to breed more and pass on their less-desirable genes. An overpopulation of female deer also wreaks havoc with buck signs. When there are too many does, bucks leave fewer rubs, make fewer scrapes, and wander the property less often. All these factors result in fewer sightings and shooting opportunities for hunters.

Any experienced biologist will support the fact that a certain amount of female deer should be harvested to establish a healthier and better-balanced deer herd. The best way to achieve this goal and know exactly how many does should be taken on your land is to hire a biologist to survey your land and advise you. Sometimes game departments offer this service for free.

A healthy doe population will definitely establish a more balanced resident adult buck populace. It will help draw neighboring adult males to your land, as they will find the property particularly female friendly during the rut. Younger bucks that are dispersing from other lands and looking to establish a new area to call home are drawn to the land, too.

Homesick Bucks

Research has documented that bucks who travel a few miles to search for does, even if they move out of their home range, shouldn't be gone for an extended period of time. The evidence strongly supports that adult male deer who wander from their usual haunts during the rut will return to their home range area sooner, rather than later.

Another fact about ABD is that a study in Maryland acknowledged about 70 percent of extended movement by adult bucks from their home range to other areas happened during daylight hours. More interestingly,

Research studies document that 70 percent of adult males will return to their home range sooner rather than later.

the study discovered that 70 percent of this movement occurred during the primary rut. During the other phases of the rut, ABD movement was much less. During the pre-rut, only 15 percent of bucks moved during daylight and, through the late rut phase, 30 percent of bucks traveled during daylight hours.

The study identified another key point. The Maryland researchers noted that while some adult buck movement happened from 8 a.m. to 10 a.m., there was a steady increase in movement during daylight after 10 a.m. As I have mentioned countless times in my seminars and articles, hunting from 10 a.m. to 2 p.m. is key to seeing and bagging mature bucks. The study only further supports my belief that it is a worthwhile investment to hunt during this off-hour time frame.

A combined Maryland, Mississippi, and New York research project also suggests that a buck who has wandered from his core area and spent the night seeking out receptive does is likely to amble back to his home range at any point during daylight hours. A buck from the neighbor's land may also end up walking through your land while heading back to his home range. Both scenarios can culminate, allowing opportunities for hunters to take a mature buck.

A hunter should remain on stand as long as possible to escalate the chances of killing a trophy-class buck. This advice is particularly true during the rut, when adult bucks wander the most. However, I strongly recommend to hunters that they should not remain in the same tree stand the entire day. It is nearly impossible to stay in one hunting location without having human odor permeate the entire area. Hunters will also find it hard to remain totally focused on the hunt over that long of a period of time.

Instead, post in a favorite stand from dawn to about 9:30 a.m. Then get down from the stand and head to another prime hunting location. A good choice would be where active rubs or scrapes are located close to heavy cover or near a known buck bedding area. Hunt from that location from 10 a.m. to 2 p.m. If a buck doesn't make an appearance during the off-hour time frame, either go back to the original stand or select yet another prime location, perhaps a heavily traveled doe trail, and hunt it from 2:30 p.m. until sunset. This single tactic will help you to get more opportunities at mature bucks.

Young Buck Dispersal

In order to separate the two annual buck dispersal movements, I would like to cover what YBD entails. In many studies, particularly the 1994 study in Maryland, researchers came up with some fascinating findings regarding how to maximize the adult male population on deer managed properties. This is one specific goal all deer managers work hard to achieve.

In 1994, Dr. Chris Rosenberry led a YBD research study in Maryland on a 3,300-acre area. The study concluded that immature bucks disperse from their home range just prior to the rut. It also determined that young bucks travel one to thirty-five miles to set up their new digs.

Photo Credit: Ted Rose

The renowned Maryland research program was conducted on a 3,300-acre area in 1994 by Dr. Chris Rosenberry and other researchers. The study stated that most YBD takes place just prior to the rut. During the study, the researchers captured seventy-five fawns and yearling bucks and fitted them with radio collars. Of the seventy-five bucks, fifty-one of them were kept tabs on until they either died or the study ended. What they found was that 70 percent of the yearling bucks dispersed off the study area. Thirty-five of the fifty-one bucks traveled from one to five miles to establish a new home range of their own. One buck traveled an unbelievable thirty-five-plus miles, crossing a wide variety of terrain, including streams and rivers from the original study site.

If young bucks dispersed from that large of a tract of land, how realistic is it to think they would remain on small parcels of two hundred to several hundred acres in size? Many would say it doesn't seem worthwhile or practical for hunters who practice deer management to protect yearling bucks only to have the animals leave their lands. It appears that young bucks have little chance of turning into mature bucks on the land they were born on. No matter how much they are protected, they are naturally inclined to find new home ranges because the mature bucks that want to reduce competition for estrus does often chase them out. Many believe protecting young bucks would increase the number of yearling bucks for other landowners, which does little to boost the numbers of mature bucks on their own land.

This is why it is so important to try to get bordering neighbors, and even nearby property owners whose lands do not border managed properties, to become involved in a deer management program. Their participation helps your management efforts immensely, especially since some of the six- to eighteen-month-old bucks born on their land may end up making their home range on your land. There is a great possibility your neighbors' bucks will become your adult bucks in the future and vice versa. Therefore, through cooperative management efforts of protecting fawn and yearling bucks, everyone involved experiences better adult buck hunting.

October Lull

There are several other forms of buck movements, including times of the year, social or staging area transitions, and movements between food sources. Let's begin with a transition often referred to as the October lull. Many deer hunters are befuddled and depressed by this particular buck behavior. It is caused by the dual personality of adult male deer that begins during the first phase of the rut, known as the pre-rut.

Up until early October, an adult male deer's behavior and feeding patterns are somewhat predictable. As I have mentioned, adult bucks become elusive during this period not because of brainpower, but because they grow up being paranoid recluses who are frightened by their own shadows. They spend much of their time slipping from one piece of heavy cover to another. Just catching a glimpse of a mature buck before mid-October is hard to do, except as he makes his way to a food source just prior to sundown or back to his bedding area before sunrise.

By mid-October, during the lull, mature bucks have forsaken their predictable summer behaviors and patterns. While they still visit their

Photo Credit: Ted Rose

Locating an adult buck, such as this fella, during the October lull can be frustrating. This time of year, bucks become reclusive and stay in heavy cover more often.

favorite food sources, they will seldom do so until they have the safety of darkness. They also return to their bedding long before sunrise. It is during this time frame that most adult bucks are seen less often than they will be seen all fall.

By the third week of October, a buck's daytime movement is reduced considerably. This often leads hunters to believe that bucks seen earlier have been spooked by small game hunters, deer scouting, hunters setting up tree stands, and even early season bow hunting. The fact is no one can really explain what causes the behavior.

I have found that the best and quickest way to find a good buck during the lull is to locate a deer stand close to what I call a social area, also known as a staging area. Deer social areas are usually located in semi-dense cover that is about one hundred yards from reliable feeding sources. This is where a buck will feel most comfortable approaching a food source during the last thirty minutes of light.

Buck social areas are often defined by a group of rubs made close together. The rubs will be facing both to and from the food source. Those made on the sides of the trees going to the food source are the evening trails. The rubs facing away from the food source are the morning trails. Set your deer stand according to the time you want to hunt from it and in good wind currents. Other deer signs associated with social areas include lots of deer scat, tracks, and, most importantly, some scrapes. They are easily found by first identifying what deer, bucks in particular, are currently feeding on.

What is most interesting about hunting social areas is that you can approach them during an afternoon hunt without being overly concerned about spooking deer, as they are all still lying low in the beds. Leaving the stand after the hunt can be a problem, as the deer will be feeding nearby. Having an exit route planned that won't take you in the direction of where the deer are feeding will allow you to leave with the least amount of disturbance and keep them from sensing your presence. It is crucial to remember that staging areas are sensitive to hunt. If you spook a buck once, he may avoid the area for several days. If he is scared off twice from his social area, the chances of taking him in that spot are reduced significantly and he may even abandon the area entirely. I have found the best opportunity to hunt a social area is prior to a heavy rainfall or when a cold front is moving in, especially after a warm spell.

Food Transition and Other Forms of Buck Movement Patterns

The next type of buck movement is entirely motivated by available food sources. Nothing is more important to deer, other than the need to reproduce, than food. Despite what has been said about how a buck will stop eating during the rut, this theory is mostly an old wives' tale.

Photo Credit: Ted Rose

Adult Buck Dispersal can also be attributed to bucks leaving their home range to find other food sources. Deer seek them out no matter how far they have to roam but remain away only temporarily.

No matter where whitetails roam, the food sources within their home range ripen at specific times. The deer know exactly when the plants they prefer mature and when they are most abundant. Deer will seek them out enthusiastically, albeit temporarily, even forsaking other food sources.

In agricultural areas, deer will stop eating some of their most preferred foods, such as alfalfa, corn, wheat, oats, and other highly regarded foods, as soon as the mast, or acorn, crop begins to ripen and fall to the ground. They will gorge themselves on acorns, particularly white oak, until they have eaten all they can find. In other types of terrain, the same behavior takes place with other food sources they prefer.

This activity is referred to as a food transition movement pattern (FTMP). Both bucks and does are affected by the abundance and ripening of food sources and will move from the places they usually feed to seek current preferred foods. Many hunters have witnessed this type of FTMP behavior by whitetail deer.

During late summer and early fall, bucks can be seen dining on clover, corn, alfalfa, etc., in agricultural fields during the last hour before sundown. Suddenly, it is nearly impossible to spot a buck and, at times, even a doe feeding in fields. It is FTMP that accounts for their temporary absence, as both bucks and does have located one or more other types of appealing foods. These foods, such as acorns, apples, berries, grapes, sumac, pears, and fallen maple leaves, can be in the forest or in orchards. Particular farm crops are also sought out as they ripen. Through the scent of mature crops, such as soybean, corn, and oats, deer instinctively know which foods are limited to a particular season and, therefore, are only available at certain times of the year. If you're hunting farmlands, keep in contact with the farmer and ask him or her to let you know when particular crops will mature. By knowing when crops ripen, you can adjust your hunting locations accordingly and intercept a wily buck waiting for sunset in a social area before entering the field.

Hunters who take advantage of FTMP will increase their buck and doe sightings and harvests. Remember that even during the rut when male deer are said to stop eating (they actually eat less but continue to feed), estrus does will continue with the FTMP behavior and often have rut-crazed bucks on their trails as they seek out preferred food sources.

During the rut, setting up outside of bedding areas along trails that lead to current food sources, especially for estrus does, is a top-notch tactic. By taking full advantage of FTMPs, savvy hunters can boost their odds

Food transition movement patterns (FTMP) are a major cause of deer suddenly disappearing from agricultural fields from late summer to early fall. They leave to eat fruit, acorns, and other natural vegetation.

to take a good buck while other hunters are watching over food sources that deer have temporarily abandoned.

Knowing what motivates different buck movements will make you a more informed deer hunter. You won't be left wondering what has happened to your bucks. Rather, you'll be a hunter who knows exactly what behavior is taking place and will adjust your whitetail hunting strategies accordingly.

Are Buck Management Practices Really Practical?

The reality about understanding all the elements it takes to keep bucks on a particular piece of land are too numerous to cover in a single chapter. There are a lot of differing opinions, conflicting ideas, and variances in research on this subject. What should be done to provide better buck management on deer management lands, then? I wish I could be more encouraging, but there is no easy answer.

The 192 acres owned by Kate and me, the 110 acres owned by my cousin, and the 130 acres owned by a third party in our area encompass a total of 432 contiguous acres, one-third of which is split by a road. We have

To shoot larger antlered deer, a management program should be implemented that is designed to protect yearling bucks. Even a spike buck can grow antlers with eight or more points if he is given the time to mature.

practiced deer management for twelve consecutive years on our lands. What we have learned about our general deer management goals, particularly our buck control objectives, has been both unexpected and gratifying.

When we first began our deer management, we thought it was absolutely necessary not to shoot our button or yearling bucks. We firmly believed that by adhering to this practice we would create better opportunities for these bucks to remain on our land and become our mature 3½-year-old or older whitetail bucks. After several years, I came to the conclusion that no matter how well we managed our land, the practicality of producing and holding mature bucks on a year-round basis on 192 to 432 acres is impractical and caused me to consider if achieving our goal was even possible.

It also doesn't help us achieve our management goals when a majority of our neighbors, including those who border our land, are not likeminded. Some are downright unfriendly about our planting practices and eight-point antler restriction program. This surly attitude holds true, despite many neighbors reluctantly admitting that their overall hunting experiences have changed for the better since we began practicing deer management.

There is no doubt that our overall hunting experiences have improved tremendously from when we first bought the land. During the past twelve years, many of my surrounding landowners have had opportunities to harvest mature bucks. This single fact helps me continue with our deer management plan, even though others who disagree with it and refuse to partake in a similar practice benefit equally from our hard work and dedication.

Deer management is a key reason to understand YBD.

There are many biologists who believe YBD is chiefly caused by social forces of female deer. Studies have suggested that the mother of a young buck, as well as other related adult females within her group, will constantly harass yearling bucks. The purpose of these does' continual aggression is purely instinctive and is designed by Mother Nature to prevent inbreeding through dispersal.

This aggressive behavior causes young bucks to seek more peaceful areas in which to live. This theory suggests that if adult females cause dispersal, the increased harvest of does will lower YBD rates. Other studies suggest that breeding competition among bucks is the chief cause of YBD. If so, another hypothesis is that an increase in the buck age structure might reduce yearling buck participation in breeding and therefore reduce YBD. Confused yet? Don't be. As I said earlier, there are many varying opinions as to why ABD and YBD take place. Just understanding a little about why they occur will help your deer hunting and any deer management program in which you become involved.

HUNTING
TACTICS

———

Chapter Five

How to Make a Mock Rub and Score

In 1988, I accidentally discovered the effectiveness of luring in a buck by making a fake buck rub. It happened a few years after our outdoor television program, *Woods N' Water Big Game Adventures*, launched nationally on a network called TEMPO (the Outdoor Channel of its time).

I considered taping a deer hunting segment on a 16,000-acre tract of private land called Sterling Forest in southern Orange County, New York. The property was covered with steep mountains, cliffs, and ledges and was as wild and breathtaking as any place I had hunted. Sterling Forest allowed hunting and fishing as long as you purchased a rather expensive seasonal permit, which was the prime reason few people hunted there at the time. Sterling Forest in those days was as pristine as the Adirondack Mountains. The land was a first-rate place to hunt for whitetails, bear, turkey, and other game.

After a few early scouting trips in late September, I selected an area to hang my tree stand. The bow season opened in mid-October, and after several weeks of hunting the stand I had seen plenty of does but I only saw several immature bucks with antlers ranging from spikes to six-points. I decided to change the stand's location before the firearm season opened. I placed it just off the top of a ridge that overlooked a deep, narrow draw that was a natural funnel. It was definitely a hot spot, and I probably missed seeing it during the entire bow season because it was hidden from view during my scouting trip by the dense leaves and vegetation. Not

In 1985, Woods N'Water *was featured on the front cover of the TV guide of a large New York newspaper, the* Times Herald Record.

only was the end of the draw close to my stand, I also had a view of the ridgetop's plateau, which was covered with white oak trees with leaves that had begun to fall as the firearm season approached. I hunted the stand about every third morning before I went to work.

A few days after the opening morning of the firearm season in November, I got started later than usual. I left the main hiking trail at my usual spot and walked roughly halfway through the woods toward my stand, which was about three hundred yards from the trail. I spotted a good buck about one hundred yards in front of me. I watched the buck for several minutes as he contently fed on white acorns and slowly made his way from the top of the draw toward the plateau. However, he was walking through a tangle of second growth of young oak trees that prevented me taking a shot at him. He passed within forty or fifty yards of my tree stand. The combined excitement of seeing the buck so close to the stand and the fact that he was a 135- to 140-class ten-point buck sent my anticipation levels soaring. Rather than risk spooking the buck, I decided to hunt him another morning. I quietly backed out of the area and went to work.

Two days later, I was in my stand long before light. Shortly after daybreak, I was about to make a few soft grunt calls when I heard hunters noisily walking down the trail, talking and snapping twigs underfoot as they made their way to their respective tree stands. I could clearly hear their footfalls as they passed by the spot where I left the main trail and continued on until I couldn't hear them any longer. Several more times on my morning post I could hear them, from the moment they noisily shut the truck's doors and began walking along the hiking trail, which was a considerable distance from me.

The next time I hunted the area, I was walking along the main trail just before dawn, when I rounded a turn and saw the hunters just ahead of me. I was still a couple hundred yards from where I departed the trail and was surprised that they actually arrived earlier than I did. I decided it would be wise to stop and let them get a good distance from me before moving on. Just as I leaned on a tree along the trail, one of the two saw me. They both stopped and looked back at me as I pretended to fix my daypack. I was sure they thought I was going to leave the main trail where I was and head to my tree stand. To stall and hopefully give them the opportunity to keep moving, I continued to fiddle with my pack.

Before going on with this story I have to explain a point. What I'm about to write isn't meant to sound self-important, or, worse yet, bigheaded or conceited. I assure you that the only reason I'm mentioning it is to give you some background about this particular incident. In 1988, I had been hosting my television show for several years. *Woods N' Water* was one of a handful of nationally aired hunting television shows at that time. Four years prior to that, it was the only big game hunting program that aired on Time Warner Cable locally throughout several southern counties of New York and New Jersey.

Because of my television program, I was seen as somewhat of a local celebrity. The notoriety brought with it both benefits and disadvantages. One of the latter was that it added competition to the places I hunted. If my truck was in an area I was hunting, especially if it was a new spot, the next time I hunted there I would often find other hunters' vehicles parked there as well.

Peter Fiduccia prepares another episode of "Woods and Waters" for Group W Cable in Warwick.   Record photo by Eleanor Martin

The ins and outs of local TV shows

By ELEANOR MARTIN

Spotlight on cable TV

WARWICK — "Eww-w-w. What's in that truck?" Office workers at the Warwick Group W Cable Television Station ran to the window.

Six deer seemed to be gazing at them from the back of a pickup truck.

It was Peter Fiduccia arriving at the station for the taping an episode of "Woods and Waters," his outdoor show for hunters, fishermen and nature-lovers that is televised Monday and Thursday at 6:30 p.m.

"I've got to borrow some jumper-cables," he said. "Truck didn't start too well this morning. We'll get out there and I won't be able to get back."

Kevin Nelson, who is the show's producer, director, editor and cameraman, also served as a cable procurer on this bright fall morning, and soon they were off, a pickup truck loaded with six mounted deer heads and a van with Group W Cable emblazoned on its sides. Inside was all the equipment Nelson would need, a camera and three bags containing sound equipment and extra tapes.

"Working at a small station is fun," said Nelson, as he bounced behind the steering wheel over the back roads of southern Orange County. "You can be creative. It's a real training ground."

Nelson, 27, has been the Warwick cable TV station's cameraman for almost a year. He says he was "really lucky" to get the post after 10 months of job-hunting in the television field. "Guys like me are a dime a dozen."

Nelson majored in communications at Ramapo College after he'd spent four years in the Navy. He says he's a little behind in his climb up the career ladder because of those years in service, but he also says he "really knows" what he wants to do.

At a big network television station he'd

get paid four times what he gets here, he said. But he'd be "stuck doing one thing — like audio, just audio all the time."

Instead, Nelson gets to shoot such programs as Fiduccia's "Wind and Water," plus local high school football games, a half-hour of daily news, and commercials. "You can really be creative with commercials," he said. "Most advertisers around here have no experience producing for television. They're eager to use my suggestions."

Colleagues and friends

Nelson suggested that the outdoor show should be shot outdoors, where the inexperienced Fiduccia would be more comfortable, than in the studio, where he did a lot of stumbling over his words. After taping and editing five shows the two men have become friends — a working team that produces surprisingly polished programs using only a shoulder-balanced camera and Fiduccia's enthusiasm for his subject.

In proposing the show to station manager Tom Halsey, Fiduccia took advantage of a little-known proviso in most cable TV franchise agreements with the towns they serve that they must provide public access to any member of the community who can come up with a reasonable, workable program of local interest.

Group W's franchise covers 10 towns in southern Orange County and northern New Jersey. It has 11,300 subscribers who get their local programs on Channel 12.

Judy Lekoski, Channel 12's nightly news

anchorwoman for the past three years, gave her last news broadcast from Warwick in the fall. She said she'd learned all she could at the tiny station and that there was no place for her to go but away. At 27, she was getting ready to move into network news broadcasting, where she could see a future for herself. When last heard from before Christmas, she was still looking in a tough field where searchers outnumber the jobs.

She said cable television has the potential for creativity and innovation in local broadcasting, but she doubted it would ever realize that potential.

"There's not much commitment to local broadcasting," Ms. Lekoski said. "Most cable stations are run by businessmen. That's the way cable began. If you get a manager who's really interested in local programming, you can do anything. It depends upon the people."

The best local news programming in cablevision, she said, is in remote areas far from big cities. But Warwick, she said, is too close to New York City.

Halsey, who has a dual post as station manager and advertising manager, said the Warwick station has always had a commitment to local programming. Such a commitment originated with its founder, Ed Klein, who also owned a local newspaper and radio station.

Local access, said Halsey, is divided into two parts. For educational and governmental access, the station is not allowed to charge a fee. For public access, it may charge, either for use of the studio and equipment if someone wants to produce the show at the studio, or for the expenses connected with showing a tape produced elsewhere.

Broadcasting is expensive, even on a small basis, Halsey said. "A single camera costs from $7,000 to $9,000. Tapes are $20

(Continued on page 45)

A television program about hunting big game was so unique in the early eighties that major newspapers carried featured articles about Woods N' Water. The stories appeared in papers across New York including the Times Herald Record, The New York Times, *the* Daily News, *the* Post, *and others. The exposure attached a small degree of "celebrity" to me.*

So when the two hunters saw me, to my disappointment, they turned and walked back toward me. I continued adjusting my gear as they reached me. They nodded hello and one of them said, "Hey, how ya doing? Have you seen any good bucks in the area?"

I thought for a second and replied, "Yes, I've seen a few bucks during the bow season. How about you guys?"

"We haven't had much luck in the spot we're hunting, so we thought we'd move to where we found a tree stand below a ridge yesterday afternoon."

"Oh," I said, "I hope you have better luck hunting the stand than I did."

I suspected they knew it was my tree stand. My name was printed in large letters on the underside of the wooden footrest. I knew at least one of them was planning to hunt from the stand, and the other guy would probably be close.

Then, one of the dynamic duo asked, "Where have you been seeing the bucks?"

I knew my choices were limited. Either I had to tell them the truth or I could tell them a half-truth. I quickly opted for the fib. "Well, after several hunts from my stand that you found off the ridge. . ." (I wanted to make that point clear.) ". . . I only saw several young bucks." But the other day I saw a real good buck from a different stand I was heading to this morning. It's not far from here. He's a definite keeper!"

"Wow, no kidding. Really?" they asked.

"Yup," I replied.

Then, the taller and older looking one of the two said, "Well, good luck. I hope you get 'im."

Then, without further conversation or explanation, instead of turning back toward the direction they just came from, they walked past me and back along the main trail as if they were heading out. After seventy-five yards or so, I heard them crunching leaves as they both entered the woods on either side of the trail. I thought, "Wow! That takes some nerve." I figured they were going to use me to drive deer to them as I walked to my stand. I smiled and actually whispered to myself, "I've got a game plan for you guys."

Unfortunately, that morning I had to hunt from the area where I met the other hunters. I wanted to make sure they thought that was the location where I saw the big buck. I spent the morning watching several does and a few turkeys eating acorns. Around 9:30 a.m., I left. I purposely made just enough noise for them to hear that I was done hunting in the area and heading back toward my vehicle. I even kicked a few rocks along the trail to complete the pretense.

Photo Credit: Fiduccia Ent.

This is one of the several bogus buck rubs I made in an attempt to lure the hunters away from my area.

That night, I spent hours thinking how I could distract them from hunting at or near my ridge stand. Finally, I got an idea. Since my stand was off the left side of the trail, I would make one large fake buck rub and several smaller rubs to create a natural-looking rub line on the right. I planned for the decoy rub to be least five hundred yards from where I entered the woods to get to the ridge stand. As the hunters walked along the trail, they would see the big decoy rub and spot the line I made, all of which were meant to lead them in the opposite direction of where I was hunting. "This is a purely genius plan," I thought to myself.

Late the next day, I made the fake rubs around noon, when I was sure the pair was out of the woods. After creating the fake rub, I stepped back took several photos of the rubs I made and admired my handiwork. I had to admit, the rubs looked realistic enough to fool me. The next morning, I arrived early and hid in a thicket of laurels to wait for the duo come down the trail. I heard them approaching long before I saw them. When they reached the fake rub, they stopped on a dime.

I could hear the excitement in their voices as they whispered back and forth. When they spotted the second rub, which was about ten yards from the first, one of them instantly took off in that direction. When he found the third rub, he couldn't contain his excitement any longer and called to his buddy to look at it. After sighting the next, they began laughing and giggling. One of them walked back in the direction they had just come from, while the other walked along the rub line.

I almost laughed out loud. It took all my willpower to contain myself. "What a freakin' genius I am," I whispered to myself and quickly made my way to my stand even though it was after 7:30 a.m. I thought that even if my buck had already passed the area, he might come through later than usual. Or perhaps the two would-be buck killers might push something my way.

As it turned out, I didn't even see a deer that morning, never mind the ten-point buck. At about 10 a.m., I had to leave to go to work and planned to return to my stand around 2 p.m. for the evening post. I was walking down the trail when my heart skipped a beat and I almost vomited. There, along the trail, were the hunters. To add insult to injury, attached to one of my products, a Peter Fiduccia Lifetime Deer Drag, was the ten-point buck. "Holy $^&*!" I thought. "This can't be happening!"

Before either hunter even greeted me, the first words out of the taller one's mouth were, "How the hell did the big deer hunter miss those rubs along the trail this morning? You know what? We almost didn't go hunting this morning. On the way in, I saw a fresh rub off the trail and quickly set up my stand. Around 8:30, this bad boy came sneaking along the rub line and stopped to freshen up the last rub. That's when I flipped the safety off and took my shot."

The second hunter said with a big grin, "Not a bad morning's hunt, huh? You gotta read fresh buck signs."

Holding back my frustration and tears, I managed to reply, "No, not a bad morning at all." I did my best to congratulate the hunters and offered to help drag the buck out—thankfully they declined. Despondently, and that's putting it mildly, I continued down the trail, ridiculing myself with cuss words that have yet to be invented. My self-deprecation ended with one last important question, "So your plan to trick the two hunters backfired, eh?"

This is the hunter who bagged the buck I was hunting. The old adage what goes around comes around certainly applied to my premeditated Machiavellian plan. The face is blackened for obvious reasons.

Photo credit: Fiduccia Ent.

On the drive home, I kept envisioning the antlers on the dead buck. The fact that he was actually attracted to the fake rubs amazed me. I kept thinking about how I created an ass-kicking, buck-killing tactic that worked for the guys I was trying to deceive. How's that for turn-around-fair-play? From that day forward, I promised myself I would share each and every tactic I ever thought of, created, used, or read about with any and all deer hunters who cared to listen. Now, are you ready to listen and benefit from creating a mock rub to bag your next buck?

Since that unfortunate day during the firearm season in 1988, I have used my mock rub tactic successfully many times (I count that buck shot by the other hunter as one of my successes). Like any other deer hunting tactic, making a fake rub to lure in a buck doesn't work every time. However, it has worked often enough over the years for me to consider it a worthwhile skill. Mock rubs will work well for you once you decide to include them as one of your deer hunting strategies.

WHAT ARE RUBS?

A natural buck rub acts as a travel indicator. It clearly states the direction of both the day and evening travel patterns a buck is taking. Let's imagine you're hunting near the top of a ridge and above is a bedding area. Below are feeding sources, such as corn or soybean fields, apple orchards, etc. While walking up to the ridge, you happen to see a rub that is facing you. If you were to walk fifteen to twenty yards above that particular rub, turn around, and carefully look back down the ridge thirty to fifty yards to either side of the rub you found, you will discover more rubs on the opposite sides of the trees. What you have just found are the morning and evening travel routes of a buck moving to and from his bedding and feeding areas.

This might seem like it is an insignificant finding, but it isn't. The rubs unmistakably designate where you should set up for a morning or evening post, based on which side of the tree the rub is facing. The ability to recognize this buck sign will help you maximize your hunting time by setting up a stand along a trail that a buck will be using at a particular time of day.

Let's take a more serious look at what it takes to make a fake rub work to lure in deer, mainly bucks. First off, you have to accept that deer, particularly mature bucks and does, survive within their daily environment not through the power of intelligence, but from instinctive behaviors.

Photo Credit: Fiduccia Ent.

This rub faces a thick bedding area in our refuge. The opposite side of the sapling faces our food plots. Knowing the directions of the bedding and feeding areas, I knew that this rub was on the buck's evening travel corridor.

Deer do not have the capability to reason, accumulate brainpower, or store long-term memories. You must accept that deer are not smarter than you. They are simply much better than humans at surviving by using their extra-keen sensory abilities.

To be the best deer hunter you can be, you must believe in yourself and your deer hunting capabilities. I have written and talked about this point many times. The truth of the matter is that many of you are better deer hunters than you allow yourselves to believe. With that said, many hunters make basic mistakes that foil their deer season hopes. I will mention just one mistake that has more than likely kept many a deer hunter from killing a buck: texting on a cell phone while on stand. If you are guilty of this ridiculous error, you must read the chapter "STOP!" Every deer hunter, professionals included, makes mistakes during deer season. I know I have made enough mistakes in my forty-five years of hunting whitetails. The difference is that most professional hunters quickly learn from their mistakes and rarely repeat them. Keep your confidence level high, open your mind to new and varied tactics, and trust your gut decisions. You will increase your buck and doe hunting success beginning the next season.

MAKE IT NATURAL

Burn this next information into your memory about deer decoy tactics. When a hunter uses deer calls, scents, antler rattling, a full-size decoy, a natural deer tail, a mock rub, or a mock scrape, he or she is using a lure to attract a deer. As any angler knows, for a bass to strike a lure or trout to take a floating fly, the presentation must look, smell, and sound natural.

Photo Credit: Buck Stop Scents

When making a mock rub or scrape, one of the key scents to include is buck urine. As the rut progresses, I also like to add tarsal and other glandular scents when creating mock rubs or scrapes.

It is no different with deer. If you want a deer to respond to your decoy tactics enthusiastically, your presentations must be made to smell, look, and feel natural to them.

The deer's instincts must convey to the sensory portion of its brain that what it is interested in is safe to inspect. Deer don't investigate a decoy because they have the power of thought that says, "Hey, I think I'll check out that deer." Rather, they respond by what can be described as a compulsion, reflex, or urge, all of which are parts of its instinctive behaviors. It is these forces that drive deer to investigate many different elements in their surroundings. The only thing that stops a deer from investigating something they are interested in is if their combined senses set off an alarm.

If you want to put this logic to the test, take several apples and rub them hard with your hands. You want to make sure you get a lot of human scent on them. Then, place them on your lawn or somewhere easily accessible to deer where you can hide. Deer will approach them because of their visual attraction, but when they sense your odor, they will hesitate because they've encountered a sensory warning. After some time

has passed, however, and the deer don't smell, see, or hear danger, they will cautiously eat the apples. After a few days, place some apples on your lawn that you have not touched with your bare hands. As the deer approach the apples, begin talking and step into their line of sight. They won't wait to pick up your scent before they take off in high gear. They have received all the danger

Rubs represent many things to deer. A rubbed tree mostly functions as an olfactory scent marking post. They also serve as visual stimuli because bucks impulsively need to investigate rubs within their home range.

Photo Credit: Ted Rose

signals they need to run for safety. The point is that deer are inquisitive and will investigate anything that interests them as long as it smells, looks, and sounds natural.

Visual stimulation is what attracts or alerts deer about every element in their environment. For more than thirty years, I have attracted deer using a natural, sparingly scented deer tail attached to fifty yards of cord that is hung over a low branch twenty-eight inches or so off the ground. It has helped me not only kill whitetail bucks and does, but this tail has attracted a bull moose, elk, and other game.

Unfortunately, not enough is written or said about how eager deer are to react to visual stimulation. I can assure you, it is a powerful force in the world of the whitetail deer—more than most hunters believe. When used correctly, a visual decoy is one of the most effective tactics. Deer can be instinctively forced to investigate something they see when they really shouldn't. Therefore, a mock rub is one of the top visual stimuli to ignite this type of behavior. The buck is drawn to the decoy rub because his instincts communicate to him that it is natural looking and, therefore, can be safely investigated.

Hopefully by this point, you have picked up on the word natural. I emphasize it because when you make a mock rub, fake scrape, use any type of scents, rattling, deer calls, or decoys, you must create the entire illusion of whatever tactic you are using to encourage a deer to respond. The illusion includes sending the message to the deer that it is natural and safe to investigate. Trust me when I tell you that it was worth driving this point home. Making a mock rub is one of the best tactics a hunter can use to lure in even the most cunning buck to a gun or bow. In fact, it can be the one strategy that enables you to kill the buck of a lifetime.

When a buck, whether it is immature or an older animal, sees a freshly made natural rub, he instantly recognizes the highly visual object (deer can see rubs from long distances) as an olfactory sign. Deer are naturally and characteristically curious about rubs, and they have an inherent need to investigate them. The buck's senses tell him he must inspect and mark the rub with his scent to communicate his presence and status to other bucks and does within the area. As long as nothing happens to set off an alarm, he has practically no choice but to inspect the rub because his instincts are demanding he do so. Not a lot of deer hunting tactics work on such basic sensory and instinctive levels.

I should mention here that mock scrapes are excellent decoys, too. However, when a buck responds to a natural or fake scrape, he does so with some degree of caution. He knows other bucks may be lurking in nearby cover, often closely watching primary scrapes. So mock rubs generate more response than mock scrapes do, but both are effective tactics when used correctly.

DO BIG BUCKS MAKE BIG RUBS?

There has been a lot said about the age class and antler size of a buck that makes a large rub on an equally large tree. Mature bucks make big rubs. Small bucks make small rubs. While those statements are mostly true, they aren't always the case. I have seen and recorded on video many large-antlered bucks rubbing sapling trees and many small-antlered deer, even four-points and spikes, rubbing large trees. I mention this only to make a point—almost nothing about a whitetail's behavior is written in stone. That is worth remembering in any whitetail hunting you do.

Researchers have documented that many 3½-year-old and older bucks often rub small saplings. Many start this during the first stages of the pre-rut, which is usually around October 10th, give or take several days.

Photo Credit: Ted Rose

This adult buck blows away the myth that big-antlered deer always rub big trees and small-antlered deer rub small trees. As I have stated many times, nothing about deer hunting is written in stone.

Most times, a rub can provide more information about buck's age class, body size, and the antlers than a buck scrape can. When you find larger than normal false and secondary scrapes, it isn't indicative that one mature buck made them all. A large scrape may only mean that several bucks attended it and pawed it into its ever-widening size. The old belief that only one buck makes a rub and scrape and uses them is an absolute

Genuine dominant conduct occurs within certain species of animals. It is designed to allow only the alpha male to mate with females. If a lower-ranking male, even if it is the second-raking beta animal, breaks the rule, the reaction by the alpha male is swift, harsh, and sometimes violent enough to cause severe injury or death. This behavior does not exist in the world of the whitetail deer.

fairy tale. Rubs and scrapes are olfactory and visual signs in the world of a deer. As such, they are often used by several bucks and sometimes does within a given herd.

Most pre-rut rubbing is carried out by what many biologists and hunters refer to as dominant bucks. I would like to clarify that definition. There is no such animal as the dominant buck. Not in the true sense of the meaning of dominance in the whitetail's world, anyway. True dominance is found in animal groups like wolves (canines), lions (felines), and other animals that urine-mark the borders of their territory. If another of their species trespasses on the area marked as their turf, they immediately react by physically engaging the violator, many times with enough prejudice to kill the intruder. If the transgressor is not killed, he is severely beaten up and chased until he departs across the scent line that marks the dominant animal's territory. This is a more accurate way of describing dominance among animals.

Since the early 1980s, when I began taping the behavior of whitetails, I have recorded dozens of scenes where young bucks are breeding does directly in view of older bucks. In a world of true dominance, this is simply not allowed to take place. The dominant animal would knock

Wolves and other canines display genuine dominance. Like this coyote, canines urinate along a defined border to establish clear olfactory territorial boundaries that warn potential intruders to trespass at their own risk.

the snot out of any other male that threatened his rank and, subsequently, breeding status. Have you ever seen what happens to a beta or even lower-ranking gorilla, wolf, or lion when he tries to mate with a female? The dominant animal teaches him lessons he won't soon forget. Take the word dominance out of your whitetail vocabulary and replace it with the more accurate terms of pecking order, social hierarchy, current rank or status, or the top rung on the ladder of clout.

According to researchers, when the rut begins, high-ranking (note that I didn't say dominant) bucks make fewer rubs and concentrate more on making and attending secondary and primary scrapes and licking sticks and overhanging branches. Researchers discovered that the intensity and seasonal pattern of rubbing often reflects the age class and social hierarchy among bucks of a given herd. Biologists also say that the amount of rubs in the early fall, for example, reveals the presence of one or more older bucks that rank high in the pecking order. Seeing signs in an area that has many rubs does not necessarily mean they were made by a lot of different bucks.

KEY FACTORS ABOUT MOCK RUBS

So by now you're saying, "Alright already, tell me how to make a false rub." Here we go. When making a mock rub, it helps to create the complete illusion if you make it near a natural rub. The natural rub can be recently made or even one that was made last season. Bucks have favorite trees and areas they regularly use to make rubs. So even if the rub is an old one, you can make your mock rub near it. Once you locate a natural rub, walk about thirty yards and select a tree similar in circumference and height.

You do this for two reasons, the first being to make your mock rub look as similar to the natural rub as possible. Second, you never want to create a rub that appears to be made by the biggest buck in the woods. As with all hunting tactics, make them smell, look, and sound as if they were from a younger, submissive buck. You will have more response if you do.

Yes, I know, you have read and heard that to draw in the top-ranking buck, you must attract him by making yourself sound aggressive. That is total nonsense. Even the most aggressive buck that occupies the highest place in the pecking order doesn't want to get an unnecessary injury in an altercation with a bigger buck. It is natural behavior for bucks to

*When you discover a natural rub, make sure your fake
rub matches its length, height, and is placed on a tree of a
similar size.*

Photo Credit: Fiduccia Ent.

avoid harm as much as possible. So, they are more inclined to respond
to something that looks or sounds like they can chase it off with body
language rather than risk a physical altercation. Most fights that end
with one or both bucks seriously injured or dead happen when one
adult transient buck from a different home range is found trespassing
by a resident adult buck. Your mock rub must not suggest to a buck, no
matter how large its antlers are, that it was made by a bigger and more
aggressive deer.

As I have said, bucks will establish their pecking order while they
are in bachelor groups long before they shed the velvet from their antlers. By fall, prior to the rut, they establish which buck is, for the time
being, sitting at the top of the hierarchy and which occupies the bottom. Pushing and shoving matches (and even more serious fighting) only

occur between rivals in the group closely matched in body weight, antler size, and age. Therefore a 2½-year-old buck will seldom pick a fight with a 4½-year-old buck, especially one he knows from his bachelor group. He realizes the fight might injure him and avoids the conflict instead of risking a serious wound.

A natural buck rub and mock rub act in the same way to any buck you are trying to lure. The natural rub's mere presence and odor tells another buck about the potential size and status of the buck that made it. Therefore, when a buck sees a rub that is substantially larger than the surrounding rubs, he is immediately put off by its size and becomes cautious about investigating it. He will avoid it rather than be attracted to it.

When making a mock rub, it is not possible to include all the scents a buck deposits on a natural rub, but using what scents are available commercially will work well to lure a buck. However, the scents should be used in moderation to make their odors smell as natural as possible. Using too much of any scent will lessen your chances of success. When you are ready to make your first mock rub, you will need several products and tools.

MOCK RUB TOOLS

Commercial Deer Scents: One bottle each of plain buck urine, tarsal scent, interdigital scent, forehead gland scent, and All-Season Deer Lure, which is a combination of hide and body odors of deer.

Gloves: A few pairs of thin gloves, such as the kind doctors wear. Latex or similar gloves will help avoid leaving too much human odor at the mock rub tree site. Eliminating all human odors is impossible, so don't go crazy trying to.

Zip-Top Plastic Bag: A medium-sized zip-top bag. Use it to carry several large bore cleaning patches for applying the scents.

Natural Deer Antler: One small natural deer antler that has six to eight tines, including the brow tine. The newer the antler is, the better.

Handsaw: In lieu of a deer antler, use a small folding handsaw.

Nail Punch: If you use a handsaw to make your rub, you will need a nail punch with a flat tip and a small hammer.

Measuring Tape: A small six-foot measuring tape, which you can sometimes find in a dollar store or hardware store.

Pencil and Paper: A pad and pencil to jot down the length of your mock rub. This is a critical aspect to the success of your mock rub tactic. Don't forget it.

CREATE THE ILLUSION

When you are in the woods and ready to begin, take your tape and measure the size of the natural rub from top to bottom on the tree. Write the measurement down. Do not try to record it by memory. I will explain why soon. If you forgot paper and a pencil, you can use your cell phone.

It is important to note that I have gotten a slightly better response by creating a false rub when it's near a natural rub, but it isn't always necessary to do so. I have had nearly as much success by making a mock rub without placing it near a natural one, as demonstrated by the anecdote at the start of this chapter.

Make your mock rub two or three inches smaller than the real rub. Remember, you are creating an illusion that the buck that made the rub is lower in the pecking order than the buck that made the real rub. You don't want your mock rub to look like it was made by the King Kong of deer, right? Its length, shape, and trunk

After finding this fresh rub, I created a mock rub about thirty yards away from it. Two days later, I shot a nice eight-point buck as he investigated the bogus rub.

Photo Credit: Fiduccia Ent.

size should suggest that it was made by another buck that can be easily intimidated.

Once you select a tree for your mock rub, you can use either a small folding handsaw or a natural antler. I prefer to use a natural antler, as I'm a big fan of creating the most natural replication possible. There have been times, however, that I have used either a handsaw or synthetic antler to make a false rub. The natural antler, though, adds an element of realism by leaving the scent of bone on the tree, no matter how dissipated it might be, which is detectible to deer.

If you're creating the mock rub next to a natural one, be careful not to rub so vigorously that you exceed the height of the latter. If you are creating the illusion without a natural rub nearby, contain your eagerness so you don't make your fake rub too large. Using a natural antler requires more elbow grease than a handsaw. Press the antler firmly against the bark and begin to make forceful up and down strokes. It takes a little practice to learn how to peel the bark off, but after a few rehearsals you will learn to do it so it looks natural. Make your mock rub face in the same direction of the natural one. Don't remove any peeling bark. Let it hang or fall naturally while you are rubbing the antlers on the tree.

If you use a small handsaw, its teeth should be fine. Large teeth are too destructive and will make the rub look unnatural. After the rub is made with a saw, use a fresh natural antler to rub up and down the tree trunk. It will leave the scent of bone to make the rub more inviting to a buck. Remember, do not rub all around the trunk of the tree, stick to one side.

Once your mock rub is finished, step back and see if it compares closely to the length, shape, and size of the natural rub. If so, go to the next step. If not, make any necessary adjustments before continuing. A key point is to make sure your rub is slightly shorter in length than the natural rub.

Take the antler and press a single tine point into the trunk just forcefully enough to create a small dent in a few places high and low within the rub, as well as a few in the bark above the rub. This duplicates the penetration made by the rack of a buck as he rubs a tree. If you don't have an antler to do this with, use your small nail punch. With the hammer, gently tap the nail punch to make indentations to simulate an antler tine. If you used a handsaw, use a flat-tipped nail punch.

Now take commercially made forehead scent and place several drops on a clean bore cleaning patch. Rub the patch along the entire portion of the rub. Put a couple drops of All-Season Deer Lure on another clean patch and dab it along the sides of the rub. At the base of the tree, squirt several drops of pure buck urine. Then add a single drop of interdigital scent. Those of you who think more than one drop will work better will find out the hard way that it won't. The buck will avoid excess interdigital scent. Then put down a couple of drops of tarsal scent around the tree. Two drops will do nicely, but more won't.

Walk back from your mock rub about ten yards and place ten to fifteen drops or a few good squirts of the buck urine on the forest floor. Make it spray, as a buck would, in several directions but not all over the place. A doe would urinate in a single spot, but a buck's man part will dangle from side to side while urinating and dribble urine in a wider pattern. Be sure the urine pattern is in line with the way the rub is facing. Create the entire illusion.

You have completed your mock rub. Now waste no time in setting up your tree stand or ground blind. The first buck to happen through the area will see and smell the rub and have no choice but to check it out. Unless he catches wind of you, sees, or hears you, he will go toward the mock rub, stop, stare at it, smell the buck urine, and then urinate over it or close by and move to the rub. He will go through all the traditional sniffing, licking, and rubbing behaviors in an attempt to discover which buck made the rub and let him know who is refreshing it.

Photo Credit: Ted Rose

Note there are two other rubs near the large fresh rub. A buck will often bed close to a big rub whether he made it or not.

To be perfectly clear, this tactic doesn't work all the time, but it does work enough of the time to be high on my list of strategies. My records also indicate the most successful dates are from October 31st through November 13th. But I have had success with this tactic through the third week of November and occasionally during the post-rut of December. Like all tactics, it has its moments of huge success and days of no response at all. You can also use deer calls like soft grunting or an estrus doe blat in hopes that a buck you call sees your mock rub. Rattling also works but not as often as deer calls.

No matter what strategy you decide to use, be it a sit and wait ambush, deer calls, rattling, or a combination thereof, when a buck responds to your mock rub it will feel like your heart is about to pound out of your chest. The excitement is that intense—I promise you.

MOCK RUB FOLLOW UP

If after two or three days you don't see a buck, it is time to reevaluate the spot. This is where your tape measure and the measurement you wrote down come in handy. You did jot it down, right? After three days without anything happening, measure your rub. If it is the same length you made it—what was that number again? Wait–let me check my paper. Oh, 13¾ inches and it is still that size. If that's the case, it is time to move on and try the tactic someplace else. Eventually it will work.

If your 13¾-inch rub has turned into 15¼ inches, you will know the rub was indeed visited, but not when you were there. You can spend another day over it. If you had been hunting during the morning and afternoon posts, try hunting it during the off-hours of 10 a.m. to 2 p.m. If it doesn't produce, move to another location at least two hundred yards away.

Now you have one of my better and more successful strategies. This tactic has proven to work best by creating all the elements I mentioned above. It is important, however, that I tell you I have made mock rubs while hunting without all the scents and other items I mentioned. On a few occasions, I have come across a large fresh rub and made a mock one with nothing more than my handsaw and some buck urine with reasonable response. That said, you will get the best response when you create the entire illusion.

If possible, use a leaf blower to clear a trail. It will make the job quicker and easier.

Chapter Six

Blow and Rake to Bag Your Buck

In 1964, I developed my first deer hunting strategy during a frustrating but illuminating hunt. I was hunting on lumber company property (International Paper Company) in the Adirondack Mountains of New York. During a scouting trip the day before the opening of deer season, I found an area with a fresh rub line that was in a thicket overlooking two heavily used, intersecting deer trails. That evening I sat in the blind to see if any bucks passed by.

As luck would have it, around 4:15 p.m. I caught sight of a racked buck with his nose tightly pressed to the ground heading along one of the deer paths. He passed within fifty yards of my blind and was totally unaware of my presence. I watched him trot along the trail until he disappeared into a thick stand of evergreens.

This buck closely resembles the buck I saw and what he was doing during my evening hunt in the Adirondacks.

Excitedly, I left the blind as quietly as I could. As I walked, I marked the trail on the way to my vehicle to help me reach the blind without getting turned around the next morning.

Long before daylight on opening day, I headed into the woods in total darkness. The temperatures had plummeted overnight and there was a hard frost on the ground. As I picked my way along the trail, the frost made my every step sound like a freight train. On top of that, I realized it was unusually dark for that time of morning.

I decided to stop where I was and wait until the first rays of dawn provided enough light for me to see what was underfoot. I hoped my plan would prevent me from making any further crunching noises by stepping on frost-covered leaves and other debris. At the first hint of dawn, I moved toward the blind. After carefully picking my way along, I saw my double marker, which indicated the blind was close—no more than thirty or forty yards from me. I continued heading slowly in the blind's direction, but when I reached the halfway point, I stepped on a dead twig that broke louder than a snapping turtle's mouth slamming shut. I froze in place, but not before hearing a series of alarm-distress snorts (which are discussed later) and seeing an antlered buck bolt for cover.

Totally frustrated, I sat in the blind watching and hoping either another buck would walk down the trail or the first would return. I spent the time thinking of what I could do to avoid getting to a stand without making noise from stepping on frosted leaves or, for that matter, accidently snapping a twig or kicking a rock in the dark in good weather conditions. Then I had an epiphany. I thought to myself, "Why not rake a trail from an entry point all the way to the stand?" By removing all leaves and other debris, including twigs, branches, and loose rocks, I would be able to get to any stand quietly. It would also make it easier to find the stand even in the darkest of situations.

The problem would be that the trail must be cleared completely, from entry point to the stand, no matter how long it might be. Another problem would be if I was hunting public land, a cleanly raked forest trail would probably be seen and used by other hunters. But if I got there before anyone else, my raked trail theory would work to get me to the stand as quietly as a church mouse. I decided raking a trail would be worth the risk.

By 9 a.m. on opening morning, I was in the Tupper Lake hardware store picking out a heavy-duty leaf rake. Minutes later, I was driving the thirty miles back to the International Paper Company land in Childwold. At 10 a.m., I was raking a trail from where I parked my vehicle to my ground blind. I finished the task at about noon and went back to the vehicle to change my clothes and eat lunch. I was comfortably tucked in my stand by 1:30 p.m. The evening post resulted in seeing several does.

The next morning, I made my way quickly and quietly along the trail and settled into the blind before dawn. About an hour later, I heard the unmistakable sound of deer hooves crunching leaves. Within moments, several does accompanied by a six-point buck ambled down the deer trail. I put the scope on the buck and squeezed off a shot. To my surprise, the buck whirled and ran off into the surrounding cover. I searched the area for more than two hours before coming to the realization that I had missed the buck cleanly. For the record, this was my first year of deer hunting and the first buck at which I had ever taken a shot. I was overwhelmed with disappointment.

My only consolation was that my first deer hunting strategy worked and, as far as I was concerned, it was totally responsible for me getting to my stand without making enough noise to spook deer. Seeing the does and the six-point buck walk calmly along the trail that morning enlightened me. I was absolutely hooked and completely believed that raking trails to stands would benefit me in taking bucks for many years to come.

Over the next several years, this tactic proved to be the primary reason I was able to kill many bucks. Over the past five decades, creating debris-free trails to my stands has helped me sneak quietly into places that deer feed and bed. It has even allowed me to penetrate buck core areas without my approach being revealed by the crunching of fall leaves or inadvertent snapping of an unseen twig or dead branch. This is especially true in the darkness before dawn and, more importantly, when I change stands to take advantage of hunting between 10 a.m. and 2 p.m, which I refer to as off-hours. This one tactic has improved my sightings of deer tremendously over the years and helped me kill bucks and does that I would have otherwise spooked long before I saw them.

Since those early days of raking trails, my tactic has undergone some technological changes. Now, I use a heavy-duty leaf blower to remove most, if not all, of the leaves, small twigs, and other debris. I only use the rake to remove wet leaves, heavier branches, or remaining debris. I also carry heavy-duty pruning clips to cut away any annoying branches hanging over the trail that could catch on my clothing and make noise. I also remove the stems or branches of thorn bushes so I don't get stuck in the face or eyes as I walk to my stand in the dark. Pruners also come in handy to cut those aggravating tree roots waiting to reach out and grab your feet, sending you tumbling to the ground. So, while I have added some tools in addition to my leaf rake, they have all helped to improve my strategy over the years.

Using a leaf blower makes the job go more quickly and easily. It can be done along or as seen here, with friends. We like to rake our trails soon after all the leaves have fallen. Quiet trails significantly increase sightings and kill ratios. The key is to keep conversations to a bare minimum. Adult bucks will tolerate the sounds from the blower and raking but not the sounds of human voices.

There are other benefits of raking trails to your stands that can prove to be worthwhile. How many times have you gone to a stand you are familiar with, only to discover that it has seemingly disappeared? Though most of us immediately get the sinking feeling that it has been stolen, you eventually find it, but not before you have wandered around and crunched many more leaves, twigs, or frozen snow.

You've not only made additional noise trying to find the stand, but you have also wasted valuable hunting time. Add to this equation the fact that if the stand is on a mountainside or in thick cover, you sweat up a storm as you look for it. All these elements, when combined, will result in a frustrating morning of hunting.

IWhile a gas-powered blower quickly removes leaves, a sturdy leaf rake removes twigs and branches to put the final touches on a trail, allowing for a quiet approach to your stand. From left to right, part of the Nerd Gang: Eric Schultz, P. Cody Fiduccia, and Dr. Victor Schultz.

Raked trails serve more functions than allowing a hunter to access his or her stand quietly and quickly. Interestingly, deer begin to use them within a half-day of being cleared. They will often follow the trail for its entire length before leaving it. Time and time again, I have witnessed this over the years I've been raking trails to stands.

I have also noticed that as soon as one deer uses the trail, other deer begin to use it, as well. Within a short period of time of raking a trail where no deer signs have appeared before, the area is soon covered with prints and dung. When I have raked in thick, overgrown areas where bucks like to hang out, I have discovered that there, too, the deer often prefer to use the raked path over their usual trail. I don't know exactly why they do this, but it could be because they realize it is quieter to walk along or it provides a path of least resistance. Either way, they like using the raked paths.

Of course, there are downsides to raking trails. They take time and work to create. A trail made over muddy or wet areas will on occasion freeze and make just as much noise as a debris-ridden trail when walked over. However, that scenario is rare and doesn't happen enough to preclude the use of this strategy.

If you hunt on public ground, a cleared trail can lead unwanted hunters to your stand. In the days when I hunted public areas exclusively, I prevented this from happening by taking advantage of the unsuspecting hunters. At the halfway point of my cleared trail, I would hang a large blaze orange ribbon on a tree branch. Then I would either use smaller blaze orange ribbons or luminescent thumbtacks to mark off a trail through the woods for one hundred yards or more. This trail, of course, was not raked. Hunters who saw the ribbon and other markers almost always assumed that the markers led to a tree stand or blind and continued along the marked but noisy trail.

Cleared trails also help the deer move along, reducing the sound of their approach almost entirely. Often, deer using a cleared trail seem to magically appear without any warning. Because of this, it is important when hunting along raked or blown trails to be extra diligent for any sign of movement and pay meticulous attention to the slightest sounds, or you will miss opportunities.

Of course, blown or raked trails work best on land you own or lease. Once you have tried this tactic, you will find it to be one of the most effective strategies you can use to get to your stand quickly and quietly. It can also help you get noiselessly to the edge of woods that overlook a food plot, apple orchard, cornfield, or soybean field. These are areas where a deer in a field can often pick up your noise as you approach. The act of clearing trails has proved to be a chore worth its weight in gold.

The key is not to think that any trail is too long to rake or blow, or it isn't worth taking the time to create. If you think this, you are thinking incorrectly. Clearing a trail of the debris that leads to a stand will improve your sightings and bag limit the very first season you try it.

Photo Credit: Fiduccia Ent.

Here are the tools needed for your trail raking task. Missing from this photo is a roll of evil blaze orange tape.

Tools Needed:

- Heavy-duty leaf rake
- Leaf blower
- Quality pruners
- Work gloves to prevent blisters when raking
- Daypack with water and snacks
- A roll of devious blaze orange tape—you know what for.

Chapter Seven

STOP!

There are many mistakes, big and small, all hunters make that end up limiting their chances to kill a buck, particularly an adult buck. The blunders include a wide array of slip ups, including ignoring scent control, choosing poor stand locations, not paying keen attention to wind currents, heavy footfalls, walking to and from a stand along the same trails every day, and, the most serious of offenses, not having the right mind-set during a hunt.

Wade Boggs shot this dandy buck while hunting with me in New York. Boggs hunts deer like he played baseball—with total concentration and dedication to the task at hand.

There are a lot of different phrases that can be used to refer to the correct mind-set. They include having your head screwed on right, being in the zone, keeping your eye on the prize, grabbing the brass ring, and staying at the top of your game. All these expressions refer to the participants paying total attention to the job at hand, particularly if they expect to be consistently successful at their sport (or anything else in life, for that matter).

For example, a professional athlete works diligently to stay on top of his or her profession. Only when some outside element affects their concentration does their performance level drop and ability to perform suffer. They are said to be in a slump. Actually, it would better be described as a loss of attention due to one or more external factors. They have lost focus on the job at hand due to an evident or not-so-obvious element.

A baseball player who steps up to the plate thinking about getting traded usually falls into a hitting slump. A football lineman thinking about something as mundane as his displeasure for cleaning his garage is asking for the opposing lineman to flatten him on the snap. Once, a professional bass angler I know had the worse season of his career because he was launching a new clothing line. In other words, there are many elements, both big and small, that can seriously change the outcome of an important personal event, from winning a tennis match to bagging a buck.

Success is basically a three-part head game that includes confidence in your abilities, concentration on the job at hand, and being aware of what is going on around you. When you put that recipe together, you have a formula for consistent success no matter what you are engaged in.

When it comes to deer hunting, there are too many external diversions that can wreak havoc in ending with a successful day afield. They range from being bored on stand and daydreaming to talking on two-way radios about unimportant hunting-related matters. Conversations between hunting companions should be limited to "I just fell out of my tree stand and can't get up," or "I just shot a buck and could use some help dragging it out."

However, with cell phone technology growing exponentially, unfortunately a new and devastatingly unconstructive distraction has snuck into the deer hunter's ability to concentrate on the job at hand, which is the taking of a buck or doe. By name, the culprit is texting. It has

Photo Credit: Fiduccia Ent.

When hunting our land, we only use Motorola two-way radios to communicate essential or urgent messages. Discussions about the temperature, how many deer were seen, and other trivial conversations are frowned upon.

curled its ugly electronic fingers around the necks of countless deer hunt-ers across North America, who are hell-bent on talking to their hunting companions about general conversation while posted on stand. Countless hunters, professional guides, and relatives I hunt with have done this over the past several years. They simply can't help themselves. Someone texts them and, like a buck responding to the sight of a new rub or scrape, they are instinctively drawn to reply.

What I have noticed about this behavior is that a hunter's addiction to texting causes them to totally deny the fact that staring down and read-ing a message on their cell phone and typing back a reply has damaging effects on their hunt. That type of denial is completely absurd. Of course

Photo Credit: Fiduccia Ent.

Texting on stand diverts a hunter's undivided attention from the job at hand—watching intently for deer. If you text on stand and do not see deer on a consistent basis, STOP!

it has an adverse effect on the hunt—it distracts the hunter from observing his or her surroundings.

It only takes a buck, specifically a mature buck, seconds to slip by a deer stand undetected while your head is down and you're reading or typing a message. As you're paying attention to a text, the buck you've been praying to see walked by your stand and was allowed to escape unnoticed because you thought it was more important to be texting on stand.

STOP the madness, please. STOP is the acronym I created. It stands for Stop Texting on Post. If you're dedicated to killing a buck year after year, you have to be in the game. You can't have distractions, however small, complicate your ability to bag a buck. I can personally guarantee that fact. In 1991, I was dealing with a problem that severely limited my ability to concentrate on hunting over two consecutive seasons. Not only did I fail to take a buck while hunting in my home state, on many hunts

A deer, especially a mature buck, can slip quietly by a deer stand faster than most hunters realize. STOP! Don't allow yourself to get distracted with sending texts on stand.

I never even saw a deer, never mind a buck. When I did see deer, I wasn't even expecting them.

Another interesting sidebar is that hunters who constantly text on stand are the same hunters who end up not seeing or bagging a buck over the hunting season and then complain about it. Yes, sometimes texting hunters are successful. These are usually men or women who hunt extreme backyard bucks or bucks that travel highly restricted corridors to go from bedding to feeding areas. They have no choice but to move on their very visible trails that make them accessible to even the most novice hunter. These hunters get away with texting because they would have to do an Irish jig on stand to miss these deer moving through. There are some other hunters who text that get lucky, as well. They finish texting, and when they look up they happen to catch a buck moving by their stand.

No matter what type of hunting you engage in, be it stalking, posting, driving, trailing, decoying, calling, or rattling, you will increase your success by tenfold by eliminating texting on your cell phone. You can take that advice to the deer hunting bank.

Photo credit Ted Rose.

Chapter Eight

Weather or Not

———

Hunters can control many elements that directly affect the success of their efforts to bag a whitetail buck, including personal scent control, accurate interpretation of deer signs, proper stand placement, a combination of hunting strategies, and even the discretion of taking or passing on a prospective buck. However, there remains one important factor that not even the most experienced buck hunter has any control over, and that's weather conditions.

Depending on where you hunt, your idea of perfect deer hunting weather can vary to some degree. In the Midwest, seasoned deer hunters tend to favor clear, crisp mornings in the upper 20s or 30s with a heavy frost on the ground at daybreak and temperatures warming to the mid-40s by noon. Out west on the High Plains, consistently successful whitetail hunters pray for a light snow, while in the South they tend to take what they can get and keep their fingers crossed that there isn't foul weather late in the season. In the Northeast and New England, hunters expect the weather to be anywhere from frigid to cold with just enough snow to make for perfect tracking conditions. But what about deer hunting when, in your mind, the weather is less than ideal?

Contrary to what some hunters read or are told by their older peers, hunting deer in foul weather can be unexpectedly productive. Of course, there are times when especially foul weather conditions dictate that any sensible hunter should sleep in. After more than five decades of experience stalking whitetails across North America, I have learned that when the weather turns sour, a hunter can still bag a dandy buck, even in heavy rain or snow.

Photo Credit: Ted Rose

Deer will continue to move in rain, snow, or even a mix of both weather conditions. Only the heaviest or most severe weather conditions will force deer to remain in their bedding areas.

After evaluating the records I keep, I've discovered that deer, especially mature whitetail bucks, will often move more in a heavy rain storm than during a clear, sunny day. I can assure you, I have seen more big bucks while hunting in dismal weather than I have during cloudless skies.

Exactly what do deer consider bad weather? Well, it covers a range of different conditions, such as ice storms, heavy prolonged rain, hard-blowing winds, excessively deep snowfalls, thick fog, long periods of extreme cold, and even extremely hot or arid temperatures. Each of these environmental circumstances acts as a trigger for different activity levels and responses from whitetails. The savvy deer stalker learns how to capitalize on each of these conditions and, by doing so, ends up with more success than his or her peers.

Except for the most extreme weather conditions, such as twenty-four- to forty-eight-hour snow blizzards, severe and long-lasting ice storms, or twenty-four-hour torrential downpours, deer generally don't bed down for long periods of time, contrary to what some old-timers say. By the way, at sixty-seven years of age, I guess I'm part of the old-timer fraternity now, so I can use that term freely.

The fact of the matter is that whitetails just can't stay holed up for extended periods of time without foraging for grub. They are ruminants and have four-chambered stomachs. Each of these stomach compartments is shaped differently, has a unique lining, and serves a different purpose in the digestion of the wide variety of forage and grasses consumed by whitetails. From the moment of ingestion and storage of the roughly chewed food in the first of these compartments, it takes approximately twenty-four to thirty-six hours for an adult whitetail deer to pass the food as scat. That being the case, it becomes clear that whitetails cannot stay bedded for much longer than that before they are instinctively compelled to get up and look for food in spite of foul weather.

I want to assure you that so-called bad weather conditions often end up giving an edge to deer hunters. For instance, many times during an especially windy day, I have used the gusts to cover my scent and footfalls, enabling me to sneak up undetected on deer that were bedded behind a windfall, in tall grass or thick laurels, or as they fed at the edges of fields or in the woods.

Photo Credit: Ted Rose

Two does moving about during a snow storm. Deer generally don't bed down in foul weather as much as hunters believe they do, unless the conditions become severe.

During times of foul weather, such as strong winds, heavy rain, or snow, whitetails lose their ability to detect danger, as their senses are not as acute as during calm weather. It becomes difficult for deer to pick up sounds and smells that could provide an early warning of an approaching predator or hunter. Gusty winds will also disperse scent molecules more quickly, which vastly reduces the effectiveness of a deer's olfactory abilities. The bottom line is that during inclement weather conditions, all three senses that deer depend on to avoid trouble—their sensitive sense of smell, acute hearing, and sharp eyesight—are all less effective, thereby giving an advantage to the hunter.

Photo Credit: Fiduccia Ent.

I tracked this buck along a ridgetop during the tail end of a snowstorm. I caught up with him on the backside of a steep mountain as he headed toward an apple orchard.

The quandary for most deer hunters is that they don't believe deer will move during inclement conditions and end up staying home instead of going hunting. This is most likely based on their own comfort levels— many hunters simply prefer not to hunt in heavy rain or deep snow. To be a consistently successful foul-weather whitetail hunter, you must motivate yourself to get up from a warm, dry bed and hunt in rain, wind, snow, fog, or other unpleasant situations. Sometimes, for all of us, this is easier said than done.

Without this type of self-determination, however, the hunt is over before it has even begun. Once you have made the choice to hunt during foul weather, you must also commit to being prepared mentally and physically to remain in the woods as long as you would if the weather were clear. Hunting during bad weather demands this type of strength of mind and body. The vocabulary of a consistently successful foul-weather hunter includes words such as determination, willpower, resolve, fortitude, grit, resilience, and, most of all, staying power. If hunters make a commitment to these descriptive adjectives, it will regularly pay off in big dividends.

This type of mental attitude was referred to in a formula I wrote in my first book, *Whitetail Strategies: A No-Nonsense Approach to Successful Deer Hunting*. It especially applies when hunting in foul weather.

CONCENTRATION + POSITIVE THINKING + CONFIDENCE = CONSISTENT SUCCESS!

This principle applies not only to deer hunting but also to life in general. I promise you, if you eliminate one element of this equation, you will seriously diminish your chances of being a consistently successful hunter. This is even more relevant when it comes to hunting in foul weather that can be wet, snowy, windy, and, the absolute worst (to me, anyway), bitter cold. Without adhering to these fundamental components, foul-weather hunting is an exercise in futility.

One of the most unusual behavioral traits I have noticed over the years that is brought on by foul weather is deer activity during times of the day when deer are not supposed to be moving, or what I refer to as off-hour travel patterns. While a majority of adult bucks will move less during dawn and dusk as hunting pressure increases, they will move more

Photo Credit: Fiduccia Ent.

Kate shot this doe in foul weather at 10:30 a.m. It rained heavily the first few hours of daylight, then it turned into a wet, heavy snowfall. With snow rapidly accumulating on her scope, Kate killed the doe as it meandered by her blind at thirty yards.

between the off-hours of 10 a.m. to 2 p.m. They will also travel just before or after a severe storm front is approaching during these hours. This is even more likely if extremely bad weather conditions have held the deer stationary for a long period of time.

While a wide variety of tactics will work, including deer calls and rattling during foul weather, stand and still hunting offer the best opportunities for tagging a buck in stormy weather. Another interesting point I have discovered about hunting in adverse weather is that you can't expect to see just a little movement here and there. During inclement weather, hunters can expect to see either a lot of deer or none at all. It's the old feast or famine analogy. If they are moving, however, you can bet they will move throughout the day. If, after a few hours on stand, you haven't seen a deer during stormy weather, it is time to leave your stand and start still-hunting. Stalking in heavy rain or fresh snow often provides the hunter with an excellent opportunity to slip up on a bedded buck or doe undetected while they are hunkered down trying to escape the unpleasant weather.

When the wind is howling at about forty-five to fifty-five miles per hour (these are known as strong and whole gale winds) and a storm has

Photo Credit: Ted Rose

During snow or rain, don't expect to see just a few deer moving. You will either see a lot of deer movement or none at all.

been raging for several hours, chances are that deer will remain bedded until the winds subside or hunger forces them to begin foraging. Winds that are less than forty-five miles per hour are ideal times for still-hunting. Concentrate on areas of heavy cover, such as big stands of overgrown evergreen trees, closely knit cedar thickets, dense patches of laurels, and blowdowns, or areas where the wind has knocked down trees. During these times, bucks will not bed in their usual fair-weather spots.

Time and time again, I have found that bucks will bed in only the densest of cover during heavy winds mixed with some other inclement weather. It is usually the most impenetrable cover they can find in the area you are hunting. Don't pass by standing fields of high grass or corn—bucks and does see these timber-free places as ideal hiding spots. I have kicked out many a good buck from a standing cornfield during inclement weather. Some I have been able to get a shot at, others were unintentionally moved to hunting buddies, and some remained bedded as I spotted them.

Remember, it takes more to stop a deer than what I refer to as a casual wind, or winds that blow between one and twenty-four miles per hour. Even stronger winds, from twenty-five to thirty-five miles per hour, will not put deer down and keep them there. As I mentioned previously, this is primarily attributable to the fact that two of the deer's strongest senses, hearing and smell, are significantly reduced during these conditions. Deer try to make up for this deficiency by relying on their other prime sense, sight. To do so, they must stay on the move and continuously scan their surroundings for danger. Even this becomes more difficult when everything in their environment is moving, snapping, and creaking from blowing winds. But it takes a lot of wind to keep deer down, often more than forty-five miles per hour. Sitting up in a stand on the fringe of heavy cover during very windy days often proves to be an effective hunting method.

In fair, inclement, and even stormy weather, I go deer hunting and recommend you do, too. This is especially important in states with short hunting seasons, such as New Jersey's one-week shotgun season. If you let a few days of bad weather keep you out of the woods during one of these short seasons, you could lose a major portion of your hunting time, odds of being successful, and, therefore, your opportunity to take a buck. Hunters wait about ten months to go hunting, so when the season arrives, don't let foul weather steal your time. Instead, go hunting, foul weather or not.

The most authoritative, informative, and well-written book I have read on this subject is *Trophy Bucks in Any Weather* by Dan Carlson, a former professional meteorologist and avid deer hunter. The book is published by Krause Publications, an imprint of F&W Publications. It has 271 pages of color images and is jam-packed with useful foul-weather tactics and general weather information you can use on your next deer hunt. I strongly recommend it.

Although hunting during such winds is not recommended or likely to be successful, this chart is provided to give you a clear comparison of wind speeds, designations, and descriptions.

The Beaufort Scale

Wind Speed (mph)	Designation	Description
13–18	Moderate breeze	Small branches move
19–24	Fresh breeze	Small trees sway
25–31	Strong breeze	Large branches move, wind whistles in wires
32–38	Moderate gale	Whole trees move, walking slightly affected
39–46	Fresh gale	Twigs break off trees, walking slightly difficult
47–54	Strong gale	Slight structural damage, high waves, branches break
55–63	Whole gale	Trees uprooted, considerable structural damage, very high waves with crest

The Beaufort Scale

Wind Speed (mph)	Designation	Description
64–74	Storm	Widespread damage, extremely high waves, sea covered with white foam patches
75+	Hurricane	Severe and extensive damage, visibility of sea greatly reduced

Source: *The Audubon Society's Field Guide to North American Weather* by David Ludlum

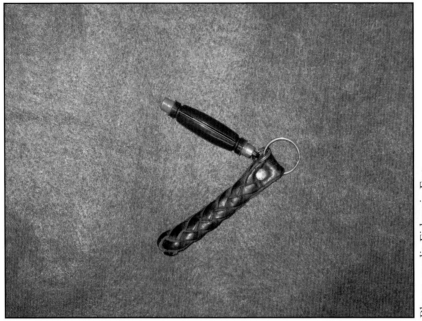

Photo credit Fiduccia Ent.

Chapter Nine

The Best Damn Call Ever: The Snort

———

Anyone who has successfully attracted a buck or doe by imitating any of the four primary deer vocalizations knows three things for sure. First, all the sounds that deer calls imitate work well to lure deer to the hunter's location. Second, when calls are made incorrectly, they can instantly spook deer, particularly mature bucks and does. Lastly, most deer calls, including the grunt, adult blat, and fawn bleat vocalizations, have smaller windows of opportunity during the season to coax deer into the gun or bow than a snort call.

While the primary grunt or any of its four sub-cadences can seem to work like magic during the rut, bucks are generally overly enthusiastic about responding to a grunt call for fewer than ten days of deer season. The fawn bleat is also an effective call, but it, too, has its time restraints in attracting bucks and does. While the adult blat and its varied sub-sounds will attract deer for most of the season, the sound falls short of generating consistent responses. There is one deer vocalization, however, that can be used the entire deer season. More importantly, deer have no choice but to respond to it every time it is used. The reason is that they have learned from the time they were fawns that if they ignore three of the four cadences of the primary snort, it could cost them dearly (sorry, I just had to write that).

Seriously though, deer have come to recognize that when they hear the sound of alarm, alarm–distress, or a snort-wheeze, there is a real and present danger nearby. From the crack of dawn on opening day to the last rays of legal light at season's end, all four cadences of the primary snort can be used anywhere in North America. This makes a snort

Deer instinctively respond to the snort vocalization. Does have taught fawns that the snort vocalizations can warn of immediate danger.

call the most useful and effective call a hunter can use during the entire deer season. There is no doubt a snort call will provide a hunter with an opportunity for an increased success ratio. Anyone dedicated to improving their deer hunting should never be in the field without a snort call hanging around their neck or kept in an accessible outer pocket. To do so would be a critical a miscalculation that will end in fewer opportunities to kill the buck of his or her dreams.

Lohman discontinued making the snort (and fawn bleat) calls. I am looking into manufacturing a snort call. Check www.deerdoctor.com for updates.

Regrettably, because a majority of hunters associate the sound of a snort with deer fleeing, the snort call is one of the most misunderstood and rarely used deer calls. Understandably, many have little faith that using a snort call can be an effective hunting tool, which is unfortunate because it simply isn't the case. Once you learn how to decode the meaning of each snort variation, you'll not only be surprised at how effective each cadence is, you will also increase your deer hunting success.

Photo Credit: Ted Rose

Many hunters find it difficult to get past the notion that a snort call frightens deer. Most believe if they use it, all they will see is the raised flag of a fleeing buck or doe. Unfortunately, that conviction is entirely incorrect.

VARIATIONS

There are five variations to the primary snort vocalization. Four can be used to attract, hold, stop, and even draw deer to a specific location. Some experts say there are six snort vocalizations, but I'll address that later. One of the most astonishing snort cadences can be used to intentionally frighten deer from areas where they are seeking security. I have accumulated more than four decades of experience using this particular variation of the primary snort. During this time, I have used this sub-vocalization to intentionally startle or frighten deer into involuntarily revealing themselves from a wide variety of cover including clusters of blowdowns, fields of standing corn, trenches in farm fields, ledges overlooking thickets of mountain laurel, swamps, thick stands of evergreens, and anywhere else a buck might conceal himself.

For many years, I have used the snort to intentionally frighten deer from secure cover. My favorite places to use it are standing cornfields, blowdowns, and in thick swamps.

I can say with extreme confidence that the alarm–distress cadence, when done correctly, is one of the most exciting, effective, and amazing deer calls you can add to your hunting tactics. This variation of the primary snort vocalization will definitely cause a buck or doe, no matter what type of area they are hiding in, to reveal themselves. They have no choice because they respond to this sound intuitively. This is especially true with mature bucks. It is common knowledge that adult bucks will hide in cover and hold tight as hunters pass within feet of where they are laying rather than risk abandoning the cover to run away.

In order of my preference and the call's effectiveness, the variations of the primary snort include:

1. The Alarm–Distress Snort
2. The Alarm Snort
3. The Social Snort
4. The Aggressive Snort

5.   The Snort-Wheeze
6.   The Snort-Grunt-Wheeze

Each of the variations to the primary snort, or any primary deer vocalization for that matter, communicates a specific meaning to other deer in different circumstances. That is why it is so important to learn each sub-sound and practice long before deer season begins. If you use the wrong cadence in a situation, the result will either be that the deer will ignore it, move away from it, or, in the worst-case scenario, flee. Here are the two best variations of the snort call. Learn these and you will have a greater chance for success this fall.

ALARM-DISTRESS SNORT

As I have said many times in magazine articles, on our television program, and at my seminars, the alarm-distress is by far my favorite deer call and preferred snort cadence. Why? This call affects deer on an instinctive behavioral level, though some biologists say it is a learned behavior. Either way, deer react to this sound quickly and without second-guessing what it communicates to them—immediate, life-threatening danger.

The alarm-distress snort can be used when you are hunting alone or a hunter can use it to drive deer from cover to hunting companions posted at potential escape routes. No other deer call is better to use when it comes to hunting a wise old buck. This is particularly true when you are still-hunting, walking to a stand, or planning a deer drive. Locate thick cover, such as a cedar patch or swamp, then post hunters along the networks of trails that are escape routes. The call sounds like this, "Whew—whew—whew—whew, whew, whew, whew." Make the first three snorts loud and hesitate about a second between each sound. Then, make the next four snorts quickly without any hesitation. To help create the entire illusion, you can also stomp your foot on the ground a few times. Wait a minute or two and repeat the sequence. If there are deer in the cover, the sound of the call should make them sneak out along the routes where the other hunters are posted.

The alarm-distress call can also be used when you are hunting alone—I have had the most success with this cadence when I do. I use it to roust deer from cattails, ledges, brush piles, small woodlots, laurels, and standing corn. In addition, I have been successful with this call when walking through blowdowns. Used alone or in conjunction with other hunters, the alarm-distress cadence will help you see bucks you may have walked by otherwise.

Photo Credit: Fiduccia Ent.

Many years ago, I used an alarm-distress snort to get this buck up from his bed—a thick patch of thorn bushes bordering a New York apple orchard.

ALARM SNORT

The alarm cadence of the primary snort is the most recognized vocalization that deer make. I can even tell you when and where you probably encountered a deer making this sound. Often, a hunter walks along a logging road or makes his way through the woods to his stand and jumps a deer. When the deer does not see nor smell the hunter first, it only reacts to the hunter's noise. If it had sensed the hunter first, it would have quietly snuck off or blown the alarm-distress call as it made a hasty retreat.

In this instance, however, the deer is confused and blows an alarm call. It doesn't really know what alarmed it, and it often remains standing or slowly walks away a short distance and blows the vocalization again. The deer that makes this sound can be easily lured back if you know exactly what to do.

When you encounter a deer unexpectedly, the deer may respond by blowing a single snort, then running several yards, stopping, and blowing a second single snort. "Whew . . . Whew." It is alarmed, but it has not been able to pinpoint why. It knows it is safer not to run any further until it can determine exactly what made it nervous to begin with.

This is where you either make or break your opportunity to call this deer back. I have learned through trial and error that you must stop in your tracks when you hear this snort. Immediately blow a single snort at the deer in return. Be careful here—if the sound you heard seems to be fifty yards or closer, one single snort is all you dare make or you risk being discovered. If, on the other hand, it sounds as if the deer is more than fifty yards away, you can make two single snorts. A snort, followed by a few seconds of silence, then another single snort, "Whew . . . . Whew."

By blowing back at the deer with the alarm cadence of the primary snort call, you stimulate the deer's curiosity. Often, after hearing what it perceives to be just a call from another deer, it decides to slowly make its way back toward the location where it first encountered the perceived danger.

As long as the deer remains at a distance and continues to blow one or two snorts, you can keep blowing a single snort. Continue to do this as long as the deer does not walk toward you. The second the deer moves in your direction, stop calling. Even if the deer continues to snort, you must let its curiosity build. By doing so, it will eventually walk to within shooting distance.

You will find the alarm snort to be the easiest snort to learn and use. Keep in mind, however, that the critical aspect when using a snort call is to not blow an alarm snort to a deer that is vocalizing an alarm–distress snort. You must know the different cadences of each call for them to be effective. To learn more about the snort call and how the variations are supposed to sound, you can get my calling DVD *Tactics for Talking to Deer* at Amazon or on our web site, www.deerdoctor.com.

By learning all the different types of snort vocalizations, you will be able to create hunting opportunities you would not have without using this call. I guarantee that this one call will be more effective than the grunt, adult blat, and fawn bleat.

Photo Credit: Fiduccia Ent.

Cody shot this buck in 1999. I stopped the buck as he trotted past our blind by using an alarm snort. It was Cody's first buck.

When you plan your deer hunting strategies, be certain to include the use of a snort call and all its variations. While there are many different tactics I use and recommend to bag your deer, using a snort call is one of my favorite strategies. It might end up being the tactic that provides you the most opportunities to take deer. For me, it is definitely the most valuable and effective hunting tool I own and, after using it, you may feel the same way.

Chapter Ten

Dressed to Kill

In 1990, I hunted whitetails in Lamar, Colorado. At that time, the area was a well-kept secret regarding its ability to produce trophy-size bucks, some of which could be classified as Boone and Crockett class. I came away from that hunt with two thoughts. The first was that I was sure that sometime in the near future, Colorado would produce a buck that would challenge my long-time friend Milo Hansen's world record. While no one has surpassed Milo's incredible buck to date, several bucks taken in and around Lamar, Colorado have come close.

In the mid-70s, I lived in Crawford and Vail, Colorado. During that time, I mostly hunted for mule deer and elk. Back then, an average mule buck would have a twenty-eight-inch inside spread and it wasn't uncommon to see thirty-inch wide mule deer roaming the more rural areas of the Gunnison Mountain range and other areas of Colorado. Outfitters that operated in towns including Crawford, Paonia, Delta, and Hotchkiss regularly had clients that took thirty-inch wide bucks that scored 170 inches plus. The elk population back then was healthy and it wasn't unusual to see 5x5 or 6x6 bulls with heavy antlers and long tines.

However, back then no one hunted for whitetail deer in Colorado. Whitetails were rarely seen along the eastern border of Colorado and Kansas. The bucks that were seen hardly had the headgear that would interest any westerner. Outfitters in these areas didn't even bother having clients hunt them.

As time passed, more and more transient Kansas whitetails began to migrate into eastern Colorado, but were still all but ignored by an overwhelming majority of deer hunters. These deer grew and multiplied unmolested for many years. Then, in the late 80s, hunters began shooting

Photo Credit: Ted Rose

This would be a typical trophy-class eastern Colorado whitetail buck. Their antlers get this large because they get the time they need to mature into adult bucks.

some dandy whitetail trophies, with some measured for consideration in the Boone and Crockett record books.

It didn't take long from that time on for the secret to leak out. Soon, many whitetail trophy hunters became aware of their excellent chance to take a trophy-class whitetail buck from the eastern plains of Colorado. News spread that the farms along the miles of the Arkansas River bottom just east of Lamar harbored some monster bucks.

Today eastern Colorado, particularly Lamar and its surrounding areas, are well-known hotspots for hunters looking to score on a trophy whitetail buck. Some say the area offers the best whitetail buck hunting in the Midwest. Success for taking a bruiser whitetail buck in this area is achieved by patience. Hunters spend days in strategically placed tree stands or ground blinds that overlook bedding and rutting areas along the well-traveled corridors coming from the Arkansas River bottom to the multitudes of bordering farmlands.

Outfitters I have hunted with place the blinds to take advantage of big buck movement patterns. Blinds or tree stands are usually placed in known adult buck staging areas and along routes that take them to and from established sheltered areas. They also put stands along trails that lead to and from secure bedding zones to feeding belts of agricultural crops.

Many of the Colorado outfitters boast of excellent buck-to-doe ratios. When there is a balanced buck-to-doe population, bucks leave more signs, including rubs, scrapes, and sign post rubbings. I know friends who have hunted in Colorado say they had "terrific success" (i.e. buck response) when they used rattling, calling, and decoying tactics. When I hunted whitetails in Colorado, I know I found the deer to be receptive to deer calls and antler rattling. In areas where the population is balanced, bucks will also act more aggressively. They fight more and, many times, travel throughout the day in search of receptive does.

A majority of the Colorado whitetail outfitters do not allow hunters to harvest immature bucks. In fact, many of them assess additional kill fees to hunters who take bucks that score fewer than 125 inches. So, if you want to bag one of Colorado's monster monarch bucks, make sure you have the mind-set to take an adult buck and know how to score a buck on the hoof.

In addition, be sure to dress properly. No matter where you hunt for whitetails, but particularly in the western provinces of Canada and the western states of the Rocky Mountains, the weather plays a huge role in your success. You must be able to remain in your stand as long as possible to increase your opportunities to see and harvest a trophy-class buck. After my Colorado hunt, I promised myself I would never again hunt in bitterly cold conditions without dressing to kill and having an arsenal of cold-weather hunting tactics to help me bag my buck.

Over the years, I have developed a better routine for staying warm and key tactics for bagging deer in extremely cold weather. Here are some tips that will put a big buck in your sights in cold conditions and keep you warm, too.

Photo Credit: Fiduccia Ent.

A wool Filson Cap protects the neck and ears. Keeping the head and ears warm and frostbite free can make or break a hunt. This is true, particularly when hunting in the frigid conditions common to the Rocky Mountain states and many western Canadian provinces.

BITTER-COLD HUNTING TIPS

1. While hot coffee or tea will help keep you warm on stand, a thermos of beef or chicken broth will keep your body temperature higher and make you more comfortable every time. The broth offers nutritional

value and will kick-start your internal body temperature to generate body heat, which coffee and tea don't.

2. When the temperature drops, plan to hunt near areas where deer will seek food. Deer need extra energy in bitterly cold weather and will search for high-energy foods to get it. Food sources that are high-energy include corn, sorghum (milo), winter grains (such as wheat, triticale, rye, oats, and barley), and other cold weather crops, such as brassicas (swede, turnips, kale, etc.). Find and hunt near these foods or the trails leading to them, and it won't be long before you are sitting by the camp's fireplace recounting the hunt, no matter whether it is out west or in the east.

3. Have you ever noticed while driving along a highway after a snow-fall that one side of the road is bare of snow and the other isn't? South-facing slopes can be as much as fifteen degrees warmer than north-facing hillsides. When you're afield, keep this in mind. South-facing slopes are where you will see the most deer activity and be warmer, as well.

4. When the temperature is frigid, some gun oils and lubes might slow your firearm's action down considerably. During the coldest part of the season, use a solvent to remove the present oil and lube. Then relube your firearm lightly using a high-viscosity oil.

5. On the coldest days, I carry two heat seats to my stand—one thin and one thicker one. I place the thinner Therm-a-Seat inside my jacket over my kidneys. I stand on the thicker one. With my kidneys and feet warm, the rest of my body stays comfortably warm, too.

6. If you have staghorn sumac on the land you hunt, plan to hunt near there when temperatures fall. This plant has a higher fat content than any other native forage. Deer instinctively (there's that word again) know this plant helps them generate high levels of body heat and seek it out. They do this especially when the temperatures plummet into the single digits. Staghorn sumac is easily identified by its bright red seed clusters and gnarled branches. It stands two to six feet tall and grows in thick groves.

7. When the weather gets too cold to bear, go to a backup ground blind instead of suffering in your tree stand, especially during snow, ice, or sleet-filled days. On our farm, we have more than a dozen shooting houses to retreat to when the weather turns sour. The ground blinds also enable us to hunt in heavy rain.

8. Biologists say that some of deer's favorite foods in winter also include white cedar, red maple, mountain maple, aspen, and sumac. Find out if you have any of these trees on the land you hunt and hunt near them, especially just before and after storms.

9. On cold days, it is not wise to bring your firearms, optics, or other equipment into a warm house, cabin, or tent. Condensation, fogging, and other problems are sure to happen if you do. Leave your gear on the deck, in your vehicle, or outside on a free-standing gun rack.

10. Ever have trouble starting your vehicle or ATV at deer camp after a cold night? Ever have it parked the wrong way when you need a jump? When you park your vehicle after the day's hunt, make sure it is facing the direction you want to go the next morning. You may also want to keep the transmission in first gear and the transfer case engaged. This will enable the engine to kick over easily in the morning.

11. As mid-winter approaches, the circadian rhythm, or daily activity cycle, of deer shifts. During this time, deer don't move a lot at dawn and dusk. Rather, they move about more midday, from 11 a.m. to 3 p.m. The best tip I can share is to hunt these off-hours. Most times, it is way too cold to stay on stand all day, so sleeping in until 10 a.m. is a welcomed break. Head to your stand around 10:30 a.m. and you'll get there during the peak deer activity period.

12. In heavy rain or snow, place a piece of tape or a small rubber cap over the muzzle of your rifle to prevent snow and sleet from going down the barrel. This is even more important in the case that you fall or slip. You can shoot through the tape without worry about loss of accuracy.

13. In driving winds, deer might bed on hillsides or in the middle of thick cover.

14. When the weather has been cold and a warming trend is predicted, you can bet you will see an increase in deer movement. Keep in mind a warming might be only a few degrees above what the temperatures have been the last few days. For instance, if it has been in the mid-teens and the temperature jumps only five degrees higher, that's a warming trend for the deer and they will be on the move.

15. When the weather turns really cold on our farm, we look for deer in the swamps. Swamps are located in lower elevations than the surrounding land and are more protected from cold blasts of northerly

winds coming off ridges or across open fields. Lowlands, swamps, and bogs can be as much as ten degrees warmer than higher ground that is only a few hundred yards away.

16. When harvested crop fields are covered in snow, don't think the deer will not feed in them. I have seen deer paw through several inches of snow, as long as it hasn't frozen on top, to get to old corn or other vegetable or legume spillage left in the field after the harvest. Deer can easily smell the food under the snow.

17. When you're still-hunting or staging drives, concentrate on thick groves of cedars. When packed tightly, cedars are the preferred bedding for whitetails. They're also a favorite cold-weather food, and deer don't have to spend energy traveling long distances from bedding sites to feeding areas.

18. In frigid weather, deer will move with the sun. You'll find them bedded on east-facing slopes in the morning, south-facing slopes during midday, and west-facing slopes in late afternoon. You won't find them on north-facing slopes.

19. A dry, cold day does not stop deer from moving as much as a damp, cold day will. If the relative humidity is higher than normal on a given day, don't expect much deer movement.

20. There are numerous brands of portable heaters on the market that burn odorless (I use Mr. Heater). They can be used for waterfowl hunting and deer hunting. They work to warm your whole body when used in a ground blind, or you can put them between your feet when you're in a tree stand to keep your feet warm during severely cold weather.

21. When a storm is approaching, the barometer begins to drop rapidly. Deer will quickly head to thick cover to bed. A rising barometer signals the storm is over, which causes the deer to leave their beds and head to feeding areas.

22. An old but true adage is that if you want to stay warm, wear a warm hat. The head and neck region is where most body heat escapes. Keep your ears and head covered and you can last at least two more hours on stand on a cold day.

As additional information to this chapter, I included whitetail outfitters that offer quality hunts. The following outfitters have been favorably recommended to me by friends or industry contacts★.

Rocky Mountain Safaris—Lamar, Colorado: Owned and operated by Michael Palmer and his son, Michael. Rocky Mountain Safaris hunts for adult bucks in the towns of Lamar and Holly, Colorado. In the Lamar area, they hunt ten miles of prime riverfront property. It is a seven-day hunt that offers five full days of hunting.

Photo Credit: Ted Rose

Adult bucks of this size are more common in the northern ranges. Sitting for eight plus hours in a blind requires the hunter to have the ultimate patience, concentration, and the proper clothing. Leave any one element out, and the success rate drops dramatically.

Hunters can book to hunt whitetails during archery, muzzleloader, or regular firearm seasons. Hunters lodge and eat locally at their own cost. Archery hunts are $3,500, muzzleloader hunts are $4,000, and regular firearm hunts are $5,500. Seasons run in October, November, and December. The November timeframe includes the primary rut when bucks are running does. The late-season hunt takes place in December and is an equally prime time period to kill a large buck.

According to the elder Michael, "This is the time to see a Booner-class buck looking for does during the late rut. It is also a prime time to see some of the largest bucks staying in the agricultural fields a little later in the mornings and coming out feed earlier in the evenings. The weather is cold, and it keeps them moving and active."

For more detailed information, contact Michael Palmer at Rocky Mountain Safaris at (719) 332-0044 or visit their website at www. rockymountainsafaris.com.

Dahl Creek Outfitters—Hudson Bay, Saskatchewan, Canada: Owned and operated by Arnold Holmes. Don't expect to be hunting agricultural crop fields at Dahl Creek Outfitters. They operate in a wild and remote area containing about three hundred square miles of wilderness in northeastern Saskatchewan.

Guests hunt from safe and spacious permanent tree stands, ground blinds, or commercially made portable tree stands. All blinds are strategically located overlooking key runways and travel corridors.

The hunt includes five nights and six days, plus all meals once you are at camp and transportation during your stay. For more information, contact Arnold at (306) 865-2097 (home) or (306) 865-7288 (cell), or visit www.dahlcreek@sasktel.net.

Eagle's Nest Sporting Camps—Dorrington Hill, New Brunswick: Owned and operated by Arnold Drost and his family since 1987. They offer four hundred square miles of awesome hunting in zone fifteen, located in southwestern New Brunswick. This magnificent area is known for its wide mix of forest, lakes, and streams where big whitetails roam.

Eagle's Nest offers a unique combination deer and bear package and the main lodge includes all the amenities. Both bow and firearm hunters are welcome at Eagle's Nest. The hunt is five days long. The area is known for producing heavy-bodied bucks with thick antlers.

Contact Arnold at (506) 279-2114 or visit his website at www.eagle-snestcamps.com. While you're on the site, don't forget to look at the size of the bodies and antlers on the deer.

*Note: I have not hunted with any of the above outfitters. However, they come recommended to me by others. Use due diligence before booking a hunt.

Photo credit R. Jaskolski

Chapter Eleven

Using Scents Sensibly

—————

The buck held his head high, raised his upper lip, and breathed in deeply. In the frigid morning air, I could see his breath as he exhaled. My hands were shaking from being both cold and nervous, and I couldn't draw back the string on my stick bow.

What happened next made me tenser, and things quickly progressed from bad to worse. The buck slowly stretched his neck out to try and capture the estrus odor scent I placed on a tree near my deer stand. In doing so, he caught sight of me in his peripheral vision and was gone before I could react. I was torn between the excitement of the buck being drawn to the scent and the total letdown of him running off, when all of a sudden there he was again, slowly sneaking back toward the hanging scent wick.

With a lot more caution than he came in with the first time, the buck carefully stepped toward the wick. Every now and then, he would glance in my direction and then toward the wick sprinkled with doe estrus.

It took him a long time (more than ten minutes, but for all I know it could have been thirty—I was too excited at the time to know), but he eventually made his way to the exact spot where the wick was hanging. He turned slightly and, with his back to me, stuck his nose out and whiffed the scent wick. This was his fatal mistake. I mustered all my will-power and yanked the string of the bow until it came to full draw.

What seemed like an hour of holding the string back (there was no let-off at that time) was probably more like seconds, and I was praying the buck would turn before I had to relax the string. Fortunately he did, and I let the arrow fly.

The two-bladed broadhead on my wooden arrow caught the buck high in the neck. (I was aiming for his lungs . . . Stop laughing. This was a very long time ago.) For a split second, I thought it was all over but as luck would have it, my arrow severed the carotid artery and the buck was dead within seconds.

That hunt took place in 1966 and was the first time I used a deer scent to attract a buck. It was also the second year of my deer hunting life. The buck was a huge four-point—I like to use the word huge

Photo Credit: Fiduccia Ent.

Love Potion No. 9 is a scent that I created in 1989. It is a mix of doe estrus and immature buck urine. It agitates older bucks into thinking they can easily chase off the younger buck that is on the trail of an estrus doe. Love Potion No. 9 is available at www.deerdoctor.com

here because in reality he was just an average, immature buck that was probably no more than eighteen months old. But the word huge had you going for a second, didn't it? It gave the story some anticipation, yes? Anyway, with that hunt I began using deer scents and, through a lot of success and even more failures, I learned the right way to use deer lures. I have continued to use a wide variety of commercially made deer scents on every whitetail hunt since that day with unwavering loyalty.

What that hunt demonstrated to me was that deer lures work. I answered a question that I had wondered about for quite awhile. It also taught me a more important lesson about having confidence in the strategies I use.

For those who have read any of my other deer hunting books, you already know how much I believe that being a confident hunter creates success in the field. Without confidence in your own hunting abilities, you might as well stay home.

As I have also said in almost every book I have ever written, I am not a better deer hunter than you. In fact, none of the other so-called pros are.

The only difference between everyday hunters and us is that we get more opportunities to hunt in prime areas.

Don't be disappointed in yourself because you're not killing the types of bucks you see on television programs. The more opportunity a hunter gets to be afield, the more chances he or she has to take game. It's as simple as that.

The problem with most hosts of outdoor television programs is that for them it's all about showing the audience how they took a big buck and very little about sharing the tactics they used. If these guys don't get good action footage, they don't have a show, so that's what they waste the entire show on—what they kill.

Most of them don't try to give the audience a valid assessment of the wide range of possibilities that can occur on a hunt. Even if a person is hunting at some of the best lodges, things can go wrong. Instead, they want to grab the viewers' attention with wrapping their show around a bow or firearm kill, which is why they spend little time on anything but video footage of the host bagging game or catching huge fish, one after another.

This helps them, they think, make the audience believe in their extraordinary hunting skills, so they focus on shooting and catching, rather than sharing information that can help viewers take their hunting or fishing skills to the next level.

The hunting shows that air nothing but huge bucks being killed are ridiculous. For an overwhelming number of deer hunters across North America, it is nearly impossible to sit in a stand for one day and see several trophy-class bucks. Unfortunately, some of the best-known celebrities of outdoor television programs do that exact thing week in and week out, while peddling their products and outfitting services to boot.

These types of shows do not serve the general hunter. They only make them feel as if their hunting skills are less than the host's. Worse yet, many hunters lose confidence in their hunting abilities because time and time again, no matter how hard they hunt, they don't get to see or shoot the types of bucks that they watch hosts shoot on television.

Believe me, if you hunted in the areas where most of these television show hosts hunt, you would be killing the same kinds of trophy animals. I challenge any other show hosts to hunt the pressured areas of the Northeast or New England. I'll bet none of them would go home with the kind of bucks you see them kill week after week on their shows.

It is important for me to mention that not all show hosts are like this. There are many who avoid this type of hype. Unfortunately, they don't get the exposure that the others do.

I don't know about you, but I am tired of seeing hosts who spar with their co-host wives on the program. Who cares that he threw her in the mud and they laughed about it? I'm especially sick of hearing the stupid, nonsensical banter between them. I could give a hoot less about which of them is the better hunter than the other.

Stop all the hype and give the audience some genuine, intelligent information and realistic entertainment. No more overdone high fives, babes with their boobs hanging out as they bend over a dead animal, or glamour girls giggling about the game they just shot. I find it insulting, and many of you have told me you and your families do, too.

Providing hardcore information, along with genuine—I repeat, genuine—enthusiasm about a successful hunt is what the overwhelming majority of the hunting and fishing audience wants to see. As a famous hunter once said, "Act like you've been there before."

Why am I rambling about this? So you don't think any less of your hunting abilities. Most of you are as good a hunter as those of us who have been fortunate enough to do this for a living. And if it weren't for folks like you who support us, we'd all be out of work. No matter what type of hunting you do or tactic you use, learn to believe in yourself and your hunting skills—I do.

Now, let's get back to how to use deer lures with consistent success. Here are the golden rules of using scent according not to Hoyle, but the Deer Doctor:

- Use sexual deer scents sparingly, despite what the directions on the bottle say.
- When combining deer scents, make sure they are naturally compatible with the tactic you are using.
- Don't hang a sexual scent too close to your stand.
- Never wear an estrus scent on your clothing. This isn't an issue of safety but to keep from attracting a buck's attention directly to you.
- To further reduce human odor, use food scents like apple and acorn, even where these foods don't grow.

Using deer lures isn't a new tactic. Native Americans and others of early hunting societies wrapped themselves in garments that had gamy aromas to get closer to their quarry. There is even evidence that they made game scents from animal extracts that served the same purpose today's scents do—they either attracted game or masked human odors.

Of course, today's hunters are inundated with a wide array of scents, including lures to attract deer sexually, imitate foods such as apple, corn, and persimmon, imitate aromas from deer glands such as the tarsal and interdigital glands, serve as cover scents such as fox urine or skunk, and a variety of unscented soaps and detergents. There are even countless varieties of human scent eliminators from which to choose. While the choices are many, they often lead to confusion for hunters on just when, where, how, and why to use deer scents properly.

Photo Credit: Buck Stop

Brian and Bonnie Johansen, owners of Buck Stop Scents, pose with two bucks. Buck Stop Scents manufactures a reliable line of scents that have consistently worked well for me for nearly five decades. (As an FYI, Buck Stop doesn't sponsor our show. I included the photo because I have used their products successfully for many years.)

Using deer scents can be helpful when used not only properly, but also with common sense. One important rule of thumb is to remember this: using too much scent will cause you problems and scare off more deer than it will attract. Also, there isn't a scent on the market, including my own Love Potion No. 9, that will work reliably unless the hunter uses the correct hunting techniques.

Anyone who has ever hunted whitetail deer knows that to be consistently successful year in and year out, you must try to reduce human and other foreign odors as much as possible. But don't be naive enough to believe that completely eliminating human is realistic. No matter what other people tell you, it isn't. With that said, however, using scent eliminators will definitely help keep your odor to a bare minimum when used properly.

By paying attention to all aspects of using scents, this element of your deer hunting strategies will immediately help you see and bag more game the next time you go afield.

Seasoned deer hunters don't doubt the whitetail's sense of smell is its key to survival. I have long said, "Bust a buck's nose and you'll bust the buck." Conversely, if a hunter doesn't pay meticulous attention to the whitetail's ability to scent humans, predators, food sources, or a hot doe, he or she is only limiting the ability to bag a deer. I promise you, the whitetail depends more on its sense of smell than any of its other senses.

Understanding wind and how air currents work is important to being consistently successful. When hunters try to lure deer in closer than usual when using deer scent, decoys, rattling, or calling, they must keep wind direction uppermost in their minds. That begins by keeping your body as clean and odor free as possible, as well as eliminating foreign odors from your hunting clothes and boots.

To help reduce human and foreign odors, you can use a variety of commercially made attracting, masking, and food scents in addition to unscented soaps.

You will find that there are three distinct opinions on using scents. Some, mostly the diehard old-timers, swear that scents are just a lot of sales hype and are vocal about them being ineffective. A second group is more practical about the use of commercially made scent and feels it has its time and place. Then, there are the overly passionate hunters who won't hunt without using some type of commercially made deer scent.

I have always had a realistic opinion about using deer scents, odor eliminators, unscented soaps, and the like. I base my support mostly on my past success when using deer scents. I also keep in mind that there is a lot of misinformation spread around by certain scent manufacturers regarding how their scent is collected and what it can do for the hunter—it's called sales hype. Unfortunately, many of us are sold on the pretty bottles and outrageous claims.

Do I believe using commercially made scents to mask human odor or attract a deer will work? You bet I do. But I temper my feelings about using deer scents with a healthy dose of good old common sense.

My number one rule about using deer scents, whether I'm using them alone or in combination, is to create the most natural olfactory illusion I can. When the scents I put out reach the nose of an interested deer, I want them to be so natural smelling that the buck or doe comes to my stand with its guard totally down. By paying attention to this statement about scent, you will have leap frogged from just a hunter who uses scent to someone savvy who understands the nuances of how to use deer scent correctly.

To begin, I can guarantee you that no matter what type of scent is used, hunters will have more success using it sparingly rather than following the directions on the labels of most bottles. Often, they suggest using more scent than is needed around your stand. Using too much sexual or glandular deer scent will almost always make most bucks approaching your stand wary.

How to Use Deer Scents

When using deer scents, don't confuse the deer's olfactory senses by using too much. Instead, place a practical amount where necessary and it will be interpreted as a natural aroma, which is what the buck or doe expects when they detect scent from another deer. By using the correct scent at the right time, hunters will see more deer responding to their scent canisters.

Read the label on the bottle. If it says to use two drops, don't empty the contents of the bottle in one place. Too much scent will spook deer away. Deer know what they should smell and how strong the smell should be.

It can be compared to when a man or woman in a cab, restaurant, or bar has put on too much cologne or perfume. Your reaction is not, "Wow, that smells nice." It is the exact opposite, "Whoa, that is way too much cologne or perfume."

In the whitetail's world, when a buck gets too much estrus scent his olfactory senses go haywire. Because he knows something doesn't smell natural, he either never comes in to investigate the aroma or gets very nervous about it. My catch phrase that I developed for the use of Love Potion No. 9 is, "Go light and he'll come in tight." With all that said, I have found that wisely using commercially made scent has always helped my deer hunting, not hindered it.

"Bust a buck's nose and you'll bust the buck" still applies today. By simply blocking, fooling, or reducing a buck's ability to pick up human or foreign odors, you are halfway to scoring your next buck.

Here are some different deer lures:

• Sexual attractive lures, such as Love Potion No. 9 or Buck Stop's Estrus Doe Urine
• Straight buck or doe urine
• Food scents, such as acorn, apple, corn, persimmon, grape, and vanilla
• Cover scents, such as pine, cedar, and earth
• Glandular scents, such as tarsal, interdigital, and forehead

Each scent has its best time to be used alone or in combination during the hunting seasons, depending on where you live and when your deer season is.

For instance, in my home state of New York, we begin our bow hunting season around October 1st each year. The season runs into our firearm season, which generally starts around the middle of November until the middle of December. During this time, different scents work when you match them up to what is naturally happening in the woods.

In October, I tend to use a combination of scents to attract deer and cover my human scent, as well as a food scent for the same reasons. This is a double whammy approach that has proven successful for me for more than forty years.

During this time, bucks make a lot of rubs and scrapes, and other deer are checking them regularly. I take full advantage of these olfactory and visual sign posts by creating mock scrapes and rubs.

I begin the evening before hunting by making sure my clothing is washed or at least sprayed with a scent eliminator. I hang the clothes outside if the weather allows. If you can't hang them outside, place them in a plastic container filled with freshly fallen leaves and pine branches. Do not use any other scent on them at this point.

I start the day of the hunt off with a shower and scrub myself and shampoo my hair with unscented soap. If I shave, I lather the soap and use it, rather than a scented shaving cream.

Next, I eat breakfast in my pajamas so I don't get food odors on my hunting clothes. Most mornings, if not all, I eat a cold breakfast to prevent the smell of bacon, eggs, butter, etc., from clinging to my skin and hair.

After breakfast, I retrieve the clothes I hung outside or remove them from their container and spray them lightly with some type of scent destroyer. Every other day, or sometimes every three days, I scrub the bottoms of my boots with a small fingernail brush, which you can buy in any drugstore. This helps remove any foreign odors on my boots that I might have picked up in the barn, on the deck, while driving, or in my home.

This is a winning tactic that has helped me control the scent left on the ground, whether I'm wearing rubber or leather boots, in the woods. However, I use common sense here. After washing the soles, I spray earth scent on them, which helps reduce any residual soap smell, no matter how

It is virtually impossible to eliminate all human odor, even when the hunter pays attention to scent control. One key factor in keeping human odor to its minimum is to shower with an unscented soap.

slight the odor might be. I know, it seems a little over the top, but it gives me confidence that I took every available measure to do what was necessary to prepare.

Once I'm in the field, I apply scents that I feel are natural for the time of year. If I'm hunting from my stand and trying to rattle a deer in, I might use a combination that matches the odors emitted by bucks, such as buck urine and tarsal.

This combination of scents helps any buck coming in downwind of me smell what he instinctively expects to smell, the urine from competing bucks and a light dose of tarsal scent. Does generally don't hang out with bucks as they spar or fight. They move a good distance away, especially when they are accompanied with fawns and yearlings, so I don't use doe urine or estrus scent at this point. Now I have, to the best of my ability and common sense, created the most natural illusion possible for any responding buck. By the way, I have found that using a heavy dose of food scent does not alarm deer like overusing other scents will.

If I make a mock rub later in October, I will use a combination of scents including buck urine, tarsal gland scent, straight doe urine, and an excellent scent that is a mixture of glandular deer scents to smell like a general deer odor. If one of my hunting buddies has already killed a buck, I will use the forehead gland scents from that buck on the rub, as well.

Photo credit: Buck Stop

During the peak chase period of the rut, things change regarding the way I use scent. I use more food lures to cover my odor than previously. Why? Common sense is why. As available food, such as apples, acorns, and corn, declines, deer are more likely to check out a food scent. It also helps keep my odor down. I always spray the inside of my hat with a food scent to help reduce odors emitting from my head, which account for about 75 percent of all human scent coming off your body.

The savvy hunter matches the types of scents used with the tactic. For example, when rattling, use buck urine and tarsal scent. It's what a buck expects to smell when approaching two fighting bucks.

Photo Credit: Buck Stop

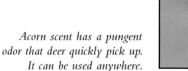

Acorn scent has a pungent odor that deer quickly pick up. It can be used anywhere.

Then I also use slightly more, and I mean slightly, doe estrus scent mixed with young buck urine. Love Potion No. 9 is the combination of a mature doe estrus and the urine of a competitive young buck. I developed this scent in the late 1980s and have used it successfully over the years. It is designed to instinctively attract mature bucks. They pick up the scent of the hot doe and, through their vomeronasal organ, they can precisely detect the rut status and age of the buck following the hot doe. They are instinctively motivated to follow the scent, knowing they can easily intimidate the younger buck off the trail of the doe, getting the opportunity to have the doe all to themselves.

You will have more success using estrus scents when used sparingly. Using too much estrus scent is as bad as not using any at all.

You can find Love Potion No. 9 on our website at www.deerdoctor. com. But no matter whose deer scents you like or buy, use this combination during the rut and it will work for you.

By now you get my meaning—when I use scent, I do so sparingly and with common sense. I always try to match what odors a deer expects to encounter in the woods and in amounts that will seem natural, especially to a nervous buck. But keep in mind, spooking a matriarchal doe can be just as devastating to a hunt.

If you would like to have more response and action this season, here is important information that you will want to read carefully.

DEER GLAND AND ORGAN SCENTS

Whitetail deer have several external glands and organs that play a significant part in their communication and behavior. These include the commonly known tarsal, interdigital, and forehead glands and the less commonly known metatarsal, nasal, and preorbital glands. Three of the least known are the vomeronasal organ, salivary, and preputial glands.

Pheromones created by these glands and organs are received and interpreted by deer to help decipher their world. The messages received via the deer's olfactory senses act to alert, calm, attract, frighten, give direction of travel, and help establish an identity of other deer in their herd by revealing a deer's pecking order, age, and estrus or rut status within the herd.

NASAL GLANDS

New facts are now available about this gland. When I first wrote about the nasal gland, biologists weren't sure of its purpose. Over the past fifteen years, however, they have discovered that the nasal gland serves multiple functions. It helps to lubricate the lining inside the deer's nose and it is also used to leave scent on overhanging branches. Some believe it is also used to leave a specific scent when a buck makes new rubs or refreshes old ones. This scent is left to let other bucks know they have visited their rubs and scrapes. Located in the nostrils, the nasal gland has been found to consist of two almond-shaped glands.

PREPUTIAL GLAND

The preputial gland is located on the inside of the buck's penal sheath. Researchers once felt that this gland didn't play a significant role regarding the rut, but that has changed. Now they believe it not only serves to lubricate the penis but the yellow-gray substance also deposits a scent when the buck urinates. The scent of this substance tells other bucks who he is and helps define his current rutting status.

FOREHEAD GLAND

The forehead gland is comprised of sebaceous and apocrine hairs. During the rut, these hairs swell up and produce a scent that the buck deposits on trees as he is rubbing. Both bucks and does use this gland as a scent marker. I have taped dozens of bucks rubbing their antlers on trees, and they all exhibited the same behavior. First, they approach the tree or sapling, smell it, and begin to vigorously rub their antlers against the trunk. After rubbing their antlers up and down several times, they pause, step back, smell the trunk, and lick it. Then, if the mood strikes them, they repeat the process over again. Obviously, this behavior is not a random act, but rather a specific behavioral routine bucks stick to when making a rub. The rubbed area often carries an odor for days.

TARSAL GLANDS

There is nothing relatively new about these pungent odor glands, which are externally located on the inside of the hind legs of all deer. The lactones of these glands are specific, and they allow other deer to determine the exact age and sex of the deer leaving the scent. The act of rubbing the tarsals together and urinating over them is call rub-urination. Bucks rub-urinate to display their current rank in the hierarchy. Does rub-urinate to leave an olfactory message for their fawns. It is also believed does rub-urinate to express their social rank within doe groups. This tan gland turns almost black as bucks continually urinate on it throughout the rut. I think the combination of the urine mixed with the preputial substance is the cause of this color change.

Deer use tarsal gland pheromones, which are mostly made up of lactones, in several ways: as a visual and olfactory signal of a mature buck, a warning, to identify individual deer, and, in mature deer, it is involved with breeding behavior during the rut. When a buck or doe is excited, the hairs on the tarsal gland stand erect and can be seen from quite a distance by other deer. All deer urinate on their tarsal glands and this contributes to their pungent odor.

To obtain optimum response from tarsal scent during the rut, put several drops of commercially made scent in a drip dispenser, rag, or pad, and hang it from a branch close by. Its scent will permeate the area and act as an attractive or agitating smell. Don't place it on your clothing—you don't want the deer's attention zoning in on you. Instead, focus his attention or aggression ten to twenty yards from you. There will be more about why I recommend this at the end of the chapter.

Although the scent from tarsal glands of harvested does attracts bucks, many hunters have had equal success attracting bucks with commercially made tarsal scent. Sometimes the odor of tarsal agitates bucks so much that they respond quickly after the scent is distributed.

When creating a mock scrape or hunting over a natural one, I use tarsal scent. I also use it when I am hunting with deer decoys or mock rubs. By placing a few drops on the inside of a buck decoy's legs, it adds an odor of realism. Remember the key phrase in all my books: Create the entire illusion. In addition, I use tarsal with estrus scents and straight buck urine when I am hunting during the rut.

Tarsal gland scent is a pungent odor. Use it only during the peak rut and sparingly. Using tarsal scent at the wrong time of year or excessively be problematic. The key to all these glandular scents is to use them during the times of year that deer are accustomed to smelling them.

INTERDIGITAL

Interdigital is a potent scent that attracts all deer when used sparingly. The interdigital gland is located between the deer's hooves. It has a waxy yellow secretion with an offensive, potent odor. Interdigital scent is like a human

fingerprint, individual to each deer. Although I don't know of documented evidence suggesting the interdigital odor from bucks and does are different, I would speculate the interdigital scent from mature bucks and does is more potent than the scent from immature deer.

Hunters can use interdigital scent two ways. The first is as an attractive scent. All deer leave tiny amounts of interdigital scent as they walk. Other deer follow trails marked with a normal amount of interdigital scent. Use only one or two drops of a commercially made scent on a boot pad. When you are about fifteen yards from your stand, remove

Photo credit: Bob Kirschner Lures

When using interdigital, remember to "Keep it light and they'll come in tight."

the pad, hang it on a bush, and wait for deer to come and investigate the odor.

Deer also use interdigital scent as a warning to other deer. When a deer stomps its hooves, it's warning other deer of danger through sight, sound, and scent. Deer that smell excess interdigital scent often refuse to continue further down the trail. They will mill about nervously for several moments, walk widely around the scent, or retreat the way they came. Deer will instinctively heed the pheromone warning left by another deer. Hunters who use interdigital scent incorrectly will definitely spook, rather than attract, deer.

Here's my favorite way to make deer move out of heavy cover. I place other hunters on known buck escape routes. I move about one hundred yards away, spread excess interdigital scent (about ten drops), stomp my feet, and blow an alarm-distress snort. This imitation of a deer sending out an alarm-distress through both audible and olfactory messages sends bucks and does sneaking down the watched-over escape routes while trying to flee the danger signals their ears and noses are receiving. Of course, you can't use this ploy too often or in more than one or two locations in the woods you are hunting—it could make deer reluctant to use the area.

To convince you of the potency of this scent, simply spread the toes of the next deer you kill and, with the tip of a knife, dig between the toes. Don't be brave enough to place the knife tip directly under your nose. You'll regret it, as it might induce the dry heave response or gag reflex. The odor is so foul it can make you nauseated. I use commercially made interdigital scent rather than collecting it from dead deer—it's much safer, easier, and practical.

PREORBITAL GLAND

The preorbital gland is located in the inside corner of a deer's eye. Deer control the gland via muscles in this area. Its main function is to serve as a tear duct. However, deer rub this gland, along with the forehead gland on bushes, branches, and tree limbs, especially during the rut. Biologists now speculate that bucks use it to signal aggressive behavior. They also say that does open the glands wide when feeding fawns but do not know why. Deer also use these glands to deposit a specific pheromone, marking certain areas and identifying deer.

METATARSAL GLANDS

The metatarsal glands are no longer as controversial as they were when I first wrote about them. In fact, I have some new thoughts, as well. This gland is within a white tuft of hair on the outside of the hind legs, just above the dewclaws. Most naturalists and biologists I have talked with believe they are atrophying, or getting smaller through evolution because they no longer serve a purpose.

There is a small camp, however, who still believe the glands emit a pheromone that is used by deer for identification. I have smelled these glands on many deer, both before and during the rut, and can say that while they do not smell as potent as the tarsal glands, they do release an odor. In my opinion, any scent a deer emits serves some type of purpose to other deer. In any event, this gland is still not well-understood.

My suggestion coincides with my philosophy about deer hunting; don't be afraid of being innovative. If you're not sure how this gland will help you during the hunting season, give it a try and experiment with it this fall.

Over the past dozen years, I have used metatarsal the same way I use tarsal. Although both bucks and does walked down a trail where the scent was deposited, for the most part they have ignored it. I may, however, be interpreting their reactions incorrectly. Instead of ignoring it, they may be more docile or relaxed by smelling it. I'm really not sure, so if you use the scent, you do so as an experiment and at your own risk.

When using deer scents, especially gland scents, be careful not to mix conflicting pheromones. For example, don't use excess interdigital with attracting scents. Excess interdigital scent is meant to warn deer of danger, not attract them. When a deer stomps its hooves repeatedly, it is sending both a visual and audible message. Researchers say the vibration from the deer's stomping hoof can be heard and felt for a few hundred yards by other deer feeding or bedding in the area. I use excess interdigital with an alarm-distress snort to help me create the illusion of danger when I'm trying to intention-ally spook deer from heavy cover. You can, however, use one or two drops of interdigital with an estrus scent, as both are attracting scents.

SEXUAL LURES

The most overused deer scent is doe estrus. Although estrus works, do not use this scent every day throughout the entire deer season. Estrus works best when used sparingly a few days prior to each peak period of the three phases of the rut.

I use doe estrus every year. However, I use it with an open mind and common sense.

When used correctly, big bucks have no hesitation in coming to investigate a scent rag or wick with doe estrus that is hung near a stand. I think estrus scent works best before the actual peak periods of each phase of the rut, especially during the peak chase periods that happen prior to the actual breeding.

FOOD SCENTS

One of my favorite lures to use is food scents. Use food scents with an open mind. I have heard some so-called experts say you can't use food scents that are not native to the area you are hunting. If there is one kind of deer hunting hype that annoys me, this is it—my deer hunting pet peeve. There are those who say you can't use apple scent in a hard-wood forest because deer will know that apples are not growing there. They are wrong at best and bull crap artists at worst. Trust me, when used correctly, food scent lures are highly effective, whether they are native to the area you are hunting or not.

If you don't believe apple scent, or any type of food lure for that matter, attracts deer where wild apples don't grow, you're missing out on a productive hunting strategy. Before hunting season, take either a couple of apples or a scent pad soaked in commercially made apple scent (food scents are the only lure you don't have to worry about using in excess). Place the fruit or pad in an area you are absolutely sure

Photo credit: Buck Stop Scents

Food scents can be used to attract deer and to help cover human scent. It is not necessary to use a food scent where the food naturally grows.

has no wild apples. I promise that as deer move through the area, they will smell the food source and investigate it.

Common sense would tell you deer instinctively check out odors from potential food sources. If they didn't, they would have a lot less food available to them. Deer have no way of figuring out if a scent pad laden with apple scent is a lure left by a hunter or an actual food item. There isn't a buck alive that would make his way through a hardwood forest free of natural apples and pick up the odor of the apple lure and say, "Aha, apples don't grow here. That must be a fake. Yikes, I've been had . . . I'm outta here!" and then run off without looking back. The fact is, they will check out anything, and I mean anything, that smells like it would be good to eat.

Apple scent is my favorite covering and attracting scent. I use it throughout the season, especially in areas where there are no apples.

Apple scent not only acts as an attractive scent, but it is also excellent as a cover to help mask your human odor. I often place several drops on my cap to help keep my human odor contained. You can also use acorn scent the same way in areas where there are no acorns. When I've hunted in evergreen forests, I've seen additional evidence that you don't have to use indigenous scents. Many deer have walked through the pines, winded the acorn scent pad, and walked over to check it out.

It's a simple matter of common sense. If you put on apple scents in an apple orchard, acorn scent in a hardwood forest filled with acorns, or corn scent in the middle of a cornfield, the only thing you would accomplish is to help mask your human odor. The food will attract the deer before the scent will. My advice is to use commercially made food scents in areas where they are not naturally present.

WOODLAND SCENTS

Natural woodland fragrances like hemlock, pine, spruce, cedar, earth, and the like can be worn on clothing without risk of attracting a deer's attention to the hunter. I use them regularly to help mask my odor. I especially like earth scent.

I treat food scents, such as acorn, apple, corn, grape, and vanilla, exactly the way I treat attracting lures. I put them twenty to thirty yards from my stand, except apple scent, which I also use on my cap to reduce human odor, as mentioned previously.

While I want to remind you that there is no way to totally eliminate human odor, you can reduce it significantly by following some important guidelines. Keep yourself as clean as possible before each hunt. Use an unscented soap and deodorant on your body and a scent destroyer spray on your clothes and boots. If you can shower between hunts, do so. During deer season, always use unscented shampoos. Scrub the soles of your boots every couple of days with a nailbrush and unscented sportsmen's soap. In addition, wash your hunting clothes at least every other day. If you can, dry them outdoors. If not, hang them outdoors for a few minutes to remove dryer odor before putting them on.

Stay away from foreign odors like gasoline and diesel fuel, and don't let your dog rub up against your hunting clothes. Avoid camp odors, such as cigarette smoke and cooking smells, as if they were the plague. Also, never get dressed and take your morning constitutional. Instead, wait until after you have relieved yourself to put on your hunting clothes. I apologize for this tacky suggestion, but it's better to say it. Finally, a savvy hunter always washes himself (not only your hands, fellows) thoroughly after going to the bathroom. Get what I mean?

Deer pick up scents from the foreign odors collected on the soles of your boots. Avoid wearing your hunting boots anywhere other than the woods. Sometimes even I'm guilty of wearing my hunting boots where I shouldn't. When I do, however, I make sure I wash the soles. If you drive to a hunting area, leave your boots in a small cardboard box filled with pine branches, leaves, and earth. Change the leaves and earth every so often. When you arrive at your hunting location, remove your shoes, put on your boots, and head into the woods. When you return, immediately remove your boots and put them back in the box. By following these suggestions, you will keep your boots free of foreign odors. I still wash the soles of my boots every few days to remove any human odor that might have permeated into the soles. By taking these scent suggestions seriously, you will eliminate as much human odor as possible and gain an edge.

Pheromones from external glands are natural, everyday odors in the woods. Used properly, they will add to your deer hunting experience. They will create deer hunting opportunities you may never have had otherwise. In addition, you will have chances to witness the amusing and interesting reactions of raccoons, coyotes, foxes, bears, and other animals when they stop and smell scents laid out for deer. By

Photo credit: Ted Rose

Deer quickly smell the foreign odors that cling to hunting boots. It is a prime reason they will avoid a trail left by a hunter. Keep your hunting footwear clean by periodically washing the soles.

using the suggestions within this chapter, you will not only have an advantage, but you will also have an interesting and exciting season watching and learning how does and bucks respond positively to scents when used correctly.

Chapter Twelve

Strategies to Take Adult Bucks

———

Before I discuss the tactics to use when hunting mature bucks, I would like to state that I'm a big fan of young buck protection programs, and we have practiced young buck protection on our farm for twelve years. With that said, we do allow first-time hunters to take any buck they care to. I also firmly believe that if a hunter doesn't want to practice young buck protection, he or she should not be criticized for taking what he or she considers to be a trophy buck in his or her eyes and heart.

WHAT IS A MATURE BUCK?

For those of you interested in regularly pursing adult bucks, I'd like to explain how researchers actually define an adult whitetail buck. Biologists have determined through numerous nationwide studies that a male whitetail deer reaches maturity when he has completed his full skeletal growth. Many biologists believe free-range male deer reach maturity at 4½ years old. Female deer develop their full skeletal growth earlier because their frame is smaller. That is usually when they reach 3½ years old.

Before bucks reach 4½ years old, most of the nutrition they eat is needed to develop muscles and bones rather than antler size. Once a buck reaches 4½ years old, however, a considerable amount of nutrition is used to develop its antlers and less is directed to the muscles and bones that are now either nearly or fully developed. Hence, when a buck reaches 4½ years old, most biologists consider him to be an adult male deer.

Photo Credit: Ted Rose

This buck has developed full skeletal growth, therefore he can be referred to as an adult deer.

Once the skeletal frame has fully developed, a buck continues to develop mass his body and antlers. At 6½ years old, all biologists consider a buck to be mature in muscles, skeleton, body, and antlers. Between the ages of 4½ and 6½ depending on where the buck lives, he will usually develop his largest set of typical antlers. Exactly which antlers become a buck's most impressive set depends on factors including habitat, genetics, quality of food sources, weather conditions, and whether the buck suffers from injury or sickness.

The antlers will continue to increase in both size and mass as the buck gets older. Once a free-range whitetail buck reaches about 6½ years old, however, his antlers may either remain typical in shape or, more likely, develop into an unusual configuration. At 7½ and older, a buck's antlers will begin to decline in mass, shape, and the number of points. This is due to the fact that from 7½ or 8½ years old (again, depending on where the buck lives), his teeth will be significantly worn down, making it more difficult for him to grind his food enough to release the maximum amount of nutrients. As a result, he begins to lose weight and his body condition, antler size, and overall health quickly decline.

Now that I have covered the biological and physical factors that define an adult buck, I'd like to share some of my tactics and strategies to hone your adult buck hunting skills. Some of these suggestions are common sense, others are known tactics, and others are some of my most successful and guarded secrets for consistently taking mature bucks year after year.

Confidence

In each and every one of the ten whitetail books I have penned over the years, I include this point as the number one component for habitually harvesting deer. Confidence is the most important thing a hunter can use as a strategy. In my first book *Whitetail Strategies: A No-Nonsense Approach to Successful Deer Hunting*, I wrote a chapter that began with the formula:

$$C + PT \times C = CS$$

(Concentration plus Positive Thinking multiplied by Confidence equals Consistent Success)

Since that time, I have altered the equation slightly to be more accurately stated. The formula now reads:

$$(C^2 + PT^{10}) \times \Delta TC = CS$$

(Confidence squared plus Positive Thinking to the tenth, multiplied by change in Total Concentration equals Consistent Success)

Yes, I'm a huge fan of *The Big Bang Theory* and obviously a frustrated would-be theoretical physicist.

You will notice an immediate and dramatic increase in your deer hunting success as soon as you convince yourself that you are a better hunter than you believe. If you don't believe me, consider this. If you live and hunt in any of the heavily hunted and pressured areas, including New York, New Jersey, Pennsylvania, or any state in New England, I assure you that you are one of the nation's top-notch deer hunters. The deer in these areas have fine-tuned their behaviors to cope with heavy hunting pressure like nowhere else in North America and have evolved to become the most wary and difficult whitetails to kill. Let no one dispute that with you.

The power of positive thinking is well-known, particularly among entrepreneurs, CEOs, investment bankers, professional athletes, coaches, and self-help motivational gurus, including L. Ron Hubbard and Tony Roberts. In the hunting genre, having confidence was brought to light by Gene and Barry Wensel in the 1980s. The point of urging you to have confidence in your hunting abilities is to help you exploit the influences of positive thinking and use its energy to maximize your hunting success (and life in general). In other words, "May the Force be with you." Yep, I'm a die-hard *Star Trek* fan who occasionally and reluctantly quotes Yoda of *Star Wars* fame—there I've admitted it.

I am sure you have questioned your tactics or the location of a particular stand ad nauseam. I can almost guarantee that while sitting on post, you allow yourself to get distracted by contemplations. When you are a negative deer hunter, you are doomed for failure. When you believe you won't see deer, you won't see deer.

The simple fact is that it only takes a deer, specifically an adult buck, seconds to slip quietly by the stand of a hunter who is preoccupied with outside thoughts or, worse yet, texting (see Chapter Seven). You must be in the game to win. I urge you to believe in your hunting skills and decisions. If in your heart you allow yourself to believe you are a better hunter, you will be.

Let Young Bucks Walk By

The first reality about being able to regularly kill adult bucks is to realize and accept that a hunter must resist the temptation to draw his or her bow or release the safety off on a firearm when they see a young buck under their stand. Instead of shooting an immature buck, let him walk by and give him the time he needs to grow into an adult. There is no other choice. It might be a hard pill to swallow for some, but it is the reality of increasing your adult buck population.

Hunters who want to hunt only adult bucks must decide not to shoot immature bucks. A spike buck can grow a set of eight-point antlers if he is allowed the time to reach adulthood.

Keep in mind that the size of a semi-mature or adult buck's antlers will differ greatly from one part of North America to another. Some 3½- to 4½-year-old bucks living in the heavily hunted areas of the Northeast or New England might have a set of antlers that measure in the high 120- to low 130-inch range and be regarded as adults. A buck with 130-inch antlers would be passed up by most hunters in

Texas, Wisconsin, Michigan, Minnesota, Iowa, Ohio, Saskatchewan, and Alberta, as well as other areas that produce large-antlered bucks from 3½ years old and older. In these areas, hunters set their goals on taking mature bucks that are no fewer than 4½ or 5½ years old.

Each hunter's definition of an adult buck (setting aside the biological standards) can be dramatically different depending on what part of the North America they hunt. I know some hunters who would give their left pinky finger to take a 3½-year-old buck with eight points that scores 125 to 135 inches. In certain areas of our country, a buck with antlers scoring in that range can be a trophy of a lifetime and rightfully so. Not all hunters are blessed with living in areas that produce 3½-year-old bucks with trophy-class antlers that score 150 inches or better.

The next strategy to learn is how to field judge the age class of male deer. A basic strategy to consistently taking mature bucks is to be able to identify a mature buck compared to younger bucks. This might sound obvious, but trust me when I say that probably 50 percent of the deer hunters I talk to have trouble identifying a mature buck on the hoof. They find it especially difficult judging a 3½-year-old buck from younger ones. The guidelines below will help anyone to recognize a mature buck quicker and easier. The information starts by identifying male deer from when they are fawns until they reach full maturity.

Buck Fawns

A reliable way to determine a fawn buck is to look for the small nubs on its head. Remember, they will barely be visible. Another good indicator is the length of the fawn's head. It will be noticeably shorter and more compact than older deer. Fawn bucks also have flat foreheads compared to the rounded foreheads of female deer. This particular feature becomes more pronounced as the season progresses. Buck fawns are more independent and, therefore, often seen traveling alone, particularly during the breeding season. They will emerge from bedding areas earlier and are sometimes seen feeding by themselves, especially in known food plots. If you want to preserve buck fawns, it is best to avoid shooting lone antlerless deer. A fawn buck's face often looks like a lamb's face.

To avoid shooting a fawn buck, take the time to closely examine the deer's skull with binoculars. Many times their antler nubs are barely visible.

A 1½-year-old buck will often have a fawn-like face and its body will lack any sign of muscular development. Its rack will generally have pencil-thin tines and be narrow in width.

1½-Year-Old Male Deer

This age class often has a petite body, young-looking face, and undeveloped neck. Its legs are noticeably long and slender, and its body resembles that of a doe. A yearling buck's antler development can vary widely from spikes to a basket rack or even a small ten-point rack. However, the antlers often lack mass and height. The length of its main beams will also be short, particularly when compared to older bucks. Another obvious indicator will be their tarsal glands. They will appear as small areas that are light tan instead of dark brown or black.

2½-Year-Old Male Deer

At this age class, a buck's body often appears to be lanky, as if its legs are growing faster than its body. It will have a thin neck, a feminine-looking face, and its stomach area will appear tight. Its antlers will get the attention of most hunters at this stage of their development. The tarsal glands will be dark brown to black, but they will still not be as visible or pronounced as an older buck's.

Photo Credit: Ted Rose

This buck represents what most 2½-year-old bucks' face, neck, and antlers look like. The rest of the body is long and lanky, but it is beginning to show signs of some body development.

3½-Year-Old Male Deer

At this age, a buck usually reaches his full skeletal maturity. His neck becomes conspicuously fuller and his chest perceptibly thicker. These are two classic features of a 3½-year-old mature buck. Its neck muscles increase, which becomes visible especially during the rut. Its chest is beginning to appear larger than its rump. Its back and stomach, however, are still straight and tight. Its neck is still five or more inches from its brisket. At this stage, the tarsal glands will be dark brown to black. It is still not as big or heavy as a fully mature 5½-year-old buck.

Photo Credit: Ted Rose

At 3½ years old, a buck's body is nearing full development. At this stage, most nutrition is now directed toward his antlers rather than body and skeletal development.

4½-Year-Old Male Deer

Bucks at this age become hard to confuse with younger bucks. Now, they have definitely attained skeletal maturity and exhibit many char-

acteristics of being a mature whitetail buck. Its rump will appear full, deep, and rounded. Its neck will be more muscular, making the deer look like a football player who has worked out. Its body looks thicker and stocky throughout. Its stomach and back will still look tight but now, for the first time, its legs appear shorter than they should for its body size. Its tarsal glands

At 4½ years old, a buck begins to have a deep chest and visible muscular development. His legs appear shorter and he looks stockier.

are clearly large and black due to continuous urinating and rubbing. Deer's bodies have reached full size by this age and they appear ripped and lean. These bucks can grow a terrific set of antlers, making them prime targets for hunters focusing on taking mature bucks.

5½-Year-Old Male Deer

At 5½ years old, most free-range bucks have reached the peak of maturity in their body, muscles, skeleton, and antler development. Usually at this age, they will sport the largest set of antlers they have ever grown. Their bodies also exhibit obvious changes. Now their stomach and back show perceptible signs of sagging. Their neck is considerably swollen in preparation for the rut. Their brisket area appears to be extremely muscular. The neck area is large, muscular, and firm. The tarsal glands will be conspicuously large and black. Many bucks in this age class have urine stains running down the inside of their legs all the way down to their hooves. Their forehead gland appears noticeably thicker and darker because of increased secretions. A 5½-year-old buck's legs will definitely look too short for his body.

All these indicators are meant to help hunters identify both immature and mature male deer. Once a hunter has the physical information concretely in his or her mind, he or she will be able to confidently identify a mature buck from younger male deer.

Bucks that are 5½ to 6½ years old have reached peak maturity. Everything about their bodies and antlers shows signs of adulthood.

TACTICS FOR TAKING MATURE BUCKS

Now I want to discuss some hardcore hunting tactics and information about bagging mature bucks. All the tactics from here on in this chapter are strategies for taking male deer 3½-years-old or older. The first strategy is one that most hunters will find unusual. But it can end a regular bow or early primitive bow or firearm season early.

Adult Bucks Act Differently

Yet another key point to keep in mind when setting your sights on taking a mature buck is that there is a marked difference in behavior when compared to a younger male deer. Almost all young bucks act the same. That is not the case when it comes to setting your sights on taking an adult buck. When you decide to hunt mature male deer, you must remember that mature bucks act totally different than young bucks and rarely abide by so-called textbook behaviors.

Therefore, it is crucial for the hunter to find a flaw in a mature buck's habits, behaviors, and travel patterns to be consistently successful. Think of a mature buck as being a skittish, nervous wreck who is inclined to be afraid of his own shadow. This behavior makes adult bucks do things according to their own mind-set more than younger deer.

Mature deer tend to move just before or just after dusk and return to their beds at or just before dawn. Many hunters believe this behavior accounts for them becoming totally nocturnal when hunting pressure starts. That is one of the biggest misunderstandings about male deer. No buck **only** moves under the protection of total darkness.

Even in heavily hunted areas, mature bucks have learned that they can move about in daylight. Through years of experience, they have become wise to the fact that they can go about their daily routine by moving during the off-hours between 10 a.m. to 2 p.m. During those four hours, a buck will get up to stretch his legs, grab a quick snack, or relieve himself. Bucks generally defecate about thirty-six times over a twenty-four-hour period or about twelve times during daylight hours. They urinate about the same number of times during the day. It is easy to figure out that between pooping, peeing, eating, stretching, and changing where he is bedded down, an adult buck moves around a lot more during daylight hours than hunters realize. When you factor in the rut, there is considerably more buck movement during daylight.

Hunt Early to Score

I'm a firm believer that the best strategy to take mature bucks is to hunt them as early in the season as possible. In some states, such as my home state of New York, game departments offer an early primitive firearm

Photo credit: Ted Rose

A key strategy to killing an adult buck, but one seldom used by hunters, is to penetrate a buck's bedding area. With the necessary precautions, a hunter can do this successfully.

or bow season that begins before the regular bow season starts. If you have an option to hunt these primitive seasons (some start as early as September) or just the regular bow season, they provide fantastic opportunities to take a mature buck. Even the most wary adult buck can be caught off guard during an early season. I first got smart to this tactic only after repeatedly noticing how often I saw buck movement during the first week of an early bow or firearm season, no matter what part of North America I was hunting. Time and time again, I discovered mature bucks can be killed this time of year before they are alerted to hunting pressure.

A key to taking a mature buck in the early season is to set up along well-traveled buck routes as close to their bedding areas as possible. I know a lot of you reading this are thinking, "What? He wants me to set up as close to a bedding area as possible? Is he nuts?" Well, it isn't a big surprise that trying to bag a buck near his bedroom is not, by any stretch of the imagination, an easy task. The fact is, it is hard to achieve and it's a downright risky tactic. Adult bucks will not tolerate repeated intrusion. This is a simple makeup of their genetic behavior. I can assure you that as few as two careless incursions into an adult buck's bedding area, no matter what time of year it is, often results in the buck moving out of that zone. However, when the strategy is used correctly and executed to the best of your ability, you will get the opportunity to bust a buck in his bedroom, and he might turn out to be the oldest and largest-antlered buck of your life.

So how do you find where a mature buck is bedding? The most practical way without blowing the buck out of the area is to locate it by using trail cameras along buck trails. Buck trails are usually not far from heavily traveled doe trails. Once you get pictures of a mature buck on the cameras, plan to set up a stand that is hidden by natural cover along the trail that leads from the bed to the currently used food sources.

Hunting adult bucks during the early season is without question the best time of year to use this tactic. All the natural ground vegetation is thick and green, the trees are still full of leaves, and the forest ground is quiet to walk on. The worst time of year to employ this strategy is fall or winter. You simply can't invade a buck's bedding when you are crunching leaves or walking on frozen snow. Under those conditions, even an immature spike buck will hightail it out of the area. An adult buck will move so quickly you would think he evaporated into thin air.

Buck Rubs are Key Clues

Once a hunter practices early season buck hunting, he or she will gain experience on just what areas attract mature bucks. This knowledge will help the hunter predict where he or she can locate adult bucks more easily with each passing year. However, one type of evidence that will put you on the right track immediately is buck rubs.

All the areas where I've bagged mature bucks during early season hunting near bedding and feeding areas contained a number of old and new rubs. At this time of year, whitetail bucks don't generally move far from their core area during their daily routines. Once you discover a few fresh rubs or a place where several trees have been rubbed near thick cover, you're probably close to a mature buck bedding area.

If you find a large rub, the odds are 50-50 that it was made by a mature buck. But don't let the size of the rub dictate whether or not you hunt an area. As I have mentioned previously, I've have taken a lot of video of big bucks rubbing small trees and vice versa. I have several video clips of yearling bucks rubbing trees with a trunk as thick as a baseball bat. A savvy hunter realizes he or she can only make generalities when it comes to whitetail behavior. As I am fond of saying, nothing about whitetail behavior is written in stone.

Another important thing to remember about early season hunting is that it is more than likely that an adult buck isn't alone. In the bachelor group, there are often immature bucks, as well. Even if you locate a few fresh pencil-thin rubs that you feel were made by a yearling buck, he could be hanging out with an older buck or two.

I once shot a 140-class buck that was accompanied by two other mature bucks and two smaller 110-class bucks. I saw the group on October 15th. When adult male bucks leave their beds to go feed during this time of year, they usually move lethargically. This behavior will allow you to take your time to look the buck over carefully and decide if he is an adult long before he gets into range. Keep this in mind, as it would be disappointing to shoot a nice eight-pointer only to see a much larger ten-pointer following closely behind him after you have taken your shot.

Lessons Adult Bucks Teach

Without question, every mature buck I have killed has taught me something about how adult bucks behave differently than younger bucks do. I'd like to share a story about one such buck with you.

Just as the first signs of dawn poked over the horizon and filtered through the woods, I heard the soft, guttural grunt I have come to associate with an adult buck. My anticipation and heart rate immediately heightened. Minutes later, I saw a buck swagger defiantly out of a swamp about two hundred fifty yards from the ledge I was on. I glassed the buck and saw he had a heavy set of antlers that sported ten points. As he walked toward me, between pine trees and windfalls, I could hear his hooves splashing through the water. With so many saplings, trees, and other forest vegetation between us, I couldn't consider taking a shot at him—not at that distance, anyway. I waited at the ready as the buck kept walking toward me. When he was about one hundred fifty yards off, I considered shooting, but only momentarily as he was facing me. I would have had to make a difficult straight-on shot, which seemed unrealistic. Again, I patiently watched as the buck kept walking toward me.

As he continued in my general direction, I could see from his body size and configuration that he was definitely a mature buck. His chest was wide, deep, and muscular. His legs appeared too short for his body. His muzzle was gray, his forehead hairs were dark brown from forehead gland fluids, and his neck was fat and rippled with each step he took. Both tarsal glands were jet-black and he had urine stains running down both legs. There wasn't a doubt in my mind—I was looking at a buck that was at least 4½ years old. I had to concentrate on not getting overexcited or I would surely risk losing him.

Minutes later, he reached the edge of the bog and stepped onto a narrow deer trail that bordered the edge of the swamp. The buck paused for a moment, taking in a long whiff of air as he curled his lip. Whether it was intentional or not, he stopped behind an old thick pine tree that protected his kill zone. If he hadn't, he would have been dead before he hit the ground. Deer, particularly mature bucks, instinctively learn to take advantage of whatever cover is available to them. Everyone reading this has probably seen this behavior and had a similar experience.

With his nose held high, the buck tried to detect the slightest scent of estrus in the air. Almost immediately, his vomeronasal organ analyzed the air and identified the odor left by a hot doe. The buck quickly turned and slowly took a few steps forward along the trail in a southwesterly direction. He took each step purposefully as he held his nose tightly to the ground, all the while keeping enough cover between us to prevent me from taking a shot. He was moving slowly but with a single-mindedness that made it apparent he had a specific destination.

Then, without warning, the buck began to walk more quickly along the trail and seemed totally focused on getting where he wanted to go. Knowing he was distracted by the estrus scent, I decided to let him get about fifty yards ahead of me. Once he did, I began to carefully shadow him. I paralleled his every movement, with a slight northwest wind in my favor. The buck seemed oblivious to his surroundings, but through many trials and errors with hunting adult bucks, I knew better. He was more than likely tuned in to everything happening around him. As he continued to make his way along the deer trail, he lifted his head occasionally to get a quick sense of the direction he was heading. My stalk was flawless and unfolding to be a rare nirvana-like moment. The wind remained perfect; the sun had risen higher to help mask my movements. I carefully placed each footfall and avoided any noise. I also luckily avoided alerting any unseen deer.

I was reasonably sure that sometime soon the buck would stop to check the estrus scent along the trail, giving me a chance to settle the crosshairs of my scope on his front shoulder. Instead, his pace suddenly quickened again and he veered slightly off the deer trail. At the same second, a smaller-racked buck stepped out onto the trail ahead of him. The larger buck's steps slowed only for a split second. He immediately pinned his ears as far back on his head as he could and, as he passed the younger buck, he seemed to intentionally bump into him with his front shoulder and pushed his way past the younger deer without even glancing at him. The older buck made his point and the smaller buck quickly ran to the security of the swamp. At that point, I did not mind if the hunt ended successfully or not—I had enjoyed what I witnessed and learned thus far.

After a long twenty minutes of following the buck, I got a sense that my luck was about to run out. I was still waiting for any opportunity for the buck to stop and offer me a clear shot when it seemed as though he realized I was dogging his trail. Even though he hadn't visually checked behind himself, he purposefully hopped off the trail and continued to parallel it while walking in the water at the edge of the swamp. In doing so, he was placing thicker cover between us, again preventing any opportunity for me to get a shot at him. The ridge was about to turn in a totally different direction in fewer than one hundred yards. I knew if I didn't get a shot at the buck soon I would lose any chance to do so. I glanced ahead, and saw a spot about fifty yards in front of the buck that offered the best opportunity for a shot. It was now or never. I carefully quickened my pace to close the distance just a little more.

With my last chance slipping away fast, I made an estrus blat, knowing he would totally ignore a grunt vocalization. At the exact moment I put the call to my lips, the buck lifted his head, glanced back at me, and quickly trotted into a thicket in the swamp. He was gone in an instant. I stood there in total disbelief with thoughts racing through my mind, "Was I too picky? Too careful? Should I have risked taking a dicey shot?" A quick mental reply answered absolutely not. I had no doubt in my mind now that the buck knew I was dogging his trail most, if not all, of the time I was following him.

He instinctively kept a safe distance ahead of me and felt secure and comfortable moving through the available cover. He wasn't going to allow me to distract his pursuit of the hot doe, but neither was he going to give me a good opportunity to kill him. A younger buck may have panicked and stopped to check his back trail, but he wasn't a younger buck. This savvy old buck knew exactly what he had to do. I learned that a common behavior of mature bucks is that they know precisely how to avoid a predator without panicking. As long as I stayed out of what he perceived as his danger zone and he kept constant cover between us, he felt comfortable enough to follow the estrus scent. The second I disturbed his comfort zone, his fight-or-flight instinct kicked in and he disappeared without a split second of hesitation.

The hunt ended in frustration but without any regrets in the decisions I made. I was content that I was able to see a terrific mature buck and learn from the experience even though I didn't get a shot at him. On that particular cold November morning, I was fine with being outwitted. Bucks in this age class develop their own personalities, habits, and escape techniques. Having information and understanding mature buck behaviors will, more often than not, help close the gap between hunter and prey.

Another important, if not crucial, fact to remember about taking an adult buck is that you have to hunt for them where adult bucks live. A hunter can waste a lot of valuable time stalking in areas that simply don't have all the components to attract adult bucks. The area might not offer the nutritional components needed for a buck to reach 4½ years or older, such as the right minerals in the soil, genetics, water, year-round quality forage, ample cover, etc. This theory also applies to hunters who set their goals on taking Boone and Crockett bucks. A buck with antlers large enough to make the Boone and Crockett record books will most often be 5½ to 6½ years of age. Therefore, hunting in areas that don't have all the necessary elements to support adult bucks in that age class drastically decreases the chances of taking a Boone and Crockett animal.

For instance, in New York, if a person hunts deer in the lower Catskill Mountains in Sullivan County, the odds of taking a trophy-class buck with antlers that would score high enough to be entered into the Boone and Crockett record books are less than good. If that same person hunted in some of the western counties in New York, however, the odds would increase dramatically. In other words, you can waste a lot of hunting time searching for mature 4½-year-old bucks or older if you hunt in areas that don't regularly produce bucks in that age class.

Research Pays Big Dividends

An important step to taking a mature buck begins with researching an area you want to hunt. Get a copy of your state's record book, such as New York's NYS Big Buck Club. Almost every state has one. If you're a bow hunter, you will also want to check out the Pope and Young record books. For those who have aspirations of killing a Boone and Crockett buck, obtain the Boone and Crockett record book, as well. These books will not only show you the states and provinces that are producing the most record-book bucks, but also the counties or parishes that offer the best opportunities. Make careful note of the dates the bucks were taken when reading these record books. That will help you select what places are currently producing big bucks as opposed to where big bucks were taken in the 50s and 60s.

Keep in mind that mature bucks come from places with well-managed deer herds. A high concentration of deer usually means there is too much competition for food, reducing the chances of producing a true trophy-class buck. Areas that have low concentrations of deer will produce bigger bucks for a variety of reasons, including one of the most crucial aspects of taking a mature buck, low hunting pressure. Low deer densities will also mean more forage for the deer living in that area. Additionally, it offers bucks the opportunity to grow to an age that produces the best set of antlers, which is 5½ years old.

Further research should include contacting the wildlife departments of potential areas you select. Talk with the wildlife manager in that area about the local deer herd. A site survey, if at all practical, is also a good bet. Visit the area during the summer and scout it. The most effective way to scout a potential area is to drive it during prime hours of dawn and dusk when deer are moving and not under hunting pressure. Spotting deer from your vehicle during this time of year can be easier and more productive.

Another adult buck hunting tips is to read everything you can about the behavior of adult bucks to broaden your knowledge. Treat adult bucks as if they were big fish—in other words, your presentation has to be nearly perfect to get an opportunity to hook one. When hunting any buck, keep as low a profile as you possibly can. When it comes to stalking and killing an adult buck, this tactic is amplified. I have also learned that an impressive majority, about 80 percent, of the adult bucks I have killed have been taken between the hours of 10 a.m. and 2 p.m. Hey, you can sleep in, go hunting later, and still end up taking a mature buck.

Core Areas in the Afternoon

An additional element that will help you take a mature buck is learning how to get close to bedding and core areas in the afternoon to intercept deer before hunting light runs out. Soon after the hunting pressure begins, mature bucks rarely walk into open fields or through open hardwoods. The exception to this is when his brain has left its original position and now occupies a space much lower in his body. In other words, only a doe in peak estrus can lure an adult buck from the security of cover and into a field or open hardwoods during the last hour before dusk.

Often, a mature buck will leave his core area or bedding spot within thirty minutes of legal light. He will slowly pick his way painstaking and very carefully through the thickly covered staging areas to places he knows does are feeding. If you hunt the staging areas, you will get opportunities to shoot mature bucks that you would not have had if you hunted more open spaces. It is necessary to mention here, however, that all bets are off when it comes to the big chase or prime rut periods. During these short but active times, even the biggest buck can throw caution to the wind.

Oddly, what I have discovered about a majority of these mature bucks is that while some of them are resident bucks, most have turned out to be bucks I have never seen in the area. They are transient male deer usually seen by hunters once or twice on their property and then never again. These animals are mature 4½-year-old and older whitetails. Some adult bucks have a wandering personality and are not content with remaining within their home range during the rut (see the chapter on adult buck dispersal). These types of bucks live by the adage "The grass is always greener on the other side of the fence." They constantly seek hot does over long distances during the rut. Other mature bucks are content to live within their home range and rarely, if ever, leave it, even during the rut.

For most deer hunters, their ultimate deer hunting goal is to see and consistently have opportunities to bag mature 3½- to 4½-year-old or older bucks. For many others, however, the ultimate deer hunting dream is to take a trophy-class whitetail buck with antlers that measure high enough to be entered into Pope and Young or Boone and Crockett record books. It is an aspiration that takes plenty of planning, patience, skill, and a good dose of luck.

In the end, taking an adult buck with a good set of antlers shouldn't be considered a walk in the park. If you want to see more adult bucks on the land you own or lease, you and your hunting companions must allow young bucks to live a couple more years. By letting younger bucks walk by, some will survive and get the time they need to grow into adult bucks with large antlers, though others will be inevitably shot by neighbors or other hunters. It also demands an unwavering commitment and dedication to stick to plans and goals to take your hunting skills to the next level. That might include staying in your stand and extra hour or two when the wind is howling, during a downpour as big bucks love to move in heavy rain, or when the thermometer drops below ten degrees and your toes and fingers feel like they are going to drop off. Total commitment to the hunt is a crucial factor for any dedicated deer stalker to bag the trophy buck of a lifetime.

When you finally make the decision to hunt adult bucks more often or exclusively, you must also be able to quickly and accurately field judge a buck on the hoof in thirty seconds or less. With practice, this is a skill anyone can master. By combining all the suggestions and guidelines in this chapter, you will greatly enhance your adult buck hunting skills and achievements. Gaining the understanding and realization that adult bucks act much differently than young bucks and knowing how to apply the tactics to take an adult buck are your steps to taking more adult bucks from year to year.

Chapter Thirteen

Antler Rattling Secrets Revealed

I have been hunting whitetails since 1964. But it wasn't until 1975 that I tried the then little-known tactic known as antler rattling. My first attempt at rattling took place in the small hamlet of Childwold, New York, tucked away in the Adirondack Mountains. Before I tell you about that first humorous, but important, story of lessons learned, I want to make an important point. The antler rattling methods I used in 1975 are no longer the techniques I use today. In 1998, I accidentally discovered how to exponentially increase my rattling success on a scouting trip in September, but more about that to follow.

My rattling methods and strategies have changed enough since 1975 that it is important for you to read this chapter, even if you have read or heard what I have said over the years about rattling in books, articles, at seminars, or on my television program. You will pick up a lot of new and useful information.

What I learned in 1999 was that there are five different types of contact that bucks engage in from as early as September to as late as December. Knowing how and when to rattle during each of the five phases will improve your odds of rattling in a buck significantly. However, each phase requires a specific technique.

I changed my rattling methods mostly as a result of firsthand experience and I learned what worked most reliably over the past thirty-eight years. With that said, the adages "Learn through trial and error" and

When I rattle antlers, I often use a deer call after I finish each sequence. The call helps to create a natural illusion for any buck I'm trying to lure in.

"Live and learn" more accurately describe the reasons for changing my rattling methods.

What I have learned about deer behavior and biology from hunting, studying, and videotaping whitetail deer has also influenced the changes I have made to my rattling tactics. But what taught me the most about rattling were the times I was unsuccessful at rattling in a buck. In fact, I became tuned in on how to take my rattling from good to better and, finally, to what is currently working best (and most consistently) for me by paying attention to the mistakes I made along the way.

The strategies I share in this chapter will help the novice hunter rattle like a veteran and provide useful information to assist long-time veterans who are old hands at this tactic. Whichever category you belong to, newcomer or veteran, you will increase your success quickly and have more opportunities to bag a buck.

I want to stress that much of what I talk about here is new rattling information that I have rarely talked about before. When used correctly, you will be able to rattle in bucks when other hunters, even those who are experienced, aren't having success with their efforts.

Rattling Works Anywhere

Even after years of reading about successful rattling tactics in outdoor magazines, seeing bucks rattled in on DVDs and television, and attending seminars on the subject, a lot of hunters still don't believe rattling works, particularly in the heavily hunted areas of the Northeast or New England. They have a myriad of excuses, opinions, hearsay, and other so-called "proof" that supports their feelings that rattling is, at best, a hit-or-miss tactic or, at worst, a total waste of time. They have little confidence that antler rattling works.

Therefore they are reluctant to believe rattling is, without a doubt, a significant and practical calling tactic. I'll bet if you put a group of hard-core whitetail hunters in a room and asked them to discuss whether they thought rattling works, the subject would be hotly debated for hours. In the end, the odds are that a majority would say rattling doesn't work. Or, at least they would say that they have never experienced much success using it.

That is most likely the reason why rattling is a calling method many hunters overlook. Although rattling works wherever white-tails roam, many hunters believe it only works in Texas or remote areas. Trust me when I tell you that rattling works anywhere in North America, even in the most heavily hunted areas.

Like all hunting tactics, antler rattling doesn't work every time you use it. It does work enough, however, to be a valuable hunting tool as long as it is done correctly. While it is not a difficult strategy to learn, the more hunters know about any deer hunting tactic they use, the more successful they will be. To be a consistently successful antler rattler, it takes a lot more than just knocking two antlers together to call in a buck, though on rare occasions even that can work.

This hunter is rattling during the late New York muzzleloader season in December. December is the fifth and final phase of the battling buck stage of buck fights.

Photo Credit: Ted Rose

Photo Credit: Ted Rose

This hunter is rattling in late November during the phase I call the clash and brawl stage.

The key to consistent rattling success is to understand how, when, where, and why to rattle. It also requires a deeper understanding of whitetail bucks' fighting behaviors and instinctive responses to other bucks engaged in a fight. Understanding these elements will help even the most experienced hunters take their rattling efforts to the next level.

Most importantly, remember that every buck has its own character. His individuality will cause him to react differently than other bucks might when responding to what he thinks are two bucks engaged in a skirmish. This is a crucial statement and once you understand its importance, you will quickly become a top-notch antler rattler.

Luck

Many of your hunting buddies will emphatically assure you that rattling in a buck is nothing more than luck—I want to reassure you that they are wrong. Hunters who believe antler rattling success is due to luck should consider what Alicia M. Soderberg, Assistant Professor of Astrophysics at Harvard University, is fond of saying about luck in relation to uncovering the many wonders of the universe, "Discovery is usually associated with serendipity, but luck favors the prepared. In the field of science you have to be prepared if you want to make important discoveries." I find Professor Soderberg's idea of luck to be a deeply philosophical statement that can be applied to any part of life, including the art of successfully rattling in a buck.

Luck has little to do with rattling success if a hunter is well-prepared. A hunter will discover that his or her ability to rattle in a buck is not by spawned by luck, coincidence, accident, good fortune, kismet, or serendipity. Rather it happens by purposeful design. Those who arm themselves with valid information and use it intelligently are successful in any endeavor they undertake. By embracing all the elements I mentioned above, you will enhance your overall rattling success.

Ralph Somma with a rattled up buck shot on our farm in New York. Ralph is a longtime successful buck hunter who strongly believes that rattling has, as he says, "Very little to do with luck."

Photo Credit: Fiduccia Ent.

My First Experience with Rattling

Rattling is an exhilarating calling method. A hunter can never be sure how a rattling session will play out in the woods. That's what makes antler rattling so much fun—it is filled with unbridled anticipation. First-time rattlers are often shocked out of their hunting boots when a buck actually responds to their efforts. I have talked with some who say they were so surprised that they froze and could only watch as the buck got away before they could get a shot.

Before I get to the nitty-gritty details of successful antler rattling tactics that can be used from September to December, I want to share with you a short story about my first rattling experience. If you have read this story before (it was included in my first book *Whitetail Strategies: A No-Nonsense Approach to Successful Deer Hunting*), feel free to skip over it and go directly to the meat and potatoes of this chapter. You won't hurt my feelings by doing so. However, you may want to refresh your memory and enjoy reading it again.

I packed my gear and headed to an area I hunted in Childwold, New York—a small hamlet nestled between Tupper Lake and Cranberry Lake on Route 3 in the Adirondack Mountains. I started hunting in the Childwold area several years earlier when International Paper Company opened their lands to hunting for the first time in more than one hundred years.

During the first few years I hunted there, I saw several large bucks that were shot by other hunters. I thought this was surely a place to try rattling. After getting off the beaten trail, I found a little knoll that overlooked a thick area and a swamp. I began to rattle my antlers together just as it became light. After several rattling sessions, I heard the unmistakable noise of crunching leaves heading in my direction. My heart beat wildly, and I expected to see a monster buck emerge from the pines behind me. As the crunch, crunch, crunching got closer, I was beginning to think it sounded too much like the footfalls of a person. Then, to my surprise, I spotted a six-foot-six Adirondack lumberjack-type man walking toward me while uttering countless profanities.

When he got nose to nose with me (and I mean nose to nose) he stopped. In a deep and threatening voice that reeked of cigarette breath (which I can recall vividly today), he said, "What the hell are you doing, stupid?!"

"I'm rattling," I said in a meek and embarrassed voice.

"You're what?" he snapped back.

"I'm rattling," I once again replied.

Then I showed him the small but sharp set of deer antlers I held tightly clutched in my hands, hoping he would recognize them as potentially deadly weapons.

"Well, I have a $%#&*^ bulletin for you, buddy. You hit those *&$#$%$# horns together again and disturb my hunting, and I'll come back here and stick them where they can't make any more noise and will cause you a lot of discomfort—get me?"

Remember, back in the early 1970s hardly anybody east of Texas had heard about rattling, and the few who had thought it was ridiculous because of all the noise it made in the woods.

With my lumberjack still nose to nose with me, all my instincts told me to run. Unfortunately, I was sure if I moved he would see that I urinated in my pants and would take that as a clue to beat me to death where I stood. So instead, I assured him I would put the antlers away and he would not have to be bothered by the noise again. As he walked away I could hear him grumbling something like, "Smart move."

I noticed with intense interest, however, that he walked off in a totally different direction from which he approached me. I'm Italian and, therefore, I'm pretty headstrong. I interpreted his departure in a new direction as a signal of total disgust, which meant that he had given up hunting in this area. I waited for about an hour—which I thought was a safe amount of time—and then mustered up the courage to start rattling again.

As lady luck would have it (or Murphy's Law), not fifteen minutes after I had made my third or fourth rattling sequence (I can't remember for sure, it was so long ago), I heard two quick shots. Then someone called out, "Hey Buddy!" (Now I was someone's buddy.) "Come here, you're not going to believe this!"

I must admit, I hesitated before making my way over to the voice. I had serious thoughts about the distinct possibility of not returning intact. But the excitement in the voice sounded genuine, so over the knoll I went. To my utter amazement, there on the ground—not one hundred yards from where I was rattling—was a magnificent eight-point New York Adirondack buck. Not twenty yards from the buck was the lumberjack-type guy yelling at the top of his lungs, "Buddy, you're not going to believe this. When you started rattling again I decided to get up and come and pay you another visit. Just as I got to my feet, that buck lying there broke out of the swamp and was heading right to you—so I thought I'd better shoot him first."

I smiled even though I wanted to stick my rattling antlers in his eyes and said, "Glad it worked for one of us."

While I was extraordinarily disappointed that he shot the buck I had rattled in, the dead buck that lay before me was solid proof that rattling did indeed work. From that moment on, I was convinced I was onto a new and exciting hunting strategy. And as long as some other anti-rattling six-foot-six hunter didn't either beat me to death for rattling or shoot the buck I rattled in, I assured myself I would continue to rattle until I rattled in and shot a buck.

Photo Credit: Fiduccia Ent.

Here is the Adirondack hunter who shot the first buck I ever rattled up. His good fate was the start to my decades of antler rattling success. His face is blurred to save my hide.

Well, I didn't rattle in another buck for the rest of that deer season. But I remained undeterred by the valuable lesson of that day and continued to rattle the next year, as well. I did, in fact, rattle in and shoot a small six-point buck. Another important thing I learned that day was, as a rattler, you have to believe that rattling works and that it will work anywhere in North America you hunt.

The above account is true to the smallest details I can recall. It will remain in my mind forever as a learning experience that was a major turning point in my hunting career. It not only taught me that rattling worked, it also demonstrated to me that being confident enough to try a new strategy, even one that at the time was highly controversial, was worthwhile.

From that day forward, I promised myself that whatever hunting tactic I tried or invented, no matter how far-fetched it seemed, I would try enthusiastically and with confidence. Many of my successful home remedy whitetail hunting tactics developed from this insight. In fact, I discovered I could rattle in a buck in September by rattling to a buck that I only thought was nearby. That anecdote is included later on in this chapter.

Have Confidence

After my encounter in the Adirondacks, I tried rattling in a buck that I would kill. To my surprise, within a week I rattled my first buck. Oddly, the more rattling success I had that year, the more I began to doubt the bucks were actually responding to my antler rattling efforts. I wouldn't let myself believe the tactic was working so well. When I rattled in a buck and he would come by my stand, I would rationalize that maybe this buck was going to pass by my stand anyway. Does this type of reasoning sound familiar to you?

One of the most troublesome elements about the tactic of antler rattling is that hunters often believe when they see a buck after they've rattled that the buck's appearance was circumstantial and didn't have to do with their rattling efforts. This can account for many hunters giving up on rattling as a calling tactic.

Once you pick up a set of antlers and rattle, if a buck passes your stand within the next hour or so, it has to be considered a buck you have rattled in. Why? Well, to be frank, it's a confidence builder, but more importantly, because it is true. Over the years I have rattled, I can say with assurance that some bucks will respond to the sounds of antler rattling within minutes, some within an hour, and still others even longer

I rattled this buck up several years after I began using the tactic. With each buck I bagged by rattling, my confidence grew exponentially—and yours will too.

than that. It becomes clear that when a buck shows up under your stand within an hour or so of rattling, he must be considered a buck that you rattled in.

Not Every Buck Responds the Same Way

Another critical point about being a successful rattler is that you have to accept that most bucks will not respond to your rattling efforts without exhibiting a certain amount of caution. The one exception to this statement is that they will show the least amount of caution during the pushing and shoving matches of September. While it is true on rare occasions that some bucks will come into rattling quickly even in open areas, that is not the general rule. Most bucks, particularly adult bucks, respond cautiously.

This might be hard to believe because many of you have seen the exact opposite on outdoor television shows. The host picks up his or her antlers, makes a short session of rattling and voila, a huge buck runs to their stand through a wide-open section of woods. Trust me, it happens this way because of the magic of editing. Don't let yourself be the kind of rattler who expects a majority of bucks to throw caution to the wind and race to your location, especially in areas that don't provide sufficient cover for the buck to hide as he approaches what he thinks is a buck fight.

Keep in mind that research has documented that about 75 percent of all game called, rattled, or decoyed escapes without being detected by the hunter. A majority of game, such as elk, turkey, moose, waterfowl, and whitetails, that respond to calling tactics, including rattling antlers, using calls, or decoys, come in slowly and cautiously.

Keep in mind, many bucks that respond to rattling will approach the area cautiously before coming to the exact spot where they believe two bucks are fighting.

It is important to note here that, of course, there are times when many bucks will throw caution to the wind and race to your stand, but the window of opportunity for that to happen is small. It usually occurs in the third or fourth phases of fighting behaviors, which I have nicknamed the Brooklyn street fight brawls and clash and battle phase.

Most bucks intuitively know to take advantage of any and all natural vegetation they can find to conceal their approach as much as possible. Almost all mature whitetail bucks instinctively stop in such cover to determine if it's safe for them to continue forward, especially if they realize they have left the safety of a thicket to cross open ground to reach the fight.

With that point in mind, another crucial element to remember about rattling is that a large percentage of bucks who respond will more often than not hang up, or remain hidden in thick cover for a period of time, before they feel secure enough to move into open areas to investigate what they interpret as two bucks fighting.

A buck hangs up for a wide variety of reasons, but mostly to determine if it will be safe for him to get mixed up in a fight before he tries to identify which two bucks are fighting. When bucks hang up, hunters think their rattling efforts were unsuccessful or, worse yet, that rattling doesn't work.

When an unsuspecting hunter doesn't realize a buck has actually responded to his rattling and is skulking in the security of nearby cover, he or she often makes the mistake of giving up on rattling too quickly and leaving the stand. All too often, as the hunter walks off, he or she is shocked and then depressed to hear a snort and see a buck race off. The fact is that the buck was more than likely standing fifty to one hundred yards away, concealed by natural cover and trying to make up its mind about moving forward. Then, when he heard and saw the hunter leaving, he left the area posthaste.

After rattling for a while without seeing a buck, hunters tend to make a lot of head movement in an attempt to locate an incoming deer. The movement is

Photo Credit: Ted Rose

This is the typical type of thick cover bucks will hang-up in prior to deciding if they want to move in closer to a buck fight.

easily picked up by a deer standing in cover or slowly moving toward the stand. Often, the buck hears and sees the movement, then escapes quietly without the hunter ever realizing he or she actually called a buck in.

I mention all of this because I can assure you that the first time you rattle and a buck responds forty-five minutes or more after you finish rattling, you will fight all logical instincts to believe that you called him in.

Instead, you will convince yourself that the buck was coming by your stand anyway. Again, that type of thinking leads to a lack of confidence that can be devastating when it comes to being a consistently successful rattler, or deer hunter for that matter.

Here's how to get over that problem. Once you decide you are going to rattle for deer, any buck that walks toward your stand within forty-five to sixty minutes after you have stopped rattling is a buck you rattled in. This is a key factor in building your confidence about rattling and, with that, you will become a more successful and seasoned rattler.

Many adult bucks will wait in cover before approaching a buck fight, sometimes for as long as an hour or more.

Look and Listen Carefully

Over the nearly four decades I have been rattling, I have had more than my share of bucks hang up on me. Sometimes they have remained hidden in cover for an hour or more. Once, an adult ten-point buck approached my rattling. When he got within sixty yards or so of my stand, he stopped behind a huge white oak tree. Only his head and rear end were visible on either side of the oak tree. He stood there for longer than an hour without ever moving a muscle. I minimized my movement to nearly nothing for as long as I could, then my back began to cramp up. Moments later, I had to bend backward to relieve what was quickly going from serious discomfort to rigid pain. The buck picked up my movement instantly and, in one fluid motion, disappeared.

Therefore, each time I finish a rattling session, I concentrate intensely on my surroundings to determine if a buck has responded but is lurking cautiously in nearby cover. I listen carefully and slowly move my head to look for a buck. Many times this has helped me spot or hear a buck in the surrounding area. Other times, bucks have snuck toward my stand, sometimes as long as sixty or more minutes after I put the antlers down.

Once I have ended a particular session (each time I rattle I do three separate sessions, but there will be more about this later), I place the antlers on the ground or hang them up on a branch if I'm in a tree stand. I do this as quietly and carefully as I can to prevent them from accidently clicking against each other and creating unwanted noise.

I also listen intently to every natural sound going on in the woods around my stand. I want to make note of both the obvious and subtle clues. For instance, I listen for soft grunts or other deer vocalizations. I also listen for the sounds of deer hooves approaching on dry leaves or even the snapping of a small twig. All these woodland noises are indicators that a buck may be motionless in cover or that he is approaching. I look and listen for the sounds of antlers being rubbed on the bark of a tree or the sudden excited chipping of a bird or squirrel. Even seeing a doe, fawn, or, especially, a yearling buck suddenly run by can mean a buck is approaching or hung up.

I also watch the surrounding underbrush, vegetation, and young sapling trees to see if I can detect any movement, especially when the wind is still. I have discovered that sometimes a buck will get frustrated by the sounds of what he thinks are two bucks fighting if he is unable to pinpoint the location and doesn't see or smell the combatants. When this happens, he often vents his irritation on the nearest sapling tree or bush, shaking it back and forth while all other forest vegetation remains still. I also look for other undergrowth, such as cattails, tall grass, or cornstalks, moving when nothing else is. All of this can be a surefire indication that a buck or doe (as they also respond to rattling) is nearby and approaching with caution even though I haven't seen its body yet.

One of the more interesting facts I have learned over the years is that there are five different buck fights during the fall. Each stage has its own level of intensity and is marked by the different sounds that deer make, both through antler contact and vocalizations, during these time phases.

A buck will respond very differently to rattling in early October than he will in early November and even during the late rut. Savvy hunters have to match the sounds that coincide with each type of fight and time of year they occur to elevate their rattling success.

Five Types of Buck Fights

As I mentioned, whitetail bucks engage in five distinct stages of fighting behaviors. Each takes place only after bucks have shed their velvet. I have nicknamed each of them to match up with the type of confrontations that actually take place. Each of these stages takes place at a certain time throughout autumn and into winter. The dates of each stage are estimates of when they occur, but they can vary by a few days. They include:

1.   The Pushing and Shoving Matches: September
2.   The Spar and Jab Period: October 1st to October 25th
3.   The Brooklyn Street Fight Phase: October 31st to November 14th
4.   The Clash and Brawl Stage: November 17th to November 28th
5.   Battling Buck Stage: December

It should be noted here that the types of fighting behaviors within the above time frames are entirely based on the breeding dates of whitetails living within the latitudes 40—45° north. These latitudes include most of the Northeast, New England and Midwest states. It also includes most of Oregon, Northern California, Nevada, Utah, Colorado, lower Idaho (south of the panhandle), a majority of Wyoming, Southern South Dakota, Nebraska, Iowa, the extreme northern tip of Missouri, the northern half of Illinois, Indiana, and Ohio, and, as noted above, a majority of Pennsylvania, New York, Northern New Jersey, Connecticut, Massachusetts, Vermont, New Hampshire, and the southern portion of Maine.

Photo Credit: Ted Rose

Two adult bucks about to engage in an October spar and jab fighting match.

The primary rut often occurs within these heavily hunted zones from November 10th to November 15th, give or take a few days. In extreme northern and southern zones, the dates will be a week to ten days earlier or later.

Forget everything you have seen on television, read, heard your buddies suggest, and experienced yourself. When is the beginning of the seeking phase? Well this is probably earlier than you think. Bucks can actively pursue does more than a month before tending or breeding season.

There is a good chance you have learned in error. Our use of the denominations pre-rut and peak-rut are prime examples. The peak of the rut to some hunters is when the deer are scraping and rubbing like crazy and chasing does all around the woods. Technically, this is wrong, as what they are describing is the pre-rut seeking phase. The actual peak is when a buck is guarding a hot doe in estrus. This is the worst time to be in the woods, as the deer, for five or six days, are locked down and nothing is happening.

For this chapter, we will use the peak of the seeking phase as the ultimate time to be in the woods. Let's clear up some of the other misconceptions before the next trip out to your stand.

All dates are accurate but not written in stone. The dates in each phase of fighting can vary a few days. With that said, however, they are the dates that my records indicate show up most for each phase of fighting.

With each progressing phase of fighting behavior, the intensity of the competition increases.

Equally important, during each of the five periods the fighting that takes place ranges in the degree of antler contact and intensity displayed by the two bucks. Additionally, the pheromone rut odors discharged by male deer from September to December also changes considerably and ranges from mild to potent. Finally, the sounds created by the antler and body contact, such as hooves moving over dry leaves, twigs, and other forest debris and vocalizations made by the bucks engaged in the fight, also differ greatly from one fighting phase to another. All the sounds must be matched as closely as possible for you to become part of an elite group—deer hunting rattlers who bag bucks year after year.

If you don't create the entire illusion of two bucks fighting, you will have less success. The more natural you make all the elements sound and smell, the more bucks you will rattle in and kill. Remember, bucks instantly recognize when the sounds and odors are out of sync or unusual for a particular time of year. When this happens, bucks know they should avoid investigating further and often sneak off before the hunter realizes they were close. It took me a couple years of using the five types of antler rattling phases (and a lot of trial and error) to learn this. Until this writing, it has been one of my most guarded hunting secrets.

Learning to imitate the five different fighting stages requires some commitment, belief, and unwavering confidence in your ability as a deer hunter. The key to your success will be how well you can make the sounds and odors of the five skirmishes fool a buck into thinking what he is responding to is actually occurring between two other bucks. I guarantee that once you understand how to rattle your antlers during each fighting phase, you will see your rattling success rate rise to the next level. When that happens, antler rattling will become your favorite deer hunting strategy.

The First Phase:
Pushing and Shoving Matches
Time Frame: September

Male deer begin making antler contact with each other as early as late August, soon after they shed their velvet. However, the pushing and

Two young bucks involved in a September pushing and shoving match.

shoving doesn't really start until the newly formed bone on their heads is hard. This phase usually lasts throughout the month of September.

These scuffles are nonviolent for the most part—they are merely meant to establish the pecking order among males living within a given herd's bachelor group. This is the first definitive sign bucks are beginning to think about what rung of the social ladder they occupy as the upcoming breeding season is approaching.

This time of year, bucks are satisfied with their newly polished and hardened headgear. They start to become full of themselves and want to test their antlers by making contact with other bucks. These skirmishes are part and parcel of early fall. They will remain low-level jostling matches until the next stage of fighting starts in October.

Pushing and shoving matches, like all fighting stages, have particular sounds and odors associated with them. Other bucks hear the September scuffles as something akin to bickering between two males. Bucks that are nearby instinctively recognize what the sounds represent and are often quickly attracted to the noises made by clicking antlers. This time of the year, however, they are mostly fascinated out of curiosity as it is the first time in a nearly year that they have heard antlers hitting antlers. Therefore, as odd as it is, hunters shouldn't be surprised that they can rattle in bucks as early as September by imitating the light antler contact sounds made by males during this phase.

The Escape Route Buck

Before I go into how to rattle during the pushing and shoving phase, I'd like to demonstrate how bucks respond to rattling this time of year with a short anecdote. Many years ago, while scouting for bucks in late September in New York, I saw several does trot out from a heavy thicket about seventy-five yards from my stand. This stand was called Bollenbach's Farm. The does weren't spooked and they ambled through a cut cornfield to put some ground between them and whatever they wanted to get away from.

The group eventually crossed the field and walked into a small woodlot. Knowing that most adult bucks I had seen on this farm didn't follow does through the open fields, I quickly focused my attention on a known escape route in thicker cover that passed behind my stand. I had two small naturally shed antlers in my daypack. I had found these on another

Photo Credit: Ted Rose

When does cross an open area, focus on the surrounding cover. Bucks avoid crossing openings and will instead stick to the security of thicker vegetation, particularly when it comes to rattling.

scouting trip a few days earlier. For whatever reason, I decided to rattle the antlers together gently to see if I could draw a buck that might be on the escape route toward my stand. I was merely trying to see if there was a buck worth hunting for during the upcoming bow season. I wasn't even sure I would get a response, but I figured I didn't have anything to lose. In the event a buck happened to be using the escape route like the does, he, too, was probably not spooked or in a hurry.

Because it was September, I decided it was best not to rattle too loudly. So, I gently clicked the tips of the antlers together and within minutes a young eight-point buck walked off the trail and under my tree stand. In my mind's eye, I could envision how the buck cautiously made his way along the escape route, heard what he thought were two bucks engaging in some antler jostling, and was curious enough to check them out. The buck was only fifty yards from the stand when I first saw him.

I tickled the antlers once more. This time, it was even more gently since the buck was close. The buck instantly responded by trotting within twenty yards of my stand. Bow season wasn't open yet, but I was so excited I pretended it was. I drew back my make believe bowstring, released my imaginary arrow, and pretended it hit the deer in the kill zone. In my mind, I saw the buck jump in the air, run about twenty yards, and crash to the ground, where I found him minutes later. With that thought, my daydream ended. However, my new rattling experience now became as plain as the nose on my face. I had just rattled a buck to my stand in September. Who would have imagined? Once more, who was going to believe it?

I can almost hear some of you saying the buck would have ambled down the trail past my stand anyway. Others of you reading this are absolutely sure he came by without any regard to the antler rattling. Well, perhaps both opinions are right but only to an extent. The buck may have indeed come along the trail and by my stand even if I wasn't rattling. But would he have come within twenty yards of my stand, which was about forty yards out of his way? Or would he have snuck by undetected along the trail instead?

My bet is the buck would have kept moving along the trail and I would have never seen him. Instead, I rattled and inadvertently imitated the early sounds of two bucks jostling, unintentionally matching what naturally happens between bucks in early fall, and lured in a buck. I was able to experience an exciting make believe hunt and, more importantly, learned that rattling worked much earlier than I (or anyone else I knew) had thought.

This took place about fourteen years ago. I had been rattling for about twenty-four years before that and had what I thought was better-than-average success. However, in 1999, the year of this anecdote, I had no idea rattling would work that early in the season. After making the connection that my rattling attracted a buck in late September, I logged it for future use as an early season rattling technique. It also spurred me to start thinking about why it worked, which was the genesis for me discovering the tactic's potential for success during four other periods from October to December. For years, I have used the September information as an effective scouting tool, as back then New York's archery season opened October 15th and only recently started opening on October 1st.

Over the years, a notable statistic I discovered is that most bucks that respond to rattling in September are usually 1½ to 2½ year old deer. Only occasionally in the last fourteen years have I rattled in an adult buck in September. Then why did I tell this story? I stated it to emphasize how

Photo Credit: Ted Rose

A typical-looking immature buck that likes to respond to the September pushing and shoving matches.

important it is as a deer hunter who uses calling techniques to be confident enough to use untested hunting theories to determine if they work. I also mentioned it to display the importance of confidence as a key factor to regular success. You must always believe you are a skilled deer hunter and any tactic you use will work. Confidence that rattling can work over a four-month period will be the chief ingredient to your success.

Male deer of all ages are accustomed to hearing antler contact noises in early autumn, and a buck does not find these to be out of place. They don't respond to them as aggressively as they do in the three remaining phases, but they respond often enough. An early fall response can work for a lot of reasons, whether it is a buck's curiosity, his comfort level, or his desire to engage in some early season showing off. For whatever reason, a buck comes in to rattling, who really cares—as long as he responds, right? In this case, having the confidence to rattle in September and early October could put meat in the freezer and a set of antlers on the trophy room wall.

Before describing how to rattle, I want to make a suggestion about how to hold the antlers in your hands when you are rattling. Whether you are right- or left-handed, or using a natural or synthetic set, hold one antler as still as possible in your less dominant hand. Then, use your dominant hand to manipulate the other antler so that it ticks, clicks, clacks, meshes, and grinds against the stationary antler.

This style of antler rattling will give you more control over how you manipulate the antlers. By holding one antler still and working the other, the realism of the sound you're creating and distance the noise travels are both increased. Also, it reduces the possibilities of scraping your knuckles and hands.

How to Imitate the Antler Sounds of the Pushing and Shoving Matches

For the best early season rattling success, two elements are necessary. The first is unwavering confidence (there's that confidence thing again) that rattling works for that time of year. Equally important is to know how to imitate the sounds and odors of two bucks making antler contact as closely as possible long before you plan to use the strategy.

To get the most consistent rattling responses during this phase, the contact with the two antlers must be kept light. As I always mention in my deer seminars, try to create the entire illusion for whatever tactic is used. In this case, I begin by placing a sparse amount of straight buck urine near my stand. I put several drops on a rag, boot pad, or scent wick, then hang it on a low branch about three to four feet off the ground.

Buck urine helps fool a buck's first line of defense, its nose. Whenever a buck is about to get into an altercation, it will urinate prior to making contact with the other buck. Because the onset of the rut is still a few weeks off, their urine doesn't contain the pheromones of a rutting buck, such as tarsal and other glandular scents. Straight buck urine helps fool a responding buck into thinking it is a natural odor for him to smell this time of year.

Before you start to rattle, hang a rag or scent wick soaked with buck urine about thirty yards from your tree stand. Often, this phase falls in the archery season, so thirty yards or closer is a good range. Once you are in your stand, wait about thirty minutes for things to settle down from the noise you made walking in and setting out the scent before you start to rattle.

Sequence One

Begin rattling by gently ticking the tips of the antlers together briefly for thirty to sixty seconds and then separate them. The sounds made by the gentle ticking imitate those made by two bucks that are about to start testing each other. Make sure the antler tips make contact, but that they don't click too loudly. Then, carefully listen and look while keeping your movements as limited as possible to detect any buck that may have responded.

Sequence Two

After twenty to thirty minutes, you can begin your second rattling sequence. Repeat the same type of soft rattling. Instead of rattling for thirty to sixty seconds, continue rattling for about two full minutes. Click and tick the antlers together gently for thirty to sixty seconds, pause for a second or two, and tick the tips of the antlers against each other for another minute, only this time make the sound slightly louder.

When you stop rattling, look and listen for about twenty minutes. Look carefully for a buck that may have responded and is lurking nearby in cover. Make sure your movements are kept slow and to a bare minimum. Try to avoid making any quick or unnecessary noises.

Sequence Three

I always try to make the last sequence include longer contact than the previous two, usually two to three minutes total. Both antlers should now be slightly meshed into one another to imitate the light meshing and grinding sounds two bucks make this time of year. To accomplish this, just intertwine both antlers so they have good contact, particularly at the base. Twist and turn them so they create a meshing or grinding type of sound, but do not get overly rambunctious or you'll sound loud or aggressive. Then stop and hang the antlers up or place them on the ground, and look and listen carefully for a buck for the next hour.

This time of year, most bucks respond to rattling without much apprehension and generally they will be highly visible when they walk in. If a buck doesn't show up after sixty minutes, you can start the entire series over again, beginning with sequence one, then moving to two and three, using the same methods in each.

You can repeat the three rattling sequences in the pushing and shoving matches a few times over the course of a few hours or so, but not more than that. If a buck doesn't respond within a three-hour time frame, you have two choices. You can either remain in the stand and not rattle again for at least a solid hour, or you can relocate to another stand two or three hundred yards away and start rattling again. I usually prefer to remain in the first location.

The Second Phase:
The Spar and Jab Period
Time Frame: October 1st to 25th

To get the most bucks to respond to your antler rattling tactics during the second stage, the volume level made by your antler contact must be louder than during the pushing and shoving match. During the second phase, bucks are more eager to test each other's place within the hierarchy. The body and antler contact becomes more deliberate and assertive than in the first stage, but not by much.

Two bucks cautiously place their antlers together before each tries to push the other backwards to win the match.

Bucks test each other more in the second phase and end up acting like professional boxers. Instead of throwing caution to the wind and rushing at each other, they jostle for good body positions and cautiously jab at each other with the tips of their tines. I have witnessed this behavior many times over the years, and it is almost the same each time.

The two opponents spar to get the best fighting position. In doing so, their antler tips act like a jab being thrown by one boxer at another. Sometimes this behavior to establish the best fighting stance may last a few minutes.

Once either buck feels confident his antlers have been placed in the best possible location between his rival's, he will twist and turn his head while applying as much forward momentum as he can to push his opponent backwards or knock him off balance.

As soon as either buck accomplishes the goal of knocking the other buck backwards with a forceful thrust or pushing the other off balance, the fight immediately comes to an end. The victor has established himself as a higher-ranking buck in the pecking order.

Two wide-antlered adult bucks jostle for position during the October 1st to 25th spar and jab period of fights.

The Swamp Buck

I can vividly recall the first buck I rattled in during the spar and jab period. I had only recently discovered that there were different intensities of buck fights and was excited to try my sparring rattling tactics out on a large piece of mountainous land I leased and posted. The property included a wide variety of terrain. I planned to rattle from a tree stand that Jay Cassell (who, at the time, was the Deputy Editor of *Field & Stream Magazine* and is now the Editorial Director of Skyhorse Publishing) and I put up only two days earlier. The stand was placed parallel to a deep ravine just above several well-used trails that ran through the bottom of it.

About thirty yards above the trails—which were obviously made by does, family groups, and 1½-year-old bucks—was a narrow deer trail that was carved deeply into the side of the ridge. My stand was just west of it. It was apparent that the area's mature bucks used it. The stand also overlooked a large swamp that bordered the Appalachian Trail in Orange County, New York. The swamp was a maze of water and thickets and was virtually impenetrable after thirty feet or so. The prevailing breeze blew from a north to northwest direction from the swamp, making it an ideal afternoon stand.

It was a promising area that had little hunting pressure to speak of, as it required a long and steep hike to get back into the spot. I had taken a few mature bucks from the area and knew that some dandy bucks were living and hiding in the impassable swamp.

I intended to rattle from the new tree stand during an afternoon hunt several days before Halloween. I had to get there before the deer began their regular movement pattern, which was about 2:30 p.m. I arrived around 12:30 p.m. and set up my drag bag in the branch of a tree fifty yards due north of the stand. I was all set for rattling action.

My plan was to wait until 2 p.m. and then begin my first session of rattling. By 1 p.m., I was itching to rattle. I took the synthetic antlers from my pack and started my first sparring period sequence.

When I finished my third set of rattling, I turned to hang the antlers on a hook in the tree. As I slowly turned back around, I heard the unmistakable splashing sounds of a deer walking through water and approaching the stand. Within a few seconds, there were the instantly recognizable sounds of hooves crunching dry leaves and walking along the buck trail from the opposite direction. Within fifteen minutes, the first buck, a dandy ten-pointer, stepped out of the swamp. His lower legs were dripping wet, covered in mud and muck, and appeared as black as charcoal. The buck quickly trotted up to the trail and began to walk toward my stand. By now, the other buck, also a ten-point but with a smaller rack, was also walking along the trail from the opposite direction on a collision course with the first buck.

When they saw each other, they immediately lowered their heads and began to exhibit assertive body posture. The next thing I knew, they were fighting just twenty-five yards from me. The initial contact was brief, perhaps less than a minute. But, I noted that the antler contact was more aggressive and louder than it is during the first fighting phase. Everything I witnessed during the fight supported what I learned over the years about how bucks fight in October.

As the bucks made antler contact again, I came to full draw. When they separated, they stood motionless for a few seconds. This was the signal to let my arrow fly. The broadhead found an artery and the swamp buck stumbled backward a few feet, sat down on his haunches briefly, and tumbled over on his back dead. Clean-cut arteries often end with a deer dying within fifteen to thirty seconds and sometimes less.

The other buck didn't know what to make of the buck lying motionless on the ground. He lowered his head, rammed the dead buck in the chest, and ran off. The entire hunt was not only a terrific learning experience, it was really exciting, too.

This is the swamp buck. It was the first buck I took during the spar and jab period.

Photo Credit: Fiduccia Ent.

How to Imitate the Antler Sounds of the Spar and Jab Period

Just like the push and shove stage, begin by hanging a scent wick soaked with buck urine about thirty yards from your tree stand (again, this fighting takes place mostly during archery season). Once you are in your stand, wait about thirty minutes for things to settle down from the noise you made walking in and setting out the scent before you start to rattle.

Unlike the push and shove match, the spar and jab period has no break between sequences one and two. In other words, you transition each sequence into the other. So it is important to keep in mind that while you are rattling for several minutes in this stage, a buck can show up anytime during the three sequences. Be on the alert the entire time you are rattling. About 50 percent of the time I rattle during the spar and jab stage, I never get past sequence one or two before an interested buck shows up.

Sequence One

Start your rattling with the tips of one antler continually ticking and clicking against the other for about two minutes. This should not be done in a rushed manner, but rather in a purposeful, deliberate way. The volume should be twice as much as you made in the pushing and shoving stage. Now, the start of the fight you're creating is meant to imitate two boxers moving around each other throwing jabs to find their opponent's weaknesses. It also helps place the boxers in the perfect position to deliver the all-important first hard blow. This is exactly what two bucks do during the spar and jab period.

Sequence Two

After a couple minutes of ticking and clicking the tips of the antlers against each other, quickly engage the antlers fully so all the tines are completely entangled with each other. Mesh and grind the antlers lightly together for about sixty to ninety seconds. Make the transition from clicking the tips to meshing the tines in as fluid a motion as you can. Use more enthusiasm than you did in the pushing and shoving phase, but don't go overboard.

Sequence Three

After meshing and grinding the antlers, while they are still entwined, lift up the antler in your dominant hand at its base by the burr so the top of that antler clicks hard, but not aggressively, against the tines and main beam of the still antler in your less dominant hand. Do this for about thirty seconds. Then abruptly disengage the antlers so the main beams and tines hit against each other as you separate one antler from the other. The last few sounds you are creating give the illusion that one buck has won the altercation and the second has pulled its antlers free to demonstrate he lost the skirmish and ranks in a lower social position than the winner. You can add a snort or grunt vocalization after breaking up the antlers, but not both.

If a buck doesn't show up after you have finished rattling, hang the antlers up and wait at least forty-five minutes before you repeat the entire process. On some occasions, I will wait seventy-five minutes, but most times I wait forty-five to sixty. In reality, how long you wait is all about how comfortable you are with choosing a waiting period. It shouldn't be less than forty-five minutes, though.

Keep your movements to a minimum, but remember not to ignore watching behind you, too. You should always try to cover as much of a 360-degree view as possible. When you are rattling from a tree stand, this is especially important as the height offers you a better view.

You can repeat all three sequences in the spar and jab period several times over the course of a few hours. When I rattle during this stage, if I don't get a response within two hours, I'll remain on stand but I don't rattle again. I may decide to use deer calls or simply wait to see if something walks in. I don't usually relocate to another stand two to three hundred yards away, but you can if you want to.

The Third Stage:
The Brooklyn Street Fight Phase
Time Frame: October 31st to November 14th

To lure a buck to your rattling during this period, the sounds must be imitated as closely as possible to the more aggressive fighting that takes

During the Brooklyn street fight phase, bucks are intent on winning the fight, even if they risk serious injury or unintentional death.

place. Like the other stages, it, too, must sound as natural as possible to maximize your success.

To be successful during the Brooklyn street fight phase, you have to mentally prepare yourself differently than the earlier two stages. Your mind-set must allow you to imagine, in detail, what exactly you must do to create the entire illusion (i.e. the sounds, odors, and sights—such as shaking a sapling back and forth when you are rattling from the ground). This is the best way to make your rattling sound, smell, and appear so realistic a buck will have no choice but to investigate.

Even though I have been rattling for nearly four decades, I still have to mentally prepare by psyching myself up to imitate what is, in reality, nothing more than a make believe buck fight. You will probably think I'm exaggerating when I explain exactly what I do to get myself ready.

Be that as it may, I'm going to put it in writing anyway. While I'm waiting in my stand for things to settle down before I begin rattling, I imagine that I'm a buck who is about to engage in a fight with another buck. The degree to which I have to psych myself up depends on which of the five stages of fighting behaviors I'm imitating. For the first two stages, it doesn't take me long to get motivated, as the level of intensity during these two stages isn't that high.

However, to get myself pumped up enough to make sounds like two bucks authentically engaged in a serious fight, it takes some commitment on my part. This is most relevant when I'm imitating two bucks involved in any of the remaining three aggressive buck fighting confrontations. Once I start to feel my belligerence levels rising, I know I'm ready to make my rattling efforts sound natural. This is an important element to your overall success as a rattler. As my saying goes, "Be the buck!"

Now that you have become the buck, begin your Brooklyn street fight in earnest. It is in this fighting period that rattling really becomes exciting and filled with uncontrolled anticipation. During the third stage of behaviors, a buck's testosterone levels are on the march upward. With each passing day, male deer become more aggressive toward one another. Bachelor groups have all but split up by now. Single bucks are on the prowl for estrus does. Their patience levels for socializing are ebbing by the hour.

Immature bucks, feeling they are made of steel, are ready and eager to fight with any buck they come in contact with from their age group and even some that might be slightly older. If they can't pick a fight with another buck, they will trash a sapling or bush. If that doesn't satisfy their belligerent state of mind, they will even start a fight with their own shadows.

Adult bucks are sour pusses this time of year. They don't tolerate any socializing from other male deer. They enthusiastically swagger their manliness around like a badge of honor. If another buck within their age class comes too close, there will instantly be intense body language to back him off. If that fails, a Brooklyn street fight breaks out.

This stage is my favorite time to rattle for a few reasons. If mistakes are made here, even to the degree of being seen by the buck, this is the time for forgiveness. Bucks are hell-bent with aggression during this time frame. I have seen them try to sneak by me, even though they are totally aware of my presence, to get to the spot where they think two bucks are fighting. I have had them exhibit this behavior even when they have a full dose of my human scent in their nostrils.

By now, you should be getting the picture that this is the time most biologists call the big chase. Bucks are running helter-skelter through the woods and fields searching for estrus does and taking on all male competition. I dubbed the big chase of the rut as the frenzy period. It is during this fight stage that you have the best chance to rattle in a wall-hanger adult buck. All you have to do is tick, click, clack, and trick him into a fight. This is the time when the most electrifying buck fights of autumn take place.

By the end of October, more precisely Halloween, bucks have splintered off from each other and are loners. The more aggression a buck demonstrates from here through the end of the primary rut, the more other male deer will acknowledge him as a high-ranking male within the hierarchy. No longer is the fighting about testing what rung of the ladder a buck occupies. This time of the year, each buck knows exactly where they belong within their herd. The conflicts are about the right to breed does. Winners mount and breed does and losers become more frustrated with each passing day.

During the Brooklyn street fight phase, the purpose is for one buck to violently knock down, flip over, push, or trip the other buck off his feet and onto the

Photo Credit: Ted Rose

An adult buck prepares to mate with a doe during the frenzy period of the third stage of fighting behaviors.

ground. When one buck knocks another off his feet, the fight should be over. But during this stage of fighting, that is rarely the case.

The standing buck immediately seizes the opportunity to try and gore his opponent in the rump or ribs while he is down. It is an intentional behavior to injure the fallen buck to demonstrate the standing buck's authority. It is a specific action that is almost entirely absent during other fight phases. By trying to gore and cause further injury to the fallen buck, the standing buck has proven to his opponent that at this time in the rut, he is stronger, more aggressive, and holds a higher rank within the social hierarchy. This gives him first dibs on estrus does, albeit temporarily.

If the loser is fortunate enough to escape being gored or further injured, he'll spring to his feet like a bolt of lightning and race away as fast as his legs will carry him. Fights like this are most often between two combatant bucks that don't know each other. In other words, one buck is a transient from another area. On occasion, however, this type of ferocious fight can happen between two bucks from the same herd.

Ten percent of the time, my records indicate this phase occurs from November 2nd to the 17th. Three percent of the time, it happens from November 1st to November 14th. The single days that have regularly demonstrated the most buck-chasing-doe activity for more than forty-six years of record keeping are October 31st and November 5th, 10th, 13th, and 14th.

As I have advised in the past, if you are driving to work on any of these days and happen to see a buck chasing after a doe or running with its nose held tightly to the ground, call in sick. Then, go back home to get your gear and go hunting.

This is the most effective time to rattle in bucks because they are actively seeking and chasing does. If they sense competition, they are eager to chase it off using aggressive body posturing or, if need be, a fight. It is also a successful time for hunters to employ other tactics including deer calls, decoys, and scent.

The aggressive fighting creates a lot more noise and scent in the woods—pounding hooves, louder antler contact, snapping branches, rustling leaves, grunting and snorting vocalizations, strong odors of urine mixed with tarsal scent, and many other rut-related odors. Now is the time to escalate rattling by several notches to copy what is naturally happening.

I have videotaped several violent buck fights over the years. During a serious fight, one buck lifted and flipped another buck over his back and into the air. When the buck hit the ground, the other buck immediately charged headlong into him, hitting him hard in the chest with his antlers. The defeated buck barely escaped without further injury.

While taping two bucks squaring off to fight in New York, a third buck raced in with his antlers held low and hit the larger of the two bucks squarely in the chest, knocking him over like a set of bowling pins. When the buck jumped to his feet, the original buck he was about to fight charged him from behind and hit him hard in the rump, drawing blood. The buck took that for the signal to escape.

My instructional rattling DVD includes some of the buck fights mentioned in this chapter. It is available at www.deerdoctor.com. Use the promo code SkyhorsePub and receive a 10 percent discount.

How to Imitate the Antler Sounds of the Brooklyn Street Fight Phase

This is the time of year you can extend your total length of rattling time to about five minutes. Make sure the antlers engage in louder contact than the previous two phases. But keep in mind that whitetail bucks don't fight like big horn sheep. Don't slam your antlers together hard one time and then repeatedly slam them several times.

While the first contact between bucks during this fighting phase imitates headlong antler contact, bucks generally, if not always, make antler to antler contact in serious fights from a distance of feet, not yards, from each other. Keep the first contact realistic. Make it much louder than you have made it during the previous two phases, but don't slam them too hard against each other or the sound will be unnaturally loud.

Just like the two prior phases, begin by hanging a scent wick about thirty yards from your tree stand, or fifty to sixty yards during firearm season. This time, use buck urine mixed with tarsal scent. You can also use a slight amount of estrus doe urine. Despite the rumor that does stand and watch a fight and leave with the victor, I have never witnessed this. Every time I have observed a serious fight between two bucks, particularly adult bucks, if there was a doe close by she took off as soon as the fight began. The reason to add a small amount of doe estrus is to suggest that one or both of the bucks involved in the fight were following a receptive female doe and clashed prior to finding her.

The doe estrus adds another natural element to the overall illusion you are creating. I suggest using a few drops of Love Potion No. 9. It is my scent and

Photo Credit: Buck Stop Scents

During the Brooklyn street fight phase, be sure to complete the illusion of two bucks fighting by using buck urine mixed with tarsal scent.

was developed to include young buck urine and estrus doe scent. This scent instinctively agitates older bucks into believing a young buck that can be easily intimidated by aggressive body language is following a doe. You can visit my website, www.deerdoctor.com, to get more information about Love Potion No. 9 and how to use it most effectively. After hanging the scent wicks on a branch or twig about four or five feet off the ground, get to your stand and let things calm down for about thirty minutes before you start to rattle.

Unlike the first two fighting phases, the Brooklyn street fight stage must include some vocalizations either before, during, or directly after the fight. I usually make a soft guttural grunt, quickly followed by a slightly deeper grunt. I keep both grunts short—no more than a few seconds each.

Sequence One

As soon as I finish making the last grunt, I separate the antlers to shoulder length and bring them together with conviction, but don't slam them unrealistically hard. As soon as they hit each other, I keep the antler in my less dominant hand still and begin robustly twisting and turning the other antler forcefully for about ninety seconds.

Sequence Two

With the moving antler, I make short jab-like motions against the still antler. It creates a clacking type noise meant to imitate when the two bucks are pushing hard against one another with their antlers. I do this for about sixty seconds.

Sequence Three

Next, I twist the moving antler over the still one, making sure that I get as many of its tines to rake over as many of the still antler's tines as possible. I do this for at least sixty seconds.

Sequence Four

Finally, I turn the still antler so that its tines are pointing up. Then I place the other antler over it so the tines of both antlers are entwined with each other. Then I begin rubbing the main beam hard (just above where the brow tines were removed and the G2s) over the base of the antler in my less dominant hand.

If the antlers have what are called perlations, which are tiny bumps normally found around the bottom portions of the antlers near the burrs, I rub the moving antler's perlations over the other antler's perlations. It helps to recreate a noise that is commonly made just prior to bucks disengaging their antlers. I do this for about thirty seconds.

Sequence Five

Next, I separate the antlers, making sure of as much contact with the tines of both antlers as possible.

You can add a snort or deep guttural grunt after separating the antlers. This is not something I do every time, but when the spirit moves me. If it feels right, I make the vocalizations. Otherwise, I separate the antlers and begin my diligent vigil of looking and listening to see if anything responds.

If there is a time when a buck will run or even charge into your antler rattling efforts, the Brooklyn street fight phase is it. But, as I mentioned earlier, the times a buck will charge in are few and far between compared to the times when he will come in cautiously.

When you rattle in this phase of fighting, it is crucial to keep in mind that a buck can show up quickly and unexpectedly anytime during the five different sequences. Be alert the entire time. On many occasions during this phase of fighting, I have seen bucks show up during different sequences. There has never been one sequence that has consistently garnered more response. Again, keep your movements to a minimum, but remember not to ignore watching behind your stand. Try to cover as much of a 360-degree view as possible.

Some say a hunter can repeat all five sequences in the big chase stage a few times over the course of three or four hours. However, I don't repeat it more than twice over three hours. I think doing it more than that can temporarily scare off the females and immature bucks from the area by creating too many aggressive fighting sounds.

The Fourth Phase:
The Clash and Brawl Stage
Time Frame: November 17th to November 28th

In this phase of fighting, you rattle aggressively, but not belligerently like in the Brooklyn street fight period. This stage of buck fighting is designed by Mother Nature herself to de-escalate the fighting a notch or two from the highly aggressive third phase. The rattling times in each sequence are shorter and the total rattling time should not last more than about four minutes.

Fights in this phase are usually between 2½- to 3½-year-old bucks. The adult bucks are tired and somewhat weakened by the previous fighting stage and many of them are recuperating during the fourth fighting stage. Although, on occasion, an adult buck will get into a fight, they do so only if they absolutely have to. During this time, adult bucks use body posturing to intimidate immature bucks more than any other time of the breeding season.

However, the fighting behavior is quite different between less mature bucks. Now they are trying to elevate their position within the hierarchy. Most 2½- to 3½-year-old bucks are now wide-eyed, ill-tempered, and, worst of

Photo Credit: Fiduccia Ent.

Jay Cassell, Editorial Director at Skyhorse Publishing, rattling during the fourth phase of buck fighting—the clash and brawl stage.

all, really love sick. Their brain functions have left the higher level of their heads and, well, you know where they have fallen to.

Things get a little haphazard in this stage—sometimes 2½-year-old bucks that have lesser antlers but more youth and strength on their side get brazen enough to take on 3½-year-old bucks. Interestingly, with nothing more than sheer strength, they can occasionally win a conflict with an older buck. This can even happen with a buck higher in the pecking order with larger antlers and twenty or more extra pounds. The younger buck then gains the rights, albeit temporarily, to breed with does that have not yet been successfully bred.

This is another stage that offers hunters a peak time to rattle. Immature bucks spend most of their time pursuing does and constantly harass them until they either stand to accept mounting or steadfastly refuse the advances. The harassment behavior toward does instigates other bucks and, before you know it, a fight breaks out between bucks chasing the same doe.

While there can be an occasional all-out fight within a buck group that only six weeks earlier was a bachelor herd, these altercations are not designed to severely injure an opponent. They are serious confrontations with strict limitations. If body posturing doesn't warn a potential opponent to back off, the other will quickly take up a fighting stance with head lowered and ears pinned back. At this point, body contact is imminent and a fight is almost unavoidable.

How to Imitate the Clash and Brawl Stage

Bucks generally make antler to antler contact after exhibiting several minutes of belligerent and antagonistic body posturing toward one another. It is time to dial back your aggressive antler rattling.

Like in all the other phases of fighting, begin by putting out scent. In this phase, hang two scent wicks about fifty to sixty yards from your tree stand. One pad should be moist with a mixture of buck urine and tarsal scent. The other pad should be damp with estrus urine. Once in your blind, let things quiet down for about thirty minutes before you start to rattle.

Sequence One

Make three or four successive, short, burp-like grunts and just before the last one, bring both antlers together while making the grunt. The antlers should make sufficient enough contact for them to clap noisily, but avoid a boisterously loud volume.

Sequence Two

Immediately twist the moving antler over the still antler, making sure as many of its tines slap and whack over and between the other antler being held in place. I do this for at least sixty seconds.

Sequence Three

Now create the sound that imitates bucks pushing enthusiastically against each other. Make short jab-like motions, stabbing the moving antler against the still antler. Do this for about a minute or so.

Sequence Four

With the antler in your dominant hand, twist, click, tick, and mesh it over and around the still antler for at least another minute. Then, pause for about thirty seconds. During this time, make a half dozen short but deep burp grunts.

Sequence Five

With authority, slap the antler in your dominant hand into the antler being held still with your other hand. As soon as both antlers hit against each other begin to twist, mesh, and grind them back and forth for about sixty to ninety seconds. Then rake them apart so the tips make as much contact with each other as possible.

While limiting your body movement, carefully study your surroundings for any signs that a buck has responded. Be on the alert the entire time you are rattling. Again, remember to watch for movement coming from behind you. Try to cover as much of a 360-degree view as possible.

Since immature bucks are actively searching for does throughout the day, you have a good chance to rattle in a buck passing by your area. The sequences can be repeated at least once every hour.

The Fifth Phase:
Battling Buck Stage
Time Frame: December

This is the last stage of fighting behavior. Because there are only a few younger does that still have not been successfully bred within each herd, bucks are hell-bent on finding them. Once a buck detects the estrus pheromones of a doe in heat, he will actively search for her throughout the day. Other bucks that pick up the estrus scent quickly follow it, which is why during this post-rut phase it is not uncommon for hunters to see a couple of bucks chasing the scent of estrus. At this time of year, the scent is most often from yearling does.

There are so few estrus does during this time that they quickly end up capturing the undivided attention of every buck within their range. Sometimes, when the doe is spotted, the bucks following her instantly come to a stop and square off against each other.

This type of fighting behavior ends up causing injuries between bucks, some of which can be serious. During this period of the post-rut, a buck's system is overflowing with frustration. Bucks of all age groups want to get a shot at breeding one last doe or, for some bucks, get their first opportunity to mate. Bucks are short-tempered, belligerent, and ready to fight anything that gets between him and the estrus doe he is after.

Photo Credit: Ted Rose

During the battling buck stage, it doesn't take long for the few estrus does left this time of year to attract male deer, particularly adult bucks.

Photo Credit: Fiduccia Ent.

Cody Fiduccia with two conventioneers dressed in Klingon costumes during an annual **Star Trek** *Convention in Las Vegas. The author extends his sincere apologies to all "Trekkies" for the* **Star Wars** *references in this book.*

This is the phase I refer to as having bucks from the dark side. They have the same temper and homicidal intentions that Anakin Skywalker had when he murdered all the innocent Jedi younglings. (My apologies to all my *Star Trek* friends for yet another *Star Wars* analogy. Please don't ignore Kate, Cody, and me at the next *Star Trek* Convention.)

All bucks in this stage are ill-tempered, aggressive, and cunning. They have become evil and often take their fighting to underhanded levels. This is the buck that will take advantage of two other fighting bucks. It will intentionally blindside the more aggressive buck, aiming to gore its belly or lung area.

The fights within this phase are often the quickest confrontations of all the fighting behaviors. Seldom do they last longer than ninety seconds.

There are many behaviors and biological changes that a buck undergoes during each of the five fighting phases that make it go from a reclusive, tolerant deer that thinks about nothing more than eating, sleeping, and drinking to the most belligerent &@$!*%# during the last fighting stage of the post-rut.

How to Imitate the Antler Sounds of the Battling Buck Stage

There are three important tactics to use in this stage other than rattling. The first is scent, the second is vocalizations, and the third is a doe decoy.

Before rattling, thoroughly soak a scent wick with buck urine and tarsal. Infuse a second wick with a natural amount of doe estrus. Hang the scent wick with buck urine and tarsal on a branch or twig. If you are not going to use a doe decoy, hang the scent wick with doe estrus on another branch about twenty yards from the buck urine and tarsal scent.

If you are going to use a decoy, put a long, thin nail at the top of the tail and hang the wick from it. Set the decoy in an area where it is easily seen with its rump facing the direction from which you feel the buck will come.

Sequence One

Before rattling, make a series of estrus doe blats. I generally make several loud blats for about thirty seconds, as this is one of the few times you can make a loud vocalization. Then make several short burp grunts for about twenty seconds. Follow the grunt calls by hitting the two antlers hard against each other, but don't make the noise so loud it is unrealistic.

Sequence Two

Without hesitation, assertively mesh and grind the antler in your dominant hand with the antler held still in the other. Make contact loud, so it sounds confrontational. Do this for about ninety seconds, then break the antlers apart so all the tines click and tick over each other. At this point, hang up the antlers.

Sequence Three

As soon as you hang the antlers up, make another series of estrus blats but don't make any more buck vocalizations. For the next several minutes, intensely look and listen for response from a buck. If you don't see or hear a buck, make one more series of estrus blats, but keep them low.

Sequence Four

If nothing has responded to your rattling, calling, and, if you choose, decoy efforts, wait an hour and repeat the entire process. I generally do three full cycles. If I don't have any response, I either move three to four hundred yards away and try rattling again, or I end my rattling and try it again the next day.

So there you have it—the five different types of fighting behaviors that will give you more time to use the tactic of antler rattling. As I mentioned in the beginning of this chapter, rattling will improve your hunting success and give you hours of anticipation and exhilaration. Even though rattling doesn't work every time, when it does you will feel incredible satisfaction and pride in taking a buck using a tactic that some don't even believe works.

Chapter Fourteen

Fertilize Oaks for Big Bucks

———

In fall, deer enthusiastically seek out acorns. In fact, mast crops comprise about 40 percent of a deer's overall diet. Acorns are an important component as fall and winter food sources. However, mast crops are unpredictable in that some years the crop is plentiful and other seasons it can be almost non-existent. In the mid–1970s, after experiencing a very poor fall acorn crop, I began thinking of what I could do to make my mast crops produce acorns more reliably.

The solution I came up with the following year didn't require a degree in rocket science. In fact, the answer was so simple I wondered why I never thought of it before. All I had to do to ensure a more consistently successful mast crop was provide the oak trees with the correct type of fertilizer, which would help them produce acorns more dependably. Over the years I put the plan into practice, I discovered that fertilizing the trees provided other benefits, as well.

When developing a long-term plan to fertilize oak trees, there are important decisions to consider. The tactic will work on private, leased, or public hunting lands. However, limit the number of trees you fertilize depending on whether you own, lease, or hunt publicly.

Your decision should also depend on the number of acres. Obviously, if it is a particularly large parcel of land that includes a few hundred acres or more, you can include more trees. If the property is small, such as one hundred acres or fewer, then two to four trees are the limit. If you own the land, no matter what size it is, spread the fertilized trees as far apart on the property as is practical. This can also be applied to leased lands, particularly if the lease is

Photo Credit: Ted Rose

Deer will abandon almost all other food sources when acorns fall. Although they prefer white acorns, they will eagerly seek out all mast crops.

a long-term one. On state lands, however, the key is to limit the number of oak trees you fertilize to one or two. It is also crucial to keep the trees you fertilize a total secret. That means you don't even share the information about what trees you fertilized with your closest hunting partner.

If you don't have white oaks on your land, fertilize any other oak trees that produce acorns. The only reason I suggest white oaks first is that deer prefer white oak acorns over all other types. As I mentioned earlier, the strategy works to its maximum potential when used on mature oak trees that have produced acorns in the past.

On our 192-acre farm, I selected four oak trees to nourish twice a year—once in early spring and again in early fall. I always plan to fertilize them when I know there is a predicted rainfall. I chose the four trees on all points of the compass, north, south, east, and west, and kept them far enough away from bordering neighbors' properties for obvious reasons. The trees are several hundred yards apart.

It is worth repeating that you need to adjust the numbers according to size. Basically, on lands two hundred acres or more, fertilize one tree per fifty or seventy-five acres. On smaller pieces of land, such as ten to fifty acres, fertilize a single oak tree, preferably in the center of the property. Use common sense on larger tracts of land that are more than five hundred acres, keeping in mind that the more trees you fertilize, the less effective the tactic will be (though it provides good nutrition for game).

When hunting public lands, it is particularly important to select a tree that is not part of a stand of oaks. The reason is that eventually your nourished tree will be accidently discovered by others hunting the area. It won't take long for them to figure out deer are frequenting a particular tree more than surrounding acorn-bearing trees. If that happens, you can bet it will be the end of your decoy hot spot. It is less likely that others will discover a single fertilized tree. Most hunters look for many acorn-bearing oak trees when hanging their tree stand, thinking the more acorns, the more deer attracted to the area.

Remember that when you fertilize too many trees, you also provide deer, bear, and turkey with too many options to visit. Instead, create just a few locations where you know deer and other game will feed. Knowing where game will dependably visit once the acorns begin falling puts you in an optimum position to select an ambush site nearby.

Once you have selected the trees you want to fertilize, your next decision is whether to use granular, pellet, or stick fertilizers. The granular fertilizer works quickly, as it dissolves the fastest. Pellets take a little longer to dissolve, and sticks take the longest to disintegrate, but they are the choice for slow fertilization.

Fertilize your trees by first making twelve to eighteen holes with a pinch bar or similar tool. The holes must be made directly below the drip line of the tree to work quickly and effectively. The drip line is directly under the ends of the longest branches extending off of the main trunk of the tree. Beneath the soil of the drip line is where the tree's feeding root system is located. If you fertilize too closely to the trunk, the benefits of the fertilizer are reduced substantially.

Poke the holes deep enough to cover the entire length of the fertilizer spike or an equal

Photo Credit: Fiduccia Ent.

Use a pinch bar to punch holes in the ground under the drip line of a tree. The pinch bar will help make fertilizing oak trees quick and easy.

amount of granular or pellet food. I use spikes because they are less work. Before placing spikes in the holes, break each spike in half, and then place both halves in each hole. Cover them with a few inches of soil. If you fertilize on public ground, cover your holes with some dead leaves or other forest debris from the area to help disguise the freshly dug dirt. As I mentioned before, fertilize the trees once in the spring and again in the fall, preferably when you know there is rain predicted within a few days.

This tactic will produce acorns that are larger, sweeter, and more abundant. You'll also discover after a couple seasons, as I did, that the fertilized oaks will begin to drop their mast later than the unfertilized trees in the area. My conclusion is that this is because the fertilizer makes the tree healthier and the acorn stems stronger. The deer, bear, and turkey will key in on this factor and record it to memory. The result is when most of the unfertilized acorns have fallen and been consumed by deer, bear, and turkey, your tree will drop its mast during the late bow season and early firearm season.

The first year you employ this strategy, the tree will respond by providing a better acorn crop. There will be a noticeable increase in the

A key benefit to fertilizing oak trees is that the trunk, branches, and stems all become healthier with each year of fertilization. Because the stems are stronger by year three, the acorns will hang from the branches longer.

tree's production in the second year. Deer and other game will quickly zone in on this. The acorns will look bigger and be noticeably more abundant. By the third year, your fertilized trees will produce bountiful crops of acorns.

Here's how to prove how effective this tactic really is. At the end of the third year, select a fallen acorn from one of your fertilized trees. After biting the fruit of the acorn, you will notice it has a bitter taste to you—almost all acorns do. Wait until the bitter flavor subsides and then bite into an acorn that has fallen from a tree that wasn't fertilized. You will instantly notice the second acorn has a more pronounced bitter flavor. Its bitterness will seem excessive compared to your fertilized acorn. Deer and other game interpret the less bitter acorn as being sweeter than the acorns they eat from other trees. Again, they will record the experience to memory and visit that tree over and over to enjoy its better tasting fruit.

If you share the location of the fertilized trees with hunting buddies, you will discover without a doubt that they will hunt the area when you're not there. If that is okay with you, then by all means let them know where it is. If you want to take a buck year in and year out at these secret locations, then keep tightlipped about it with everyone except the hunters in your immediate family.

This fertilizing strategy also works on other natural vegetation, including wild grape vines, berry-producing bushes, and a wide variety of shrubs and plants that deer consume throughout summer and fall. Find out what the deer choose as preferred plants on your land, and then ask your local farm agency what the best Nitrogen-Phosphorus-Potassium (NPK) mix of fertilizer is and apply it to the plant. It will increase the production, nutrition, and volume of the plant and its fruit, bringing the deer to it on a reliable basis.

It is probably obvious by now, but still worth saying—this tactic is equally effective for wild fruit trees. By fertilizing a few different fruit trees, such as apple, pear, and peach, you will increase the amount, size, and flavor of the crop the tree makes. The key is to use the correct mix of NPK. Your local farm agency or feed store owner can provide you with the recommendations for your area.

I have more than one hundred wild apple trees on my farm and several pear and peach trees. I fertilize one of each type. Needless to say, the deer know exactly which trees bear larger, more abundant, and better

Almost any tree fertilizer will work to improve production of mast on oak trees. However, it is best to check with your local agriculture extension for what they recommend for your area. A note: some foresters claim that fertilizing oaks does nothing to improve the mast. I beg to differ.

tasting fruit. They wait beneath the trees for the fruit to drop, which, once again, is always later than the fruit trees I don't fertilize. It is such a simple plan that provides consistent success.

Pruning wild fruit trees, vines, and bushes helps, too. Pruning should only be done when a tree is dormant. Traditionally, most people prune January through March. If you prune later than March, you could send the plant into shock and it will take a year or two to recover. I prune my fruit trees soon after the first hard freeze in the fall. Usually, that occurs as early as the last week of October or the first few weeks in November. I have had excellent success with pruning that time of the year.

Give the fertilizing plan a try. I promise you will see results the first fall. In each subsequent year, your fertilized crops will get better. It is a simple strategy and reaps huge benefits. Don't hesitate another season.

For the record, and I have researched this, I was the first outdoor communicator to write a magazine article (in 1979) about fertilizing oak trees as a hunting tactic. I have never found any evidence of any other writer covering this topic prior to that time. Thankfully, that is not the case today. There have been many articles on this subject, touting how successful fertilizing oak trees is when included in a food plot program and as a hunting strategy.

All oaks produce mast in cycles with good and bad years of production. This fertilized oak tree has consistently produced an acorn crop for several years.

Photo Credit: Fiduccia Ent.

Chapter Fifteen

Thirty-Six Tips for Success

———

Tip #1: Got Guts?

Coyote problems have become more prevalent in the past decade. This is particularly true for deer hunters throughout the Northeast. To significantly reduce the numbers of resident and, especially, transient coyotes preying on deer in your area, use this practical and effective method. It is particularly effective for those who own or lease hunting property.

If you shoot a deer, don't leave the gut pile in the woods. Carry a folded heavy-duty trash bag in your day pack and, after removing the deer's entrails, put them into the bag. Tie the bag tightly to prevent leakage. Then either stuff it into the deer's chest cavity while dragging the deer out or use an ATV to remove the bag even if you have to return to get it soon after dragging the deer out.

While the scent of the blood left behind might attract a coyote or two, they will quickly move out of the area once they discover there isn't anything to eat. By simply removing the innards, you dramatically decrease the chance of attracting a pack of coyotes.

For the first couple of years that we owned our property in upstate New York, we routinely left gut piles in the woods. The practice often ended with us seeing coyotes near or at the gut-pile site. Once we started to remove the entrails from the woods, coyote sightings dropped quickly and noticeably. Since then, the number of coyote sightings on our lands has reduced by more than 95 percent.

Deer entrails left out in the field are coyote magnets. They often attract more than one coyote, leading to fights over who gets to eat first (coyote at left is in a submissive posture). The sounds and odors left by coyotes often make resident deer nervous.

We not only remove deer innards, but we also remove all traces of turkey, small game, and waterfowl using smaller plastic bags, of course.

Tip #2: Where to Aim to Make a Quick Kill

I'm often asked by hunters, "What part of a deer's body is best to aim at to make a quick and humane kill?" There are two primary areas on a deer's body—the neck and the shoulder—that, when hit by a projectile, will cause the deer to fall immediately and expire quickly.

A shot made to the middle of the neck will almost always sever the neck vertebrae, instantly dropping the deer in its tracks. It is most effective when the deer is standing still at a distance between twenty and forty yards. When a deer is shot in the neck, there is also little loss of edible, quality meat. The remaining meat on the body is left unscathed, which provides the hunter with a delectable game animal.

It should be noted, however, that the neck of a deer is a small target area. It is not wise to shoot a deer in the neck when it is moving or if it is far from the hunter. Even when a deer is at close range, a neck shot should only be taken by hunters who are skilled and proficient shooters. This is not a shot for novice hunters or shooters.

The shoulder is another highly effective body part to aim at. It is my favorite place to aim, particularly when the deer is more than thirty yards away. The problem with this shot is that the bullet must hit the shoulder squarely in the middle of the scapula to be effective. A shoulder shot shatters the bone and often pierces both lungs, damaging them severely. This results in the animal being instantly immobilized and imparts a quick, humane kill. Like a neck shot, this is not a shot that should be taken by a neophyte. A hunter has to master the art of taking a shoulder shot, particularly at longer distances.

All serious hunters should make every effort to accurately shoot at a deer's shoulder. However, before making a shoulder shot, hunters must become familiar with the skeletal structure of a deer to achieve accurate bullet placement. Hunters who don't take the time to learn the anatomy of their quarry often end up aiming behind the shoulder. With this shot, the bullet ends up hitting the main vital area of the lungs and heart. While this hit will inevitably kill, it will not be as effective as an instantly disabling shoulder shot.

Unlike the neck shot, the shoulder shot damages meat.

Photo Credit: Fiduccia Ent.

Cody with a dandy mule buck he took at Bear Track Outfitters in Wyoming. Cody's well-placed shoulder shot took this buck down at 195 yards. Shoulder shots are reliable for making quick kills.

But, when you want to drop an animal in its tracks, it provides the best opportunity to do so. Plus, it is a larger target zone than the neck.

One last point about shooting the shoulder of big game is to make sure the bullet used is designed to break bone reliably. One excellent bullet choice is Winchester's Super-X Power Max Bonded load, available at affordable prices in a variety of calibers and bullet weights and specifically designed for whitetail deer. I also like Winchester's line of X-P 3 bullets, particularly the AccuBond CT or E-Tip; they are a little more expensive but well worth the money. Visit www.winchester.com for a complete line of deer cartridges.

Remington also makes a quality line of deer cartridges in its Core-Lokt, UMC, and AccuTip lines. The AccuTip is a super-accurate, polymer-tipped big game bullet that delivers devastating terminal performance. Visit www.remington.com for more information.

Tip #3: Urinating in the Woods

Many years ago, I did my own nonscientific research about this. For three seasons I intentionally urinated in the woods in places where I could see a deer's reaction if it passed my marking area. Sometimes I urinated close to my stand, other times fifty to one hundred yards from it.

Rather than getting into all the various reactions I noted over the three years, I will be brief and say sometimes it spooked the hell out of deer, especially if they came upon the scent when it was fresh. I noticed this was particularly true of mature bucks. With that said, however, there were times they tolerated the odor. However, those times occurred much less frequently than the times they showed concern or worry about the smell.

Since that time, I no longer urinate in the woods. If a male hunter cannot hold his urine, then taking along a wide-necked bottle to pee in is a good idea. If you do use a bottle to pee in, make sure to wash it out each day. Otherwise, pee at least one hundred yards from your stand with the wind taking the odor away from the area from which you expect to see deer.

Some hunters have told me they regularly pee in buck scrapes and it has helped to attract bucks. If it really worked, I'm happy for them, but I wouldn't recommend it.

Tip #4: Use a Decoy!

I could write at least one chapter, if not an entire book, on using decoys to enhance hunting success. Decoys serve several functions—they attract deer, hold their attention, relax them, and, during the rut, entice bucks into checking them out. Most importantly, a decoy will help distract a deer's attention from the hunter. For bow hunters, this is a crucial element because it helps them draw their bows undetected.

Used properly, a buck or doe full-sized decoy can be a useful tool to attract bucks, particularly during the peak chase period of the primary rut.

While I use full-sized deer decoys, I also include other nontraditional decoys in my deer hunting. These include fake apples and corn, a deer tail, plastic grass, a turkey decoy, and I even used a mounted doe head years ago. All these unorthodox decoys have worked to attract deer to my stand many times. Few hunters realize, or perhaps refuse to accept, their effectiveness.

Another type of decoy includes fertilizing oak trees and other natural vegetation. I also create mock scrapes and rubs to decoy deer. Some other tactics I use that act as decoys are a variety of deer scents, calls, and antler rattling.

All these decoying tactics work to attract deer. For those who want more detailed information about using all the decoys I mentioned in this tip, please visit my website at www.deerdoctor.com. You'll also find full chapters on the subject of decoying in my first book *Whitetail Strategies: A No-Nonsense Approach to Successful Deer Hunting,* and the subsequent, *Whitetail Strategies: The Ultimate Guide.*

Tip #5: Calling and Rattling

I use deer calls and ratting antlers as tactics to bring deer as close as possible to my stand. When I call or rattle, I try to make the vocalizations and noises as realistic as possible. By doing so, it creates a natural-seeming illusion and helps pacify a deer by putting it at ease.

Countless hunters think they have to use deer calls and rattling antlers loudly for a deer to hear them. Deer have excellent hearing. Mother Nature purposely designed their large, funnel-shaped ears to pick up sound waves from long distances. In one study about how far deer could hear, researchers determined that they could regularly hear rattling antlers from more than a quarter-mile away. They are much more capable of hearing sounds than humans are.

An experience I had with a buck I was watching in a field in Saskatchewan, Canada backs up what the researchers found. I blew a grunt call at him and, at a distance of about 250 yards away, the buck instantly picked up his head and looked my way. On another occasion, I called to a doe in a field on my farm that was exactly 176 yards from my blind. I made a soft blat—it was hardly audible to me—and the doe picked up her head and trotted toward my stand. I suspect that deer can hear calls

When using antlers or deer calls to attract deer, make the calls sound realistic by not making them too loud, and you will have more success.

Photo Credit: Fiduccia Ent.

for three hundred or more yards and rattling from a quarter of a mile or more away.

Because of this, a majority of the time it is unnecessary to make loud vocalizations or rattles. With that said, however, there are several variables regarding how far a deer can hear. On a particularly quiet day, this range is extended even farther. Factors that can affect a deer's hearing include wind direction, humidity, temperature, natural ambient sounds, and sounds of man, such as road noise from vehicles or passing ATVs. In suburban areas, this could also include children, barking dogs, or tool use by homeowners.

Photo Credit: Fiduccia Ent.

Kate took this awesome Texas buck using an adult estrus blat vocalization. She kept the volume low to sound natural and sexually alluring to the big buck.

Most often, however, making deer vocalizations and rattling too loudly will sound unnatural to deer. Louder than normal sounds will often lead to deer becoming uncomfortable and unresponsive to your efforts. Keep your calls low to increase your success.

Tip #6: Keep Deer Scents Fresh

If you think all doe estrous scent is collected fresh and taken from numbered estrus does, please send me your name and address—I have a bridge to sell you. I have manufactured my own deer scent, Love Potion No. 9:

This buck was taken using Love Potion No. 9. To keep your deer scent fresh, store it in a cool, dry area out of direct sunlight.

A Fatal Attraction of Pheromones, for more than twenty years. All sexually attractive deer scents contain preservatives.

Think about that for a moment. If I sold 200,000 bottles of Love Potion No. 9 to a store, such as Walmart, I would get back whatever bottles they didn't sell after deer season passed. Smaller outdoor stores usually don't have a return policy, so they keep the leftover bottles until the following season. Again, no big deal since the scent contains a preservative to prevent it from oxidizing. Most scents are also placed in amber or dark bottles to help slow oxidation. As long as estrus or other deer scents are kept in a cool, dry place, they will retain their freshness over long periods of time.

Tip #7: Ditch It

Mature bucks are wary creatures. As such, they are destined to become trophy-class animals simply because their fight-or-flight behavior can be heightened to extreme levels. They react instantly to anything new or worrisome within their environment. It is this neurotic behavior that often saves them from making fatal mistakes.

Most mature bucks will bed in out-of-the-ordinary places to conceal themselves. They will often choose an area in thick cover that is in plain view of predators. By doing so, they allow themselves a much better view of approaching danger, which provides them ample time to escape.

They seek this type of cover more often when foul weather is imminent. Places in which I have often found mature bucks bedded down, particularly in heavy rainstorms, include ditches, sloughs, or swales in farm fields, small blowdowns, high grassy areas, cattails, gullies, stream bottoms, and drainages.

When the ground is wet or damp, hunters can quietly stalk along without being heard. In these conditions, I often abandon my deer blind or tree stand in favor of still-hunting. I slip along using a crosswind to hide my scent. Most deer usually bed facing downwind, which affords a stealthy approach from the side and out of view of the buck. Rather than using a straight line of approach, meander side to side as you move along.

The key to success when still-hunting is to spot the deer before it sees you. You'll be surprised how often this ends with the hunter getting a close shot at an unsuspecting buck. On occasions, the buck may wind the hunter and spook, offering a jump shot. This type of hunting calls for either hunting with a scope set at its lowest setting or iron sights. A small, light firearm you can quickly raise to your shoulder is the best choice. This tactic works equally well for bow hunters, too.

Tip #8: Track 'Em Down

I live in upstate New York, where our firearm season often begins and ends with snow. During a fresh snowfall, I sometimes head to a piece of state land of 1,200 acres that borders my cousin Leo's farm. I look for a large set of tracks, about 2½ to 3 inches long, that leaves Leo's land and heads into the state ground and I follow them. I usually do this after the primary rut has waned. That way, I'm hopefully following a buck whose sole interest isn't chasing a doe.

When the tracks start to meander back and forth, I know I have entered the buck's core area where he will find a good place to bed down. I slow my pace and look carefully at my surroundings as I cautiously

Photo Credit: Ted Rose

A splayed, deep deer print like this one, in snow or bare ground only may indicate it was left by an adult buck.

move forward. This is when I take only a few steps at a time. Each time I stop, I remain as still as possible, only moving my eyes while I try locate the buck. Before I move again, I slowly take a peek behind me, and only then do I move forward a few more paces and repeat the whole process.

Tip #9: How Your Scent Is Carried

Researchers claim that deer can detect odors better than the average dog and, depending on what research you read, they can smell fifty to one hundred times better than a human. The nose of a whitetail has up to 297 million olfactory receptors. Dogs have 220 million, while humans max out at a mere 5 million receptors. In research, test dogs are able to detect odors from one to two parts in a trillion. A dog's ability to not only detect scent but also separate one scent from another is mind-boggling. That is why a dog can detect cancer in a human and even scent the onset of death approaching.

A large portion of a deer's brain is dedicated to analyzing odors via two giant olfactory bulbs attached to the brain that decode every aroma encountered. The bulbs weigh around sixty grams, four times as much as human olfactory bulbs. In other words, a deer's sense of smell is nearly one-third better than a dog's.

It is virtually impossible to keep a deer from detecting human odor. With that said, hunters who realize the importance of reducing their scent will see and bag more deer.

The savvy hunter will also benefit by understanding how deer use the elements to smell what is going on in their environment moment by moment. Deer constantly monitor the air to analyze particles. They can quickly separate what odors are nonthreatening and which ones indicate potential danger.

There are many factors that affect how odors are carried on air currents. They include wind speed, air temperature, and moisture. For instance, on warm moist days in a still environment, a deer's ability to smell odors from molecules is enhanced.

- Falling rain and snow force scent molecules to the earth quickly, where they are diluted at ground level by the moisture.
- Mist and fog, particularly heavy fog, also block scent molecules from being dispersed long distances.
- When the humidity is high and temperatures range from 55 to 75 degrees, these are optimal conditions for a deer to use its sense of smell. Deer often become more in tune to odors in these conditions.
- Low humidity, between 10 and 20 percent, causes the deer's nasal passage to become dry, hampering its ability to detect scent molecules.
- When temperatures are high, there is more air convection movement. The currents carry scents high into the air, making them more difficult for deer to pick up.
- Deer are also handicapped in very cold temperatures. The cold air pushes scent molecules downward, where they quickly disperse.
- Air movement or currents play a big part in a deer's ability to use its olfactory senses. An ideal scenting conditions are when the humidity is between 25 and 75 percent, the temperature is between 45 and 90 degrees, and there are slight winds of 10 to 20 miles per hour. Under these conditions, a deer will be able to detect odors, including human scent, for a half mile or more.

Tip #10: Doe Clues

Always pay close attention to a doe. Her body language is often a clue as to what is going on around her. If she constantly looks around or in one direction, she may be getting anxious about approaching deer, particularly if one is a buck.

A doe that is flagging her tail continuously from side to side as she watches her behind, probably has a buck following her.

When a relaxed doe, maybe feeding or simply ambling by, suddenly comes to an abrupt stop and cups both ears in a particular direction, something has alerted her and is probably heading her way. If she begins to eat or slowly move again, she has most likely determined the noise isn't dangerous. If you see a doe behaving this way, other deer will probably appear in short order. Sometimes, the savvy hunter gets an opportunity to spot a buck long before it gets close simply by being attentive to a doe's actions.

Tip #11: Walking on Crusted Snow

Once fresh snow becomes crusted, it is difficult for hunters to approach their stands without alerting deer to their presence. Under these conditions, the deeper a hunter goes into his hunting land, the greater the odds are that deer will flee. When quiet, soft snow turns into crunchy, loud snow, it is time to change tactics.

Instead of heading to your stand before dawn, wait until mid-morning when the sun has had a chance to soften the hard surface of the snow. It will substantially lessen the noise made by each step you take, thus allowing a stealthier approach. Select the stand that is located the farthest away from bedding areas, even if it isn't positioned in a prime location. This will help reduce the noise made by your approach and lessen the possibility of deer being spooked by your noisy footfalls.

Tip #12: Walk Out of Step

Other than the sounds made by human voices, deer are most alerted by a hunter's footfalls. As hunters walk to their stands, the sounds made by their footfalls are rhythmic and repetitive. Deer are instantly aware of the noise and recognize it as potential danger. To prevent alerting deer during your approach, change the way you walk in the woods. Make each of your footsteps land more quietly on the ground by placing your heel on the ground first. Then take a couple quick but short steps forward. Stop for several seconds before you begin to walk again. Start the next step on your tiptoes and walk slowly for several steps. Repeat this until you reach your stand. This tactic will prevent you from making a cadenced walk. It will confuse deer, providing a better opportunity for you to reach your stand undetected, or at least preventing deer from fleeing the area.

Tip #13: The Eyes Have It

To see more deer when you are still-hunting, it is important to not concentrate your attention on one specific location. Without moving your head too much, use your eyes to slowly and carefully scan from left to right and back again. You'll be surprised how often this will help you spot a motionless deer or one that is skulking away from you.

Tip #14: Other Hunters

Whenever you spot a hunter moving through your location, whether you're still-hunting or in a tree stand, it is time for you to come to full alert. Watch behind the other hunter, as well as the direction he or she is moving. Many times a buck will circle behind a hunter or try to quietly sneak off. In either case, you might get an opportunity to take a shot at a buck that is unaware of your presence because it is concentrating solely on escaping the other hunter. Over the years, I have had many hunters inadvertently send bucks my way as they walked by my hunting location.

Tip #15: Check the Cover Twice

When still-hunting, a hunter's visual perspective changes dramatically every few steps. The key to successful still-hunting is to see a buck before he spots you. Even though you may have carefully scanned the cover ahead of you and didn't see a deer, that can change with a few steps. Natural vegetation that might have hidden a buck from your view moments ago might now have changed enough to reveal a deer. The savvy still-hunter knows to check the cover ahead of him more than once.

Tip #16: Don't Walk Along the Skyline

When you're walking to a tree stand or still-hunting in steep terrain, walk below the peak of the ridge. By not silhouetting yourself against the skyline, your presence and movement will be much harder for a deer to detect.

Tip #17: Snip Dense Cover

When moving through dense underbrush, use a small set of pruning shears to snip briars, branches, and brittle twigs as you move forward. These will create noise by catching on your clothing or snapping as they break against your body. Silently snipping them will allow you to move noise-free through even the thickest cover.

Tip #18: He May Not Have Seen You

If you spot a deer that is looking back at you, remain motionless but at the ready. Many times a deer may look as if it has seen you, but it really hasn't. By standing alert and very still, the deer will not sense danger and will eventually return to whatever it was doing.

Tip #19: Take Your Boots Off

When approaching a ledge to check if there is a buck bedded in the cover below, remove your boots. Take the last dozen steps before the cliff's edge in your stocking feet. Your silent approach will give you a better chance of catching a bedded buck with his guard down.

Tip #20: Belly Crawl

Deer are masters at detecting a standing or crouching hunter, even from long distances. One of the most underutilized tactics to close the distance between hunter and quarry is the belly crawl. It will make your approach almost invisible. Crawling on your belly is a top-notch tactic when trying to get close to deer in open areas.

Tip #21: Tick, Tock

When still-hunting, forget about the time. Remove your watch and put it in your daypack. Then, you won't be tempted to constantly check to see how long you have been stalking your quarry. It will keep you focused on the hunt rather than how long you've been at it.

Tip #22: Take Boot-Length Steps

The most successful still-hunters know to move at a tortoise's pace. They don't take regular strides—instead, they keep their steps short so they won't lose their balance.

Tip #23: Walk With a Crosswind

Many hunters know to keep the wind in their face as they move along. However, walking with a crosswind is even better and will help you see more deer.

OPENING DAY TIPS
Tip #24:

The most important day of firearms deer season to be on stand earlier than usual is opening day. Plan to be settled in the stand a full hour before first light. Hunters arriving later, particularly those coming in just prior to daylight, will move deer by your location. This simple tactic can pay big dividends and could help you bag your buck shortly after legal shooting light.

Tip #25:

The savvy hunter understands the safety factor of using a flashlight while walking to his stand in the dark on opening day. If the light's beam is pointed toward the ground, it will not spook deer. For added safety, wear a red blinking light on your hat or jacket. The red light will not scare deer and it will help other hunters, even those at far distances, identify you as another hunter. After opening day I use a flashlight with a blue light and I

Photo Credit: Summit Tree Stands

On opening morning, the hordes of hunters in the woods are bound to move deer from dawn to dusk. The successful hunter gets in his or her stand before first light and leaves as late as the law allows.

always use a blinking light—even when I am hunting my own land. There isn't a deer alive worth getting shot over.

Tip #26:

Wearing a fluorescent orange cap or vest, especially on opening day, isn't a wussy thing. I wear a blaze orange hat and vest every time I walk to and from my deer stand. Once I am at the stand, I remove the hat, replace it with a camouflage cap, and put the vest in my daypack. I even do this while hunting on private property. After all, better safe than sorry. (*Editor's note: New York does not require hunters to wear fluorescent orange, but in some states it is mandatory. Check regulations in your state before hunting.*)

Tip #27:

Watching a field, food plot, or other feeding area on opening day is a worthwhile endeavor, as you may catch a buck checking them for does. Feeding areas that include apple or oak trees and other natural woodland vegetation are also good areas to post. Many bucks are caught off guard on opening day as they feed on acorns, apples, and the like while heading to their bedding area.

Tip #28:

If the area you hunt is farmland, you have a better chance of getting to your stand undetected by using a vehicle or ATV. Deer living on farms become accustomed to the daily sounds of tractors, ATVs, and trucks. Drive directly to the stand and don't risk riding around to check other areas. If you do, you will almost assuredly spook deer.

Tip #29:

I like to hunt scrapes and fresh rub areas on the opening day of bow season. You can surprise a buck at a rub or scrape site, as deer are not yet pressured by the onset of hunters. You can intercept a buck as it calmly walks along to check a scrape or to freshen a rub. As the season progress, however, bucks become more reluctant to check scrapes and rubs at dawn and dusk. Later in the bow season, set up on scrapes and rubs from 10 a.m. to 2 p.m. You'll be amazed at the buck activity that takes place during these off-hours.

Photo Credit: Summit Tree Stands

You'll be amazed at how much success you'll have when hunting scrapes and rubs from 10 a.m. to 2 p.m.

Tip #30:

One of the most crucial elements to opening day success is to be totally confident in the stand location from which you choose to hunt. By getting antsy and moving to another location, you will only join the ranks of other hunters who inadvertently drive deer to other deer stalkers on opening day. This is particularly true if you are hunting in high-pressure areas.

Tip #31:

Don't cut shooting lanes and prune branches a day or two or even a week before deer season opens for bow or gun. Deer, especially mature bucks and does, quickly become aware of changes and will avoid the area until they become accustomed to the difference in their environment.

Tip #32:

Hunters on surrounding properties often make plans to put on drives on opening day. Many times the drives take place between 9 a.m. to 1 p.m. If you know your neighbors participate in this practice, plan to take advantage of it. If the stand you choose to hunt from in the morning doesn't coincide with areas near the drives, change your stand to an area that gives you an opportunity. By being flexible, you will increase your success.

Tip #33:

If you receive permission from a farmer to hunt his or her land, remember to check when he or she intends to harvest certain crops. Nothing is more frustrating than hunting a stand on opening morning that overlooks a corn, soybean, or other crop field and being shocked when the farmer drives the tractor into the field shortly after dawn. A little preplanning will go a long way to prevent such an incident.

Tip #34:

If you wound a deer while hunting public ground or some other heavily hunted area on opening day, this is not the time to wait an hour or more to follow it. Leave the stand immediately after the deer moves out of your sight and take up its blood trail. You don't have much to lose by doing this. The odds are that the deer you wounded will end up passing another hunter anyway. The sooner you track it, the quicker the deer will bleed out. Or, you will get an opportunity to take a second shot before it ends up in front of someone else. On large private lands, this practice is not as immediate as on public hunting ground.

Tip #35:

It is always wise to have at least two or three stand options for opening morning. If you awake to foul weather conditions, such as heavy rain, bone-chilling temperatures, howling winds, or even an ice storm that makes using a climber or even sitting in a tree stand dangerous, you won't last long in an open stand. Having an option that includes a closed blind or tent circumvents this problem. You may also need to change your stand due to unsuspected hunting pressure or a last minute change in the wind's direction. Having other stand options will definitely increase your opening day success ratio.

Tip #36:

Remember the old adage dress to kill? This is a wise proverb for deer hunters. The longer you can remain on stand, the better your chances of taking game. By dressing for whatever the weather might be or change to, you will boost your chances of bagging a buck because you will be able to remain on stand.

AFTER THE HUNT

———

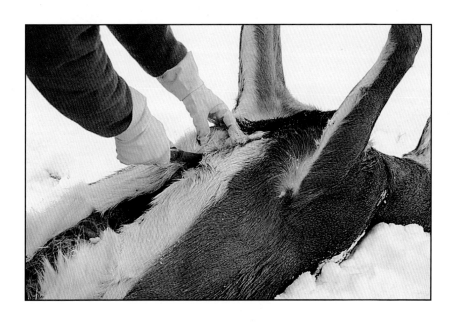

Chapter Sixteen

Field Dressing

————

To ensure the most flavorful game meat, it is essential for a hunter to know how to quickly and effectively field dress, thereby assuring the animal will go from the field to the table in prime eating condition. The tips and instructions in this DIY section will help you eliminate that gamy taste from the animals you shoot. There should be no doubt that knowing how to properly field dress deer and other big game animals is the most important element for quality, terrific tasting meat.

One of the most crucial steps in the field dressing process is removing the anal tract and bladder. The key task at hand is to do this without puncturing either and causing unwanted spillage within the body cavity. Leaky fluids and materials from a deer's anal tract and bladder can ruin the taste of game or, worse yet, contaminate the meat.

Cutting around and removing the anal canal on deer is, however, an unavoidable and necessary step when field dressing. With Hunter's Specialties Butt Out big game field dressing tool, hunters can quickly and easily remove the alimentary canal on deer and deer-sized game.

STEP #1

Photo Credit: CPi.

Turn the deer over on its back on as flat a surface as possible. The head, however, should be slightly higher than the rest of the body so gravity will help slide the entrails out of the body cavity more easily when they are cut free.

STEP #2

If you use a Butt Out tool, the next step is to remove the anal tract. Insert the Butt Out into the deer's anal cavity and push it into the anal tract as far as you can—all the way to the end of the tool's handle. Next, slowly turn the tool until you feel it catch. This is typically not more than eight to ten turns. Then, slowly and steadily pull the tool out. It will remove about a ten-inch section of the deer's intestine to the outside of the body cavity. Almost the entire section will be filled with deer pellets, or dung. Where the pellets end, the anal tract will appear white. This is where you can cut off the intestine and lay it aside. Now the rest of the field dressing process will be accomplished more quickly and effectively.

STEP #3

Make a shallow two-to three-inch long cut on the side of the penis or the udder. Separate the external reproductive organs of a buck from the abdominal wall. If it is a doe, remove the udder. Milk sours quickly in the udder, which causes a foul smell and can give the meat a disagreeable

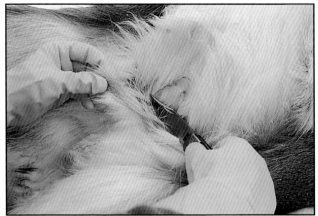

Photo Credit: CPi.

taste. However, check local game laws before removing the genitals. Some states require that they remain attached to the carcass. If they can be removed, however, carefully cut them free of the skin and let them hang over the back of the anus. It is important not to cut them free of the viscera at this point.

STEP #4

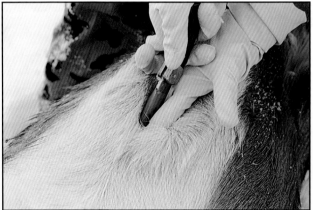

Photo Credit: CPi.

Straddle the deer while you are facing its head. Pinch a piece of skin in the belly section and pull it up and away from the body. Insert the tip of the knife blade and make a shallow slit into the muscle and skin, which will prevent accidently puncturing the intestines. Make the cut just long enough to insert your first two fingers.

Form a V with your with your fingers and carefully continue to slit a thin layer of abdomen muscle and skin all the way up to the sternum of the rib cage. As you make this cut, the intestines and stomach will begin to push out from the body cavity but will not fall entirely free as they are still attached by connective tissue.

STEP #5

Photo Credit: CPi.

If you are not going to mount the deer's head, the next step is to make a cut through the rib cage. While straddling the deer, slightly bend your knees and face the head and, with the blade facing up, position the knife under the breastbone. Hold the knife with both hands for leverage and cut through the cartilage in the center of the breastbone. Continue cutting up through the neck. If you intend to mount the deer's head, stop at the brisket line and skip step 6.

STEP #6

Photo Credit: CPi.

Once the neck is open, free the windpipe and esophagus by cutting the connective tissue. Grasp them firmly and pull them down toward the body cavity while continuing to cut any connective tissues as you proceed.

STEP #7

If you are going to mount the deer's head, you will have to tie off the gullet, or throat, push it forward as far as possible, and cut it free from the windpipe. Also cut around the diaphragm and remove the connective tissue of the lungs and other organs. Then carefully reach up as far as you can into the throat area—as high as your arms will take you—to sever the esophagus and trachea. Be aware of your knife blade, as most accidents occur during this step when you can't see what you're cutting.

STEP #8

Photo Credit: CPi.

If you haven't already removed the rectum with a Butt Out tool, it is at this point you will have to address that job. Some prefer to remove the rectal tract and urethra by slicing between the hams or splitting the pelvic bone. Others remove the anal tract first by placing the point of a knife to the side of the rectum and make a cut that completely encircles the rectum. Position the tip of the blade into the pelvic area and cut around the entire anus. Free the rectum and urethra by loosening the connective tissue with the tip of the knife blade. To prevent any leakage from the anal tract or the urethra, tie it off with a stout piece of string. The next step is the trickiest part of the whole process. Push the tied-off rectum and urethra under the pelvic bone and into the body cavity. If you choose to, you may opt to split the pelvic bone, which makes removing the rectum and urethra easier, but it requires using a stout knife or small axe.

STEP #9

Photo Credit: CPi.

Grasp one side of the rib cage firmly with one hand and pull it open. Cut all remaining connective tissue along the diaphragm free from the rib opening down to the backbone. Stay as close to the rib cage as possible. Be careful not to puncture the stomach, intestines, or any other internal matter. Now repeat the same thing on the other side so both cuts meet over the backbone.

Reach up and grasp the windpipe and esophagus and pull them down and away from the body cavity. Detach the heart and liver. Now all innards should be free of any connective tissue, allowing you to scoop out the remaining entrails onto the ground along with as much blood as possible from the body cavity.

STEP #10

Once all the entrails have been eviscerated from the deer's body cavity, it is important to cool the cavity as quickly as possible. Prop the body cavity open with a stick or the handy tool made by Outdoor Edge called the Rib-Cage Spreader.

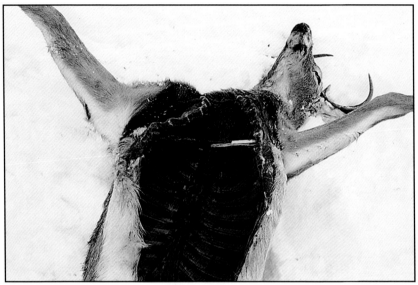

Photo Credit: CPi.

If at all possible, wash out the body cavity with water or snow. Remove as much dirt, debris, excess blood, etc., as possible. Hanging the deer right away will also greatly enhance the cooling process. If hanging isn't possible, turn it over with the open cavity down and let any remaining blood or fluids drain away.

DID YOU KNOW?

- There is no real benefit in cutting a deer's throat to bleed it out.
- A small knife with a three-to five-inch blade is the ideal size to use when field dressing a deer.
- Cooling the deer as soon as possible will help retain the overall flavor of the meat.
- To age deer meat properly, it must be placed in a refrigerated cooler with the temperature consistently ranging between thirty-eight and forty-two degrees. Hanging it in a tree to age for days or even longer only allows the meat to decay and makes it less flavorful and tender.

Chapter Seventeen

Skinning: Six Quick and Easy Steps

Once you have properly field dressed your deer, the next step for better tasting venison is to quickly remove the deer's hide to cool down the meat. This DIY chapter will demonstrate how to skin a deer using nothing more than a knife, sharpening steel, small saw, gambrel, and deer hoist. These tools are all that are needed to make this task go smoothly and help provide you with better-tasting wild game.

STEP #1

Peel the deer's skin and hide over the hind leg to reveal the large tendon located at the back of the leg. Carefully slit any connective tissue between the bone and the large tendon. Next, place the end of the gambrel between the leg bone and the tendon. Now hoist the carcass to a height at which it is comfortable to work.

Photo Credit: Cpi.

STEP #2

With the knife blade turned away from the carcass, cut the hide along the inner side of each leg. Turn the knife blade back toward the meat and begin skinning the hide around the leg. Pull hard on the hide with your hands once you reach the outside of each leg.

STEP #3

With a firm grip, pull the remaining hide down the outside of each leg until the skinned part reaches the deer's tail. Separate the tail as close to the deer's rump as possible, being careful not to cut into the meat. The tail should remain inside or attached to the hide. Continue skinning the hide along the deer's back by pulling the hide downward with your hand. Slice it free as close to the meat as possible.

STEP #4

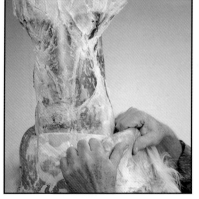

Once you reach the middle of the deer's back, grip the hide with both hands and continue to pull it down. Use the tip of your knife blade only when you need to free the hide in places where it catches, while being extra careful not to slice into or cut off pieces of meat still attached to the hide. Also, be careful not to cut holes in the hide. With your hands, continue to peel the hide down the deer's back and around the rib cage until the hide reaches the front shoulders.

STEP #5

At this point, cut along the inside of each of the front legs with your knife and peel the hide off the front legs. With a stout knife or butcher saw, remove the front legs just above the first joint, which is located slightly above the hooves.

STEP #6

Keep pulling, cutting, and peeling the hide as far down the deer's neck as possible. Once you have pulled the hide to the lowest point on the neck, cut the deer's head free of the body with a saw. Once the hide is removed from the deer, spread it out on a clean, flat surface with the hair facing down. Scrape off any remaining pieces of fat, tallow, meat, or blood. The hide is ready to be salted if it is going to be preserved.

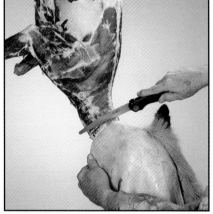

DID YOU KNOW?

• It is easier to skin a deer or other game animal while the hide is still warm.
• To make the job of skinning quicker, hang the deer by a pulley so you can raise or lower it to eye level without straining. This will also

prevent you from getting a stiff back or neck. I highly recommend the deer pulley made by Buster Greenway of E-Z Kut Ratchet Pruner.

- To prevent the hair of the hide getting on the meat, cut through the skin from the inside out. By skinning this way, your knife will slip between the hairs instead of slicing them in half and getting them all over the meat. It will also prevent your knife from dulling as quickly.
- To avoid accidently removing useable pieces of meat, use as sharp a knife as possible while skinning. Remember to touch the knife blade up repeatedly with a steel as you trim the hide from the deer.

Chapter Eighteen

Quartering

———

In today's economy, it is practical to try and save the costs, approximately $100, of taking your deer to a professional butcher to have it processed. With a little patience and information, you can easily quarter your deer at home, though it might seem a daunting task at first. To make this job a convenient and fun project simply requires understanding basic deer anatomy and the portions of the deer with which you will be working.

Many folks believe that quartering a deer at home involves a lot of expensive butchering tools, time, and working area. In reality, all the tools necessary to get the job done quickly and easily are a quality knife, sharpening steel, and small saw. With a little know-how, anyone can remove a deer's forequarters and hindquarters, tenderloins, ribs, and backstrap at home by following these simple step-by-step directions.

STEP #1

Begin by pushing the front leg away from the deer's skinned carcass. Place your sharp hunting or butchering knife with the sharp edge down and cut the connective meat and tissue free from between the leg and the rib cage. Continue cutting through this section until you reach the shoulder. The process is easier if someone holds the carcass securely while you cut it. If you don't have help available, another option is to tie the opposite leg to an anchor point to steady the carcass.

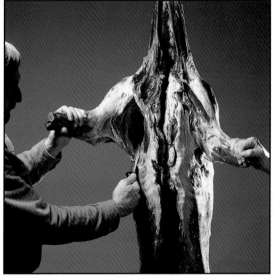

Photo Credit: CPi

STEP #2

Where the front leg reaches the shoulder, remove it by cutting between the shoulder blade and the back. Repeat steps one and two on the opposite front leg. Once both legs are off, remove the layer of brisket meat that is located over the deer's ribs.

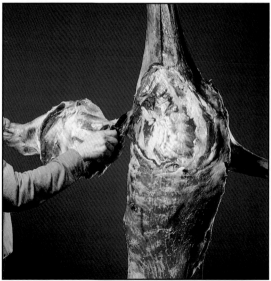

Photo Credit: CPi

STEP #3

Now, cut the meat at the base of the neck, which will enable you to cut the backstrap free. With your knife blade facing down and the tip of blade pressed closely to the bone, guide the knife slowly down toward the rump of the deer. Be careful not to cut into the backstrap to avoid leaving any of its prime meat behind. Once you have reached the rump area, you can cut off the backstrap.

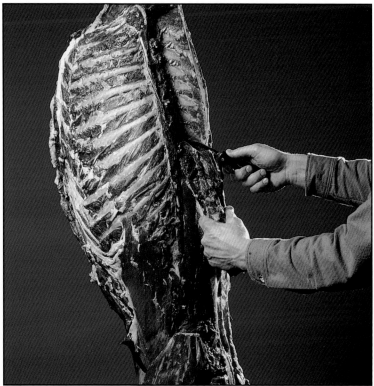

Photo Credit: CPi

STEP #4

Next, cut one of the hind legs off to expose the ball-and-socket joint. Separate the joint by forcefully pushing the leg backward until it pops apart. Now cut through the joint. Carefully work your knife around the tailbone and pelvis area until the leg is totally free. Repeat this step on the opposite rear leg.

Photo Credit: CPi

STEP #5

After trimming away the flank meat below the last rib, you can cut the tenderloins from the inside of the deer's body cavity.

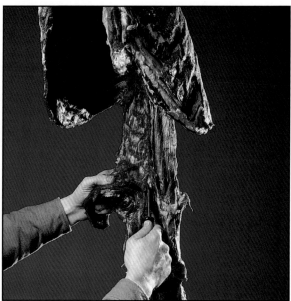

Photo Credit: CPi

STEP #6

To remove the ribs, simply saw along the backbone of the deer. Cut around the base of the neck and then snap off the backbone. Set the neck and head aside. Carefully bone out as much useable meat from the neck as possible—it makes terrific chopped meat or can be used for sausage.

Photo Credit: CPi

STEP #7

To enhance the taste and tenderness of the ribs, carefully trim away all the gristle and fat at the bottom of the rib sections. It you want to make the ribs into short ribs, saw them in half. If you prefer not to eat the ribs, don't disregard them. Instead, bone the meat and grind it into sausage or burger meat.

Photo Credit: CPi

DID YOU KNOW?

- Flank meat is often used to make jerky. The flank cut can also be ground for burger meat.
- By removing the tenderloins before properly aging your deer, you will prevent them from turning black and dehydrating. Removing them before aging will dramatically increase their flavor and tenderness.
- The primary cause of bad-tasting game meat is from not removing as much of the silver skin, or the shiny, slimy-looking connective tissue, and tallow from the meat as possible. This is how venison becomes gamy. Removing every piece of tallow is a time-consuming process. It is well worth the effort, however, to get the best tasting wild game. Fat from domestic animals imparts a tasty flavor to the meat. That is definitely not the case with wild animals, particularly antlered game.

Chapter Nineteen

Shed Hunting Tips

Shed hunting dates back to our earliest ancestors. Cavemen collected antler bone not only to make tools, but also to carve the antlers into jewelry, charms, and trinkets. Native Americans used shed deer antlers to scrape hides, as cooking tools, handles for axes and knives, and decoys. They held the antlers to their heads, as they crouched toward their quarry, such as deer, elk, moose, and caribou, to get as close to them as possible. Today, deer antlers still hold a special allure as collectibles for a diverse range of people for an equally wide variety of reasons.

Many sportsmen and nonhunters have a fascination with the antlers of all species of deer, particularly whitetails. Understandably, most hunters want to collect them while they are still attached to the buck's head, but finding a buck's dropped antler can be equally exciting. For deer hunters, shed antlers can serve as a valued trophy and an important piece of evidence. Finding them provides both confirmation and clues regarding which bucks survived the hunting season and winter.

I found my first shed antler more than forty years ago while I was repairing an old wooden tree stand that overlooked a draw of tall, thick mountain laurel. After making the repair, I took a

Photo Credit: Ted Rose

Sheds provide comforting evidence that a buck has survived both the hunting season and the winter.

shortcut back and while walking through the laurel, I accidentally dislodged an antler that was hung on a branch. It was a small antler with four points. I was overwhelmed with excitement. I held the single antler in my hands and began to imagine what the buck might have looked like with both antlers on its head. As I studied the antler, it began to look familiar to me. I never really did know if it was or not. That is the type of exhilaration, however, shed hunting can impart. From that point on, shed hunting became an enjoyable pastime for me. Every time I locate a shed deer antler it evokes anticipation, enthusiasm, and high hopes for the next deer season.

What also makes shed hunting fun is that it can be enjoyed alone or with family and friends. One of my fondest outdoor memories of our son Cody is connected to finding a shed deer antler. He was about five years old, sitting on my lap as I was taking him for a slow ride on my lawn tractor around a food plot. Suddenly, Cody yelled "Stop, Dad! I see a buck!"

Since it was early May, I giggled as I replied, "Where is he Cody?"

"Turn around and I'll show you," he said. As we drove back Cody shouted, "Look, Daddy, he's right there." I noticed he was pointing his little finger to the ground and as I followed its direction I saw a huge dropped antler. Of all the shed antlers I have collected, that one holds a special place in my heart and mind. It also told me that one of the mature bucks I hunted hard for that year survived. Having Cody find it gave me new hope and inspiration for the upcoming deer season.

When to Begin Shed Hunting

The unfortunate fact about finding shed antlers is that it isn't all that easy. There are ways however, to help increase your odds of locating dropped antlers, other than having your five-year-old spot them for you.

If you live in northern climates, don't begin to search for sheds before the snow melts. According to most successful shed hunters, the best time to start searching is late April. Over the years I have found most of my shed antlers in May while I'm planting food plots or hunting turkey. Planning a shed hunting excursion in late April and May will help you locate a majority of antlers that haven't yet been chewed on by mice or other rodents.

Photo Credit: Ted Rose

Once the snow begins to melt, finding sheds becomes much easier.

Where to Find Shed Antlers

First, locate the food sources deer were feeding on the most during January through March. Once you know where they were eating, you will be able to quickly determine where their bedding areas were. You can be assured that during that time of year, deer are primarily concerned with food and bedding. Therefore, they instinctively locate their beds as close to winter food sources as possible.

If you become a bone-head (a term I use to describe people who have become addicted to shed hunting), you may want to get more serious about ways to increase your success. By using trail cameras, you can determine when bucks begin to drop their antlers and, in some cases, actually see where a buck dropped an antler—rarely does a buck drop both antlers in the same place. Trail cameras also help identify the deer trails the bucks are using, which helps narrow your search.

Dropped antlers don't always end up falling to the ground, either. Many times a buck will pull an antler free by hooking it into a sapling and pulling away. Bucks also use thick tangles of briar and mountain laurel to pull off loose antlers. I have found sheds near cedar fence posts—I suspect bucks are attracted to the cedar and use it to knock off antlers. Barbed wire fences are also hot spots to find sheds. As the buck squeezes between the strands to pass through, an antler can get caught and pulled free.

Photo Credit: Ted Rose

Judging by the number of rubs behind this buck, he probably dropped one antler in his bedding area. Buck beds are often found near areas where a concentration of rubs are made.

Another good location to search for sheds is in evergreen thickets. If you hunt near a Christmas tree farm, consider it a sizzling hot spot. During the winter when snow, ice, and frigid winds send deer seeking thick cover, they will often head to places such as Christmas tree farms. There they spend much of their time in the shelter of the closely grouped trees and their antlers either fall off naturally or the deer use branches to free them.

Deer yards are also good locations to find sheds. Finding a deer yard can be harder than it used to be, but in some of the more northern zones, deer still yard up during the deep snow accumulations of late winter. Deer yards are one of the few places a shed hunter may end up finding a matched pair of antlers. Entering a yard while the deer are using it can cause extra stress on them at a time when they need every ounce of energy they have. For this reason, I don't recommend searching for dropped antlers in deer yards before the snow has melted and the deer have left.

I have had success locating whitetail shed antlers, as well as larger antlers like moose, elk, and mule deer, in places where they have to jump over fences or natural obstructions as they travel from one place to another. As they jump, the impact of landing on the other side can cause an antler to be jarred loose. This is also the case when a buck has to jump over a creek or stream. Find where deer are crossing a fence by locating a deer trail or deer hair caught in the fence wire. Then, search about one hundred yards along the fence on both sides, looking out from the fence about fifty yards. At creek crossings, locate the deer trail or tracks leading to the creek, searching as described above on both sides of the shoreline.

I also like to search for sheds in late-harvested cornfields. Several years ago, I was turning under a field of cut corn in early April to prepare the plot for a new crop. Halfway through tilling the field, I turned the tractor to start a new row when I caught a flash of white out of the corner of my eye. I stopped the tractor, walked over to the spot, and was delighted to find the main beam of an antler sticking up in the soil. The first few inches of each tine were buried in the soil. When I picked the antler up, it was in prime condition. I'm sure the buck dropped it sometime in the winter when he came into the plot to eat leftover corn kernels, as I leave my corn standing during the winter to provide deer with supplement.

Photo Credit: Ted Rose

I have had my best luck locating sheds when searching in harvested cornfields after the snow has melted.

Become the Shed

To be a consistently successful shed hunter, learn to think like a buck. Where would you be when it was time to drop your antlers? What natural vegetation or man-made objects would you use to help knock off loose antlers from your head? The successful shed hunter learns not only to look but rather think about how and where to find his bone-gold. Train your eyes to scan rather than stare. Look at the ground but also at trees, laurel, underbrush, and other thick cover at the approximate natural height of a buck's antlers. Look carefully for anything white that seems out of place. Don't always expect to find the entire antler lying above the ground.

Another point to consider is that a shed antler can be entirely or partially covered by leaves and other natural forest debris. It can be easily passed over unless the hunter moves slowly and carefully inspects any suspect object. Once you establish a strategy for locating shed antlers, you will develop into a champion antler shed hunter.

Tools of a Shed Hunter

Lastly, when looking for dropped antlers, bring along a backpack with shed hunting tools and essentials. You can be afield for hours, so pack drinking water to stay hydrated and a sandwich, as well as healthy energy snacks. Take a small digital camera and when you find a shed antler, take a close-up photo of it where it lays before picking it up. Then take a take slightly wider image of the location and, lastly, a wide shot of the area with the antler lying on the ground.

It pays to pack a bottle of window cleaner and a roll of paper towels or old clean cloths. You can use them to clean off any mud, dirt, or other debris from the antlers you find. Only rub them hard enough to remove the debris—if you scrub them too hard, you will also remove the natural color. Use a black permanent felt-tipped pen and, on the base of the burr, mark where the antler was found and the date. This is optional, but if you don't want to mark up the burr you should make a written note in a log. As your collection of shed antlers gets larger, the photos and the written information you record will help you recall all the details of each shed antler you discover. Include the exact location it was found, the date, time, and weather conditions. Also record how long it took before you found the shed and the condition the antler was in when you located it. All the written and photographic information will make the enjoyment and memories of your shed antler hunting adventures last a lifetime.

A New Twist to the Sport of Shed Hunting

Years ago, several groups discovered that dogs could be used to find shed antlers of all types. After all, dogs are biologically gifted to sniff out items that interest them. With some encouragement, they can be trained rather easily to become a shed-finding Sherlock Holmes—without the aid of a magnifying glass, of course. Their keen noses and instincts are hardwired for just this type of activity. If a dog can be trained to sniff out patients with cancer, they can certainly be trained to find shed antlers.

What makes shed hunting with dogs so exciting and interesting, particularly to me, is that dogs are tireless detectives who, unlike humans, are eager to search through even the most difficult terrains. If the scent of a shed reaches their olfactory senses, nothing will stop them from enthusiastically diving into deep, narrow draws, thick patches of ouchy thorn bushes, impenetrable brush, or wet areas.

Shed hunting with dogs has become the fastest growing canine sport in the country. Although the most popular breed used is the Labrador retriever, almost any dog can be trained to find shed antlers. In talking to leading authority Tom Dokken,

Photo Credit: Ted Rose

Although Labrador retrievers are very popular as shed hunting canines, any dog can easily be trained to find shed antlers.

of Dokken's Oak Ridge Kennels and Dokken's Shed Dog Products, about training young dogs to find sheds, Dokken was emphatic that the most important element in starting a puppy along the path to be a top-notch shed hunter is the "step of introduction." Dokken went on to say about his training, "an introduction program is designed to bring out and enhance your dog's natural retrieving instincts. In the program, your dog will be introduced to shed antlers, as well as an evaluation for further training. All dogs in this program are worked on a check cord to develop a retrieve. All phases of this program are positive and fun. We will not work on obedience in this program because we want to bring out the drive and natural desire of each individual puppy."

Even older dogs can be easily trained to find sheds. In fact, I used Dokken's *Shed Dog Training* DVD to start my eight-year-old lab, Kira, to find sheds. This past spring, Kira located her first shed antler. The DVD covers all the important elements of training your dog to be a shed hunting sleuth. Segments on the video include "Introducing Your Dog to Shed Antlers," "Shed Hunting Drills," "Training Equipment," "Sight Training and Scent Training," "Silhouette Training," "Using the Wind," "Where to Look for Sheds," and bonus footage from the North American Shed Hunting Dog Association (NASHDA) World Championship.

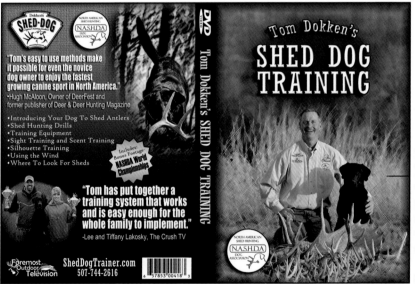

The handbook Training Your Dog to Hunt For Shed Deer Antlers *and the DVD* Shed Dog Training *are valuable tools to help train any dog. They can be found by visiting www.dokkenoakridgekennels.com or www.ShedDogTrainer.com.*

For more information to start your dog on a training program, visit www.ShedDogTrainer.com. The book *Training Your Dog to Hunt for Shed Deer Antlers* by Jerry Thoms, *Gun Dog Magazine* Field Editor and Senior Writer, provides loads of training techniques and practical teaching methods for training any dog to hunt shed antlers. It also includes advice and training drills from Tom Dokken of Shed Dog Products.

I assure anyone who likes to find shed antlers that including your dog in the hunt is enormously exciting. When Kira picked up her first shed, the enjoyment I experienced was only exceeded when Cody found his first shed twenty years ago when he was just five years old.

Shed hunting adds a new aspect to the sport of deer hunting. Whether you do it on your own, with family or friends, or with a faithful canine companion, it is a wonderful way to get outdoors and discover more about the bucks that live on the lands you hunt. Become a bone-head and join the hordes of other shed antler sleuths who have turned the sport of finding shed antlers into a whole new hunting season.

Photo Credit: NASHDA

The first place winner (the dog) and his associate (the human) of the North American Shed Hunting Dog Association (NASHDA). For more information about the NASHDA event, e-mail Tom Dokken at dokkendogsupply@aol.com.

Photo Credit: T. Rose.

ANECDOTES

———

Chapter Twenty

I Should Follow My Own Advice

Almost every deer hunter has experienced a time when they locate a big buck on their hunting grounds that they consider a trophy. The ensuing excitement of possibly harvesting the buck sometimes leads hunters into using less-than-the-best strategies, however. Big bucks have a way of obscuring a hunter's better judgment. I would like to share a story with you that took place over three deer seasons. The narrative emphasizes how a big buck can often make even a savvy deer stalker appear to be a first year novice.

The fact is that any deer hunter can become so obsessed with their quest to take a trophy-class buck that they forget to stick with their basic hunting skills and tactics, which usually ends in an unsuccessful hunt.

Though most outdoor personalities won't admit it, TV hosts, magazine writers, authors, and other celebrities are not immune to this scenario. Even we can be affected by the pressure of trying to take a mature whitetail buck and sometimes forget the advice we so ardently share in our seminars, magazine articles, and on our outdoor television programs. I reluctantly admit I have occasionally been guilty of not following the advice I diligently provide to others, but only rarely. The story I share with you, however, demonstrates that *any* deer hunter can be so captivated with their pursuit to take the trophy buck they have seen that they end up making one hunting tactic blunder after another without realizing it until it is too late. I can attest to this firsthand.

During the 2008 New York deer season, I located a trophy-class buck on our farm a day before firearm season and was captivated. For the entire season, I used strategies I would call novice at best. I hunted this buck an entire season with thoughtless abandonment of my usual tactics—mistake number one.

It started the day before the firearm season opened. While on our way to work, two hunting companions and I stopped to place a chair in a deer blind located about twenty yards from the edge of a small field called Eight-Point, near where we plant food plots. It is about one hundred fifty yards from the road that splits our 192-acre farm.

A short diversion—never buy a piece of hunting land split by a road, especially a public road that is well-traveled. This will create unwanted opportunities for peering eyes to look for deer on your land as they slowly cruise the road. It also increases the number of unsavory road hunters, who are too lazy to get out and hunt in the woods, riding around in hopes of getting a shot at a buck. Roads that split a property reduce the overall hunting area and, more importantly, create deer and vehicle collision possibilities for the deer that call your land home.

Getting back to my story, we parked the truck along the road and walked into the woods. We didn't walk fifty yards from the vehicle when we saw a good eight-point buck chasing a mature doe we nicknamed Half-Tail because half of her tail was missing. While we regularly take several does per year on our land, Half-Tail was strictly off-limits to all who hunted our property. At the time, I estimated her age to be about four years old.

The buck acted as though he was unaware of our presence, which is nearly impossible as he was no more than fifteen yards away as he ran past us. Without pausing, the buck chased Half-Tail in circles for a minute or so before a smaller eight-point buck ran from the field above us and enthusiastically entered the competition for the hot doe.

Moments after the second buck came on the scene, Half-Tail decided to hightail it (no pun intended) out of the woodlot and ran across the road to the other side of the property, with the two bucks chasing closely behind her. Mesmerized by the rut behavior going on in front of us, we weren't paying attention to what other bucks might be lurking close by—mistake number two.

As we watched the doe and the two bucks dart across the road and into the woods, we considered going back to the house to get our bows and go hunting. Obviously, the big chase phase of the rut was in full swing, as it was November 14th, one of the few major days of high breding activity during the primary rut, and yet, even knowing this, we decided it was more practical to spend at least a few hours at work. The next day was the opening of the New York firearm season and we all planned to take the entire week off. We made this decision despite the fact that I have enthusiastically preached many times, "If you are on the way to work one morning and happen to see a buck chasing a doe during the big chase phase of the rut, especially mid-morning, call in sick!" Mistake number three.

With that decision, we walked out of the woods, got back in the truck, and drove away. We went about twenty-five yards when we were shocked to see a buck with a huge set of antlers amble across the road from the side of the woods we had just been in. We quickly realized the buck was most likely standing slightly north of where the two bucks were chasing Half-Tail around as he watched the three deer and us. Once the buck reached the other side of the road, he put his head down and trotted a short distance with his nose held tightly to the ground in the direction Half-Tail had gone. He nonchalantly paused, lifted his head, and looked back directly at us as if he wanted to give us a good look at his impressive headgear. Then he turned his muscled frame and thick, swollen neck toward the hillside, threw his head back, and slipped into a small thicket of pines with his white antlers glistening in the sunlight. Our mouths hung open as we watched the buck slowly disappear.

We all agreed the buck's antlers would have scored about one hundred fifty Boone and Crockett inches. On our farm, there is little doubt that he was a shooter—not many of our bucks get to grow antlers of that size. In fact, at the time of this writing, it has taken years of strict deer management practices, including planting a wide variety of food plots and woodlot management, to achieve our goals. Our deer management includes an eight-point or better rule to give our bucks time to grow antlers that will measure one hundred thirty inches or so. I should make note here that we do allow first-time hunters and hunters who have never taken a buck to shoot any buck that has five or more points, but from that point on, they graduate to the eight-point or better rule.

With plenty of self-assurance, I told my companions I knew what direction Half-Tail would most likely be heading and that it was more than likely she and the three bucks would all end up passing at least a few of the 51-plus deer stands on that side of the land. Even though we sat there nodding our heads and agreeing with the decision, the three of us were now in the first stage of abandoning good deer hunting tactics and heading for brain-deadville. Believe this or not, we drove away feeling it was more prudent to go to work than to go hunting for what was obviously a trophy-class buck on our farm—mistake number four.

We concluded that there was a high probability one of the eight of us hunting our 432 acres of land the next morning would get an opportunity to see Mr. Big, either at first light or sometime throughout the day. We all agreed he would be caught off guard while following Half-Tail as she unwittingly lured Mr. Big back to one of her usual haunts on the west side of the property. Are you starting to see how good hunting judgment is quickly slipping away from the Deer Doctor? Mistake number five.

That night I lay awake, agonizing over where I should post on opening day and wondering to what section of the property Half-Tail would head. I finally decided to go to a stand we named Porcupine Blind because I knew it was one of Half-Tail's favorite areas. I had seen her below that blind many times and in the nearby woods, as well. I was confident she would walk by with Mr. Big in tow and I would see and shoot Mr. Big before 8 a.m. Mistake number six.

I would like to justify why I felt so self-confident I would see Mr. Big from Porcupine Blind. I was fully aware that opening day hunting pressure could cause Half-Tail to deviate from her usual routine. However, I had an encounter to take into consideration from the previous deer season. On that opening day, I was heading to Porcupine Blind about thirty minutes before dawn. As I left the field and slowly walked along the wooded trail, I saw two deer. Not thirty yards from me was Half-Tail standing in place broadside. She must have heard me approaching and stood motionless in the dark, waiting to identify what was approaching. Close behind her was a buck with a large set of antlers. Even in the predawn darkness, I could see it was an impressive ten-point buck. They both stood there as if frozen in time for what felt like several minutes, but was more likely less than twenty seconds. As they walked off, I could see the broad chest and overall mass of the buck's body. He was impressive.

I hoped that the doe would remain in the area and I would get to see him later that morning, so I continued on to the stand. As it turned out, I didn't see the buck again until three days before the regular firearm season ended. He was walking through some thick woods at the opposite end of our property that day. I never got an opportunity to take a shot at him because he moved quickly through the shooting lane in the pines near my blind. The next time I saw him was soon after the muzzleloading season ended. This time the buck was on the back border of my cousin Leo's land at the furthest distance he could be from my property. I nicknamed the buck The Traveler because of all the ground he covered.

During the thinking I did the night before opening day in 2008, I concluded that The Traveler was most likely Mr. Big. Since last season, he was a year older and his rack was a more impressive set of ten-point antlers. And that reasoning was why I was so self-confident about my plans to go to Porcupine Blind. I had a gut feeling about the spot and that feeling would be the foundation that set the rest of my season in motion.

So on opening day, all eight hunters were in blinds strategically placed throughout the lands owned by my cousins, Leo and Beth Somma, and Kate and me. We

The Darkwoods blind where I saw The Traveler three days before the regular firearm season ended.

planned to be in our blinds or tree stands long before daylight to let whatever noise we made getting to them and human odor dissipate by dawn. As we left the house, we all agreed Half-Tail, or perhaps another estrus doe, would unknowingly be our ally and lead Mr. Big past one of our stands with the lure of love in his nostrils—mistake number seven.

During the first couple hours of the morning, I was watching some does walk by Porcupine Blind, when two shots rang out from different locations. I knew one shot was from the stand where Kate was posted. Ten minutes after the rifle report, I called Kate on my Motorola Two-Way radio. "Was that you who just shot?" I asked.

"Yes, it was. I took a nice eight-point. I am going to start dragging him back to the barn."

I'm embarrassed to admit, I reluctantly offered to end my hunt and leave the stand to help. I said to her, "I'll be over to help you in about twenty minutes."

Just then, Cody's voice came over the radio, "Dad, stay where you are. I'm closer to Mom, and I'm already on my way to her stand."

"Phew," I thought to myself.

"Thanks," I replied and went back to waiting for Mr. Big to make an appearance. Not thirty minutes later, another shot rang out. This one sounded as if it came from Leo's property. That was confirmed when I heard Leo's son, Michael, on the radio saying he was heading to help Leo track his deer, which turned out to be another good eight-point buck.

Photo Credit: Fiduccia Ent.

The Porcupine Blind (in summer) where I spent almost the entire 2008 season hunting for Mr. Big.

The day passed with two bucks hanging from the game pole by the time I left the stand that evening. As I walked out of Porcupine Blind and made my way through the woods back to the vehicle, I kept thinking about where to post the next day.

That's when I decided to break one of my most hallowed deer hunting rules—don't hunt the same stand for two days straight. But I ignored the rule and promised myself I would come back to Porcupine Blind because my gut feeling was still telling me Mr. Big might follow Half-Tail through the area the next morning. I reasoned that even if he still wasn't with Half-Tail, which was likely, he could be chasing one of the other eleven does I saw that morning from Porcupine Blind. One of them could certainly come into heat, which would attract Mr. Big for sure. Without realizing it, I provided myself all the excuses I needed for breaking one of my own most sacred hunting rules—mistake number eight.

With my self-justification firmly entrenched in my mind, I inadvertently set the stage to keep making more excuses, allowing me to continue to break additional hunting guidelines in hopes of taking Mr. Big. I also decided that whether I took Mr. Big or not, I would hunt him for the entire season without regret. I would either shoot him or I wouldn't take another buck. That was the only competent choice I made that season.

Hunting for just one buck was an okay choice with me—it was a commitment I have made in the past. Sometimes, I set my sights on taking one particular buck and accept the outcome to either kill it or go without filling my tag for the season. I tell myself that I won't complain or have any qualms about the decision if I end up not taking a buck. Since I began deer hunting in 1964, this decision has caused me to end more than one season without taking a buck, even though I may have seen bucks that qualified as shooters during that time. So this wasn't something new or a rule I was changing. It was this thought process, however, that had me to return to the same stand the third morning in a row. Hunting from Porcupine Blind was now carved in stone in my mind—I would return to it one more time. At the time, I wouldn't admit to myself that this was bad judgment on my part—mistake number nine.

Now this is where the story really starts to get uncanny, at least to me. More importantly, it is where I began to admit to myself that I was becoming a thick-headed so-and-so regarding Mr. Big. Not only had I returned to Porcupine Blind for three consecutive days, I ended up hunting from the damn stand for an entire week. Yes, you read correctly, I sat in the same stand for an entire week before realizing killing this buck was seriously clouding my hunting judgment. Taking Mr. Big was clearly becoming an obsession.

Somehow, and I'm still not sure exactly how, I allowed myself to be overwhelmed by the single-minded desire to take this buck. I was captivated by a buck that lured me into using tactics I knew better than to bring into play. And worse yet, I didn't want to admit to myself that Mr. Big might be one of those rare whitetail bucks that can't be killed by a well-thought out plan or, in my case, a poor plan. Instead, a buck such as this might be the type of mature buck that meets his end accidently. He simply ends up in the wrong place at the wrong time. I was going to change my tactics, but first I would give Porcupine Blind one last chance to prove me right. I would hunt it the next morning for just one last time—mistake number ten.

So the following day, I was watching some does and a six-point buck. I did not have any luck spotting Mr. Big. I was really frustrated. I was going to make immediate and dramatic changes to my hunting tactics. I planned to start the next morning fresh and hunt from a new stand in another area of the farm. I selected a blind from which I felt I might see Mr. Big, accidently or otherwise. I felt as if a heavy rock was lifted off my chest. I could breathe again. If Mr. Big was going to meet his end, it was going to be someplace other than Porcupine Blind. I was now positive that the only way to make killing Mr. Big a real possibility would be to go to another stand.

I walked out of Porcupine Blind at 4:40 p.m. with that decision firmly in place in my mind. Slowly, I closed the door of the blind, walked through the woods and up the hill to the edge of the field above Porcupine Blind. As usual, I paused momentarily to check the field to see if any deer were in the food plots before walking across the field to the truck. As I glanced to the east, I saw Half-Tail about seventy-five yards off with her head down, contently feeding in one of my winter food plots of forage rape. I stood there and watched her, cussing her telepathically for not bringing Mr. Big past Porcupine Blind all week. By now, I was sure she had been bred, which helped me stick with my decision to abandon Porcupine Blind the next day.

I was about to sneak across the field when it happened—I saw two yearling does enter the food plot. One of the does was flagging her tail off to one side. Her body language was unmistakable, she was in peak estrus.

With her tail flicking, I attentively watched the nearby woods for any sign of Mr. Big. Not that I could shoot him if I saw him—it was well after legal shooting time. If I did see him, at least I would know he was still alive and, more importantly, where he was. Equally as important, there was a strong possibility that he might be following the trail of this hot doe and looking to breed her over the next twenty-four hours. I waited until it was too dark to see the deer any longer and then made my way to the truck.

With my heart beating in excitement, I formulated a new plan. Well, it was kind of a new plan. Yup, you guessed it—I thought, "The estrus doe might well pass by Porcupine Blind the next morning." So there you have it. Once again, the next morning I settled in at Porcupine Blind—just one more time. Come on, you have to agree that this decision was more than justified, yes? If you agree, you'd be wrong—mistake number eleven.

This story is about to get much better, or worse, depending on what side of the fence you sit. Over the remaining regular firearm season, which was more two weeks, and most of the muzzleloading season, which was another week, I returned to Porcupine Blind over and over again for a variety of perplexing, mysterious, ambiguous, and incomprehensible reasons. I justified each and every decision to continually hunt from Porcupine Blind based on a variety of reasons, including seeing lots of does each day, fresh deer signs, a few buck sightings, stubbornness, foolishness, borderline stupidity, overconfidence, and a steadfast refusal to break out of the pattern I dug myself so deeply into. (I'll bet most of you thought I would use the word rut there, didn't you?)

I was in a classic rut (there, I said it) that many hunters find themselves in after spotting a huge buck in their hunting area. You know what I'm talking about—when someone just can't leave a stand they like to hunt—mistake number twelve.

One evening at dinner, my son Cody remarked to me, "Hey, Captain Ahab, do you realize that there are only two days left of the regular firearm season? Two days left and you still haven't laid eyes on Moby Dick."

Wow, I thought. He's absolutely right. I had become Captain Ahab and Mr. Big had become my Moby Dick. That was when the light came on in my head. No, I mean it really went on. If I learned anything at all since 1964 about deer hunting it is that adult bucks do not achieve maturity by being fooled easily. They are especially not tricked by hunters who use the same stand day in and day out during the entire season.

Only a stubborn fool like I had been wouldn't have figured that out long before by now. Being a consistently successful buck hunter requires one to use a wide variety of strategies, and more importantly, flexibility in using different deer stands.

In reality, I knew that within two days of hunting season Mr. Big knew it was on. He knew enough not to be chasing does in areas he was uncomfortable using. He certainly had also sensed my hunting pressure, patterned my presence, and reacted immediately to it by avoiding the entire area around Porcupine Blind.

Over the next two days, I hunted from a different stand each day. I changed stands three times during each day as well. I went to one stand from dawn to 9 a.m. I took yet another stand during the midday hours and yet another blind during the afternoon. I was back, baby—I was back. But, it ended up being all for naught. It was too little and far too late to kill Mr. Big. He was long on to me and changing my stands wasn't going to trick him this late in the season unless I got really lucky. But anything is possible during deer season.

During my last two days of hunting the 2008 season, I did see a couple good bucks I would have taken if I hadn't committed to Mr. Big. One was a definite ten-point, a real keeper that I passed on the last day. But I didn't consider that a mistake. It was part of my pledge to take only Mr. Big and no other buck. So, I was at peace with letting the ten-point buck walk by the stand I was in, called Dot-Dot-Dash, along with the herd of does he was with.

As he passed by, I realized that even after making twelve of the most greenhorn mistakes I have ever made, this deer season was very different than any before. I went without taking a buck because I allowed a particular buck to dictate my hunting tactics and change my way of thinking, and he made me less of a hunter than I knew I could be. I simply went to pieces and lost sight of everything I know and share with others about hunting deer, especially mature bucks. So, did it teach me anything? What is the real moral of this story? Well, that's pretty simple, I learned that anyone, even a so-called professional hunter, can make mistakes—even rookie ones.

In the end, is that really so bad? Maybe, but I think not. Making all these slipups helped prove to me that even after many years of hunting, I had perhaps become a little jaded to what deer hunting is really about. It is about the heart-pounding excitement, the uncontrollable anticipation, the hopes of seeing a Mr. Big, the dreams of taking a wall-hanger, and yes, even memories of making mistakes. After all, being unsuccessful ends up being a good lesson. It all contributes to what we are and do as hunters. It also is about the most important deer hunting element—no matter when the season ends, there is always next year, especially if the buck being hunted survives through the winter. The most important lesson I learned was that I allowed a buck to outwit me or, more precisely, I outwitted myself.

Now the only thought that occupied my mind from the moment deer season closed was "Did Mr. Big survive the season?" Or did the rigors of the rut take their toll on him? That winter was shaping up to be one of the worst winters regarding snow depth that we had on the farm.

MR. BIG SURVIVED

During one of the many snowstorms in early January 2009, I was driving my ATV along the main road late at night heading to plow a neighbor's driveway. On the way, I spotted two large sets of deer tracks in the snow. The tracks crossed the road from the west side of our land, where Porcupine Blind is located, and headed east to the other side of our property. I got off the Arctic Cat to take a more careful look at the prints. Both sets of tracks were visible in the freshly fallen snow. One pair was slightly splayed more than the other and set more deeply. In one set of tracks, I saw that one hoof had a noticeable anomaly on the right side. By the size and depth of the tracks, I suspected they were made by a mature buck and, perhaps, a younger buck. The larger set of tracks left me to wonder if they belonged to Mr. Big.

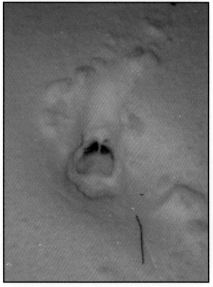

Two nights later, while riding back to my house around 11 p.m. after plowing a neighbor's driveway in yet another heavy snow storm, I was caught totally off guard by what I saw. As I approached the same area where I saw the two sets of tracks, I had

One of the tracks I found late one night during a snowstorm in 2009.

Photo Credit: Fiduccia Ent.

to quickly slow down. Standing in the road were two large deer. The snow was falling heavily and, although I was only a couple dozen yards away, I could make out that one was a buck. On this wintery, blustery, dark night with heavy snowflakes tumbling quickly to the ground, two deer stood motionless in the middle of a road. Surprisingly, they remained stationary as I slowly drove toward them.

As I got within a few yards, I stopped the Arctic Cat and turned off the engine. The headlights of the ATV shone brightly on both deer and I'm sure the lights kept them from running off. Within seconds, my question about whether Mr. Big had survived the hunting season was answered. The buck standing only yards in front of me was definitely Mr. Big.

Although I didn't pay much attention to the other buck, I noticed it had a smaller set of antlers. I stared in astonishment at one of the nicest-racked bucks I have seen on our farm. Here, on this frigid, snowy night was Mr. Big in all his glory. I would have paid a week's salary to have a camera with me.

I could see Mr. Big had lost some weight, but overall he looked healthy. His antlers were thicker than I suspected and wider, too. I could clearly see he would score in high 150s. After giving me an extended close-up look for nearly a minute, both deer walked off slowly across the road and into the woods toward the general direction of—yep, you got it—Porcupine Blind. After the deer left, I started to drive away. I thought to myself, "Those two deer are most likely heading back to the sanctuary to bed down under some of the large evergreens there."

I should mention something else about Porcupine Blind and why I became so trapped while hunting it during the prior season. The blind was purposefully placed to overlook the largest refuge on our land, a twenty-six-acre section of land with thick cover. We have not entered the area for any reason whatsoever since we established it seven years ago. Porcupine Blind is about two hundred yards from its northeast border. When I saw the bucks head in that direction, I was confident that Mr. Big spent most of his time avoiding me in the sanctuary that past season. There he would be safely hidden, as he quickly figured out I was using the northeast area day in and day out. I'll bet when he did move out of the refuge, he did so from one of the sides that wasn't being hunted, thereby avoiding detection. That's when I had an epiphany.

When creating a refuge, make the commitment to never enter it for any reason other than to recover a dead or wounded deer. Even then, only do so after 7 p.m. when the deer have left the sanctuary to feed elsewhere.

Photo Credit: Fiduccia Ent.

Maybe during this deer season, I should split my time between the northeastern Porcupine Blind and Hot-Stuff Stand, which borders the southwest side of the sanctuary. That way, I'd be able to hunt from two stands that border the sanctuary and not one. Yeah, I would be hunting from two stands—that doesn't break my rule about hunting from just one stand more than once. I promised to give that thought more consideration as I drove home. As I put the Arctic Cat in the barn, I had one fleeting thought, however, "Would hunting just two blinds and not more end up being unlucky?" Mistake number 13.

THE 2009 SEASON

Luckily, by time the 2009 deer season rolled around, I regained my senses. During the summer and early fall, I saw Mr. Big twice—once on our land and another time on state-owned hunting ground. Once again, I committed early on to hunt only him. But this year, I would allow myself an emergency plan and add in one of the good eight-point bucks I'd been seeing on the farm as my backup. I would be happy to take him if I wasn't fortunate enough to kill Mr. Big during the first two weeks of the regular firearm season. I nicknamed the eight-pointer The Backup Buck.

Three weeks into the 2009 regular firearm season (note I extended the deadline on Mr. Big by a full week), I hadn't laid eyes on Mr. Big. It seemed that up until this point, he had cleverly given me and everyone else in the neighborhood the slip. I was reasonably sure as soon as he sensed the slightest bit of hunting pressure, he quickly took up residence in our sanctuary or some other secure hideaway in his range. I'm also sure he figured out the refuge offered complete protection from hunters, understanding that he had never encountered a human presence in the sanctuary.

Regular firearm season ended without a sighting of Mr. Big by anyone hunting our farm. It was now well into the muzzleloader season and only a few days remained. Needless to say, I was hunting in earnest for The Backup Buck. On a windblown, frigid, snowy morning with three days left of the muzzleloading season, I decided to post in a blind we call Big View. The blind overlooks a twelve-acre field of various food plots, including brassica plots of turnips, rape, and kale. It also has plots of sugar beets, Kura clover, chicory, oats, and swede. I entered Big View around 10 a.m. About an hour later, I watched a dandy buck run out of the sanctuary as he chased after a doe that was feeding in a small plot of sugar beets. The buck wasn't Mr. Big or The Backup Buck. In fact, I had never seen him before on the farm. He was an eight-point buck with a wide set of antlers. It was the width of his antlers that made him a keeper in my mind, as well as the fact that deer hunting season was coming to a quick close.

As the buck chased one of the dozen does around in the sugar beet plot, I quickly put the rangefinder on him. It read a distance of 176 yards. As he stood watching a doe, he was panting hard. I placed my crosshairs on him and squeezed the trigger. The .50 caliber slug cracked and echoed across the valley as it hit the buck squarely in the shoulder. He ran about twenty yards before collapsing in his tracks in a nearby food plot of standing corn.

Only after getting to the buck did I realize how wide his antlers were. While he wasn't either of the two bucks I committed to hunt that year, I was happy to take him. It reminded me how important it is to be flexible enough to alter a deer hunting plan to end a season successfully, unlike my previous season. As I often say at my seminars, as long as the hunt itself tickles a hunter's fancy, any buck taken should be regarded as a trophy, no matter his antler size.

Photo Credit: Fiduccia Ent.

My 2009 wide-antlered buck that was shot in the sugar beet plot at 10:30 a.m.

A Big Surprise for the 2010 Deer Season

This following anecdote would not have been included in this book if I met the publisher's deadline. At the start of the 2010 deer archery season, I gathered terrific video of several bucks from our farm and on my cousin's land. Between the two parcels, there were a dozen good eight-point bucks and two good ten-points. I set my sights on one of the two ten-points as my primary target. I estimated his antlers would score about 140 inches.

I nicknamed him The Lucky Buck because of an incident on the opening afternoon of archery season—I missed him high at fifteen yards. I spotted the buck while walking to my tree stand. Three other smaller bucks were with him, and they were all in a clover field on Leo's land.

I stalked to within seventy-five yards of the deer and watched them approach as they slowly fed toward me.

When the four bucks finally got within shooting range, I came to full draw. I was so focused on the ten-point buck, I failed to notice that one of the other bucks saw me as he was walking toward me. As I released the arrow, the buck approaching me heard the string and snorted loudly. Instantly, the ten-point dropped his back, spun sharply around, and ran off as my arrow sailed harmlessly over him. Even with the miss, the prospects for a dynamic deer season looked excellent.

Over the next few weeks, I saw The Lucky Buck several times. Each time, Lady Luck was in his corner, however. Sometimes, he was either too far to take a shot at or, when he did come in close enough, his body was always covered by a tree or brush, preventing a clean hit.

On November 4th, I was rattling from the ground with my back against a stone wall that borders a neighboring farm on which we have permission to hunt. I had a 180-degree view of the woods below me. As I always do when I rattle, I was watching as many directions as possible because you can never be sure from which direction a buck will come. I looked twice to see if any deer were approaching from the field behind me—there weren't. After my third rattling session, I spotted a racked buck coming my way from a thick woodlot below me. It was The Lucky Buck.

As sometimes happens when rattling, a second buck responded to the call. As The Lucky Buck trotted toward me, I came to full draw. I gave one quick glance behind me, and that's when a deer made several alarm-distress snorts. A buck had come in directly behind me. In full stride, The Lucky Buck went into overdrive. He jumped over the stone wall going warp speed. I watched him run across the field with the other buck running hard in front of him. As I walked off, I was considering changing his name to Mr. Nine Lives.

I gave The Lucky Buck a few day's rest to calm down and decided to bow hunt my farm instead of Leo's land. On November 5th, which turned out to be the start of the big chase frenzy, I hunted from Big View, the stand where I shot the wide eight-point the previous season.

During the hunt, I saw a good nine-point buck with antlers that would score 135 or more inches after deductions. As often happens on our both our farms, neither Leo nor I had ever seen or had trail camera images of this buck prior to the day I saw him. I nicknamed him The

Kicker Buck, as he had a perfectly symmetrical eight-point rack with a four-inch drop-tine kicker point coming off the buck's right main beam.

About 2 p.m., he stepped out of a woodlot and trotted toward a doe eating in a chicory plot only fifteen yards from the window of my blind. I have often videotaped bucks and does from this blind, sometimes at even closer distances. The buck approached from about one hundred fifty yards away, giving me ample time to record him as he approached.

When he reached within fifty yards of the doe, I slowly put the camera down and with painstaking care, I picked up my bow. Somehow, the buck caught whatever slight movement I made and, within a fraction of second and in one fluid motion, he turned and disappeared back into the woods before I realized what had happened.

At that point, this buck became my primary target and The Lucky Buck dropped down to be my backup—but both bucks would take a backseat if I saw Mr. Big. Over the next couple weeks, I continued to have close encounters with both bucks. Bow season ended, however, without getting another good shooting opportunity at any of the three bucks.

Opening day of regular firearm season came and went with a couple of bucks being taken on the farm. My wife Kate had an excellent opportunity to shoot The Lucky Buck as he chased a doe along the bank of one of our fishing ponds. The buck stopped momentarily and, once Kate identified him as a keeper, she put the crosshairs on him. But before she could shoot, the doe ran off and the buck took two leaps into the swamp and was gone. This buck truly deserved his nickname.

Firearm season pressed on and, while the hunting was good, no one had a sighting of Mr. Big, The Lucky Buck, or The Kicker Buck. It was obvious they were laying low, most likely in one of our three sanctuaries. My aspirations for getting a chance at The Lucky Buck or The Kicker Buck remained high. But my hopes to get a shot at Mr. Big during the 2010 season were already begging to ebb. Even three seasons after first spotting him, Mr. Big was always someplace in the back of my mind.

If Mr. Big survived the 2009 season, he would be either 6½ or 7½ years old. I was concerned that there was a clear possibility his antlers and body size would be in decline at this point. I wasn't even sure I would recognize him if I saw him. I still held out a glimmer of hope, however, that perhaps one of us would get the opportunity to take Mr. Big this season. One thing was for sure—if one of us did get a shot at him, we would need not only hunting skills but also a tiny dose of luck. But hey, like they say, sometimes it's better to be lucky than skillful. And I was about to find out how spot-on that statement really is.

Regular firearm season ended and, as usual, we took a couple good eight-point bucks. Opening day of our nine-day muzzleloader season began on December 13th. On December 19th, with three days remaining, we had our first appreciable four- to six-inch snowfall, which was unusually late. The weather over the next few days was supposed to be cold and blustery. This was a good indication there would be increased deer movement. More importantly, according to my calculations the post-rut would kick in over the next day or two.

I determine when each phase of the rut takes place by counting twenty-eight to thirty-two days between each cycle. During the 2010 season, the peak of the primary rut took place on November 21st. By counting twenty-eight to thirty-two days forward, I figured the peak dates of the post-rut were going to fall between December 19th and 23rd. Since the muzzleloading season ended on December 21st, I only had three days left to hunt.

On December 19th, I sat in a blind called Instant Doe with a video camera. This blind lies due west of Porcupine Blind by about two hundred yards. Around 4 p.m., I saw two small bucks come out of our sanctuary chasing a doe. Minutes later, I saw a buck with a huge set of antlers leave the sanctuary to take up chase. He ran the doe hard to get her away from the younger two bucks. It didn't take me an instant to realize this buck was an absolute keeper. Unfortunately, with the snow accumulating on my scope lens, it was difficult getting a sharp image of him. The buck was moving quickly after the doe, which made it all the more difficult to get a bead on him. I opted not to shoot and I watched him run out of view. I knew one thing for sure—the following morning, which was the next to last day of the season, I would be hunting from one of our stands in this area.

I returned to a stand called Bethie-Girl the next morning and by 8:30 a.m. I only saw one small buck. They were heading toward the refuge, unfortunately, I had to leave the stand to go work. I know, I should have called in sick, but Kate knows better than that. While I was at the office, I couldn't get the buck I saw the previous day off my mind. By 10 a.m. my lack of concentration at the office was unavoidable, and with Kate away in Boston on business, I left to go hunting. While driving home, it began to snow. As I drove, I passed one of our fields and saw several does eating in a food plot of forage rape. Their bodies were already covered in snow. This field is below and to the east of another field, called Shorty Field, by about three hundred yards. It had two plots, one of turnips and the other of sugar beets.

While putting my hunting clothes on, I thought there was a good possibility that the does I saw feeding would eventually leave the forage rape plot and amble to the upper field and feed on the turnips or sugar beets. I thought to myself, "Hey, I just might see the big buck I saw the day before while he checks out some of the younger yearlings and fawns to see if they are in heat." So, I headed to my stand.

Lady Luck is a strange woman. She can treat you badly for a time and then, for whatever reason, she decides to smile on you. Today would be that day. I got to a blind called Little View around 10:45 a.m. and settled in. The snow showers had let up, and it was sunny and clear but very cold. I had to turn on the heater to get the chill out of the blind. Yes, the Deer Doctor uses a Coleman or Mr. Heater to stay warm, if need be.

By 11:30, I hadn't seen a deer when, suddenly, out of the corner of my eye I caught movement coming from the west side of the field. It was a yearling doe walking to the turnip field. What really caught my attention and made my heart race was the action of the doe's tail. As she walked along, she continually flicked her tail side to side. There was no doubt in my mind that this doe was in estrus.

I focused all my attention in the direction the doe came from with high hopes of seeing a buck following her. I carefully glassed the woodline with my binoculars to tried and locate a buck while he watched the doe from the security of cover, but I couldn't detect anything. I strained my eyes for several minutes before realizing I'd better check on the doe. I glanced back at her and saw she was now only forty yards in front of my window, pawing up turnips hidden beneath the snow. She was eating an unusually large turnip, and it seemed as if she was getting frustrated because she was having trouble chewing it in half. That's when I spotted the buck.

He entered from the south and was about twenty yards below the doe. All I could see was his head and the white throat patch on his neck. While every buck I see gets my adrenaline flowing, this buck started to make me shake. I sat totally motionless watching his every movement. He was intently staring at the doe. She was directly in front the open window of the blind and only twenty-five yards from me. Because I was in his line of sight, I wasn't sure if he saw me, too, or if he was so focused on her that he didn't notice. Either way, I decided the next move would be his. We played cat and mouse for several minutes—I made sure not to make eye contact with the buck. Every time I glanced at his rack, it elevated the game to the next level by raising my blood pressure, so I tried to stop looking at it. This buck was, without question, one of the better bucks I had ever seen on our farm.

Over the next fifteen minutes, the doe ambled one way then another, keeping her face pointed in the direction of the buck. Unfortunately, the buck just stood motionless, looking back at the doe. Because all I could see was its upper neck and face, I did not want to take a shot. Even though I was positive I could make a kill shot at fewer than fifty yards, I didn't dare take the chance. I opted to wait for a better shooting opportunity rather than risk wounding the buck.

I was hoping that the doe would change her position and cause the buck to crest the knoll. If so, I would see his body. Ten more maddening minutes passed, and then it happened. The doe started to walk off in a direction that would allow the buck to stay below the knoll, keeping him hidden from my view. I had to act quickly or chance losing him.

With the doe only a couple of dozen yards from me, I made a very soft estrus blat. The doe instantly stopped, turned toward me, and took several steps in my direction. As soon as the buck saw her move away from him, he instantly trotted into the food plot. I now saw his entire body, but the doe was in front of him. She took a few steps toward the buck and flagged her tail in his face. He stuck his nose in her rear end and took a deep whiff of the hot doe's estrus pheromones.

The doe took a few steps away from the buck. Now he was standing broadside at a distance of fewer than thirty yards. I had already lowered the power on my Swarovski 3x9x40 to four power (its lowest setting) and I quickly settled the crosshairs on the buck's shoulder. The blast from my .50 caliber muzzleloader was unusually muffled by the snow and dampness. The noise from the muzzle sounded surreal.

As the smoke began to clear, I saw the buck's legs buckle as he collapsed to the ground. I reloaded the muzzleloader, as quickly as my shaking hands and trembling body would allow me, with one eye on reloading and the other watching the buck praying he wouldn't get up.

I knew I made an excellent shot, and he was more than likely already dead. But, after reloading the rifle, I kept the muzzle pointed at the buck for several minutes before getting out of the blind and climbing down. When I got to the buck, I was amazed. His neck was swollen, his body heavy, and both ears were badly ripped and tattered.

Photo Credit: Fiduccia Ent.

This is the thirteen-point buck I eventually discovered was the buck I was hunting for two seasons—Mr. Big. Note the turnips; this small food plot was responsible for luring the doe into this field.

His antlers carried good mass from the burrs to the tips. The inside spread appeared to be at least 18 to 20 inches. I would later measure them to be 19¼ inches wide. The main beams were long and he had a typical ten-point frame. At the base of one burr was a three-inch kicker point. At the bottom of the other burr were two larger kicker points. The buck had thirteen measureable points. I stood there for several minutes staring and admiring him.

When I got him back to the barn, I hung him from the game pole. I couldn't believe how long his body was. The buck weighed in at a live weight of 193 pounds in mid-December, which means he was well over 200 pounds in early fall. (We have a farm rule to field dress all our deer in the barn so we don't leave innards in the woods, which attracts coyote.) His dressed weight was 153 pounds.

Photo Credit: Fiduccia Ent.

Mr. Big hanging on a game pole in the barn. For a short time, I thought he was an intruder.

Over the next day or so, I thought the buck was an intruder buck on our farm, such as an interloper, trespasser, or transient buck. But then, I began to think about it more. He could have certainly been the big buck I saw chasing the doe in the snow the day before. Then, that single point led me to start thinking about the possibility that the buck that hung on my game pole might not have been an intruder at all.

The more I thought about it, the more the pieces of the puzzle began to fall into place. The big buck I saw chasing the doe the day before came out of the sanctuary from the southwest corner. That would have placed him only yards from the Hot-Stuff Stand, the same stand I thought Mr. Big may have been using to evade me in 2008. I looked closely at the buck's antlers. The more I looked at them, the more they began to look similar to Mr. Big's antlers. They were as white as the antlers we saw on Mr. Big the first time we saw him and when I got the close look that night on the road.

Mr. Big had a very symmetrical ten-point rack. If you removed the three kickers from this buck, it would also have a very symmetrical ten-point set of antlers. Mr. Big's antlers had mass, were wide, and sported tines that, while they were slightly higher than this buck, were still similar in shape and size. Given all these points, I had no other option than to at least consider that the buck I shot might indeed be Mr. Big, only two years older than when I first saw him.

At that point, I was still not sure the buck was, in fact, Mr. Big. But I was becoming more convinced with each passing minute. When we all saw Mr. Big in the fall of 2008, we all agreed that he had to be at least 4½ to 5½ years old. If this buck was 6½ to 7½ years old, it would be strong evidence that he could be the very same deer. I pulled an incisor from his mouth and sent it to be analyzed to determine the buck's exact age. While thinking how important the aging of the tooth would be, I had a thought. I remembered a pertinent point about looking at his tracks the night I saw him on the road. I scrambled over to the game pole and picked up each of the buck's hooves and carefully inspected them. When I got to the last hoof up for inspection, there it was, like a bolt of lightning from the sky. I found an unmistakable chip in the hoof.

"Wow," I thought to myself, "What are the odds of this buck having so many similar characteristics to Mr. Big?" He had the same color and

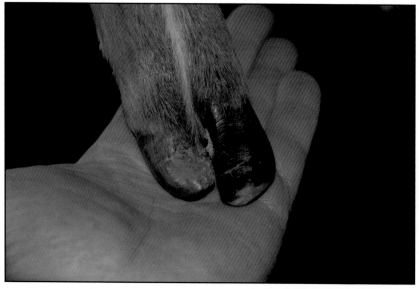

The chip on one of the toes on the rear right hoof and other similarities lead me to the undeniable truth I had finally killed Mr. Big, albeit without realizing it at first.

shape of antlers, similar width, tine count, mass, and possible age—and now both bucks had rear hooves with chips in them? At that point, it became hard for me to arrive at any other conclusion—this buck was Mr. Big.

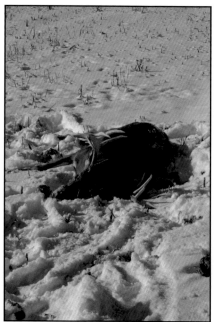

According to all the anecdotal and hard evidence, hanging from my game pole was the buck that caused my hunting tactics to go haywire in 2008. It also occupied my hunting thoughts for more than two years. In my mind's eye, I could see Mr. Big when I looked at him hanging there—I was 99.9 percent sure. The only other piece of evidence

This is the buck I shot in 2010. Soon after hanging him on the game pole, I discovered the chip in his hoof, which confirmed he could be Mr. Big.

I was waiting for to be 100 percent sure was for the forensic laboratory (Whitetail Analytical Labs, LLC) to perform a process called Cementum Annuli Tooth Analysis on the two center incisor teeth that precisely determines the age of the deer. I received that information in late January 2011. The lab confirmed the age of the buck was 7½ years old. The analysis fell exactly within the age parameters we established for Mr. Big. The results of the lab test were the last piece of evidence I needed to confirm the buck I shot in 2010 was indeed Mr. Big.

My aspirations to take Mr. Big had finally come full circle. Mr. Big made the fatal mistake that I hoped he would make during the entire deer season of 2008. In 2010, he ended up instinctively following a young estrus doe into a food plot. Through good deer tactic evaluations and a few Sherlock Holmes deductions, I posted in a blind I probably would not have hunted in that day.

A few critical elements (happenstances and assessments) fell neatly into place for me. Most importantly, I was determined to stick with my game plan to hunt from Little View Blind, a stand I most likely would not have gone to had I not seen the estrus doe in the lower field earlier that morning. In the end, my evaluations resulted in taking a terrific thirteen-point buck. A deer that, at the time, would end a two-year hunt for a single buck. As a famous news anchor of the 60s, Chet Huntley, was fond of saying about a perplexing news story, "I ask you, your thoughts?"

Cody with terrific eight-point buck taken on our land in 2011. The buck's antlers are almost indistinguishable in symmetry, mass, and tine length from Mr. Big's antlers when Mr. Big was 3½ years old. We're confident Cody's buck was sired by Mr. Big and that Mr. Big's genes will be passed on through our farm in the future.

Chapter Twenty-One

How I Got Started in an Outdoor Career

———

I included this chapter because over the last thirty years many of you have expressed that you would like to hear how I turned my hobby of hunting and fishing into a business and vocation. As I have shared with many of you, making a solo career in the outdoor industry does not entail one job or position—it's much more complicated than that.

Since the early 1980s, Kate and I have earned a living as outdoor writers, television hosts, seminar speakers, and book authors. During this time, we made our entire livelihoods as full-time, professional outdoor communicators, as defined by earning a full-time salary entirely from the outdoor industry. We also learned, however, that it was necessary to have other irons in the fire in case one particular element of our business slowed or ended.

Therefore, over the years we also developed a line of products including deer calls, scents, instructional DVDs, food plot and deer management consulting services, and Kate even developed a line of cooking sauces. We also launched a successful outdoor book publishing company that grew to including nonhunting books, though we eventually sold it. Additionally, we provided production services, such as camera work and editing, to other producers. At one point, we even owned a restaurant that included a menu for traditional and wild game. So, unless you earn a weekly salary

Making a full-time living in the outdoor industry required keeping a lot of irons in the fire to ensure a reliable paycheck. While we owned our restaurant, Kate created her wild game sauces.

by working full-time for an outdoor corporation, such as a magazine, company, agency, publishing house, organization, or group, most times it takes a lot more than just one particular occupation to earn a living from the outdoor industry—at least for us it has.

Answering the question, "How did you get started in outdoor television and writing?" will take some time to explain. Just how we went from earning a "normal" living in the restaurant and hospitality industry to making our career from hunting and fishing wasn't easy. Over the years, it had pitfalls and pinnacles, and there were many twists and turns along the way. Only through desire and steadfast determination—mixed with a dose of good business sense and a lot of good timing—were we able to make it work.

I want to be very clear here—I'm not writing this chapter to be a braggart. While some of what I have to say might seem unnecessarily long, it was written primarily to answer the hundreds, if not thousands, of folks who have asked us this question over the past thirty-one years. It was also written to emphasize some points about what it takes to make a full-time living in the outdoor industry. It includes information that demonstrates what I did to make my hobby into my career and what it takes for anyone else to do the same. Most importantly, it reveals that making a living producing a television show or being an outdoor writer requires more than just desire, experience, or persistence. It usually demands some type of personal financial sacrifice or investment, as well.

Before I relate the details, I have to set up some background information about myself. It will help you understand how I eventually ended up as an outdoor communicator. In 1962, I was in tenth grade at Fort Hamilton High School in Brooklyn, New York. I spent a lot of time in the classroom daydreaming about hunting and fishing rather than paying attention to my studies. Every parent's day ended exactly the same way, with "He's not applying himself." While I received passing grades, my errant ponderings during school about hunting and fishing stymied my academic growth and my grades.

At least once a week on the way home from school, I would exit the school bus several stops before it reached my house to stop by Fred's Store. Inevitably, I would end up spending most of the part-time salary I earned working at Louie's Butcher Shop in Fred's Store. I would buy either a Mepp's trout spinner or a Fred Arbogast bass lure. Sometimes I'd buy a gun cleaning kit, a Hot Seat, or some other hunting product, even though I wasn't legally old enough to hunt deer in New York yet.

I would end up stashing the items it away in my closet with the hope that soon I would actually be able to use what I bought.

I hardly ever missed a week of visiting Fred's store. The pleasant odors of leather boots, gun cleaning solutions, firearms, and wool clothing, and the colorful sights of the glass display cases filled to the brim with Arbogast lures enticingly displayed in their colorful boxes excited my senses. The odors and products kept me firmly entrenched in my desire to hunt and fish. For a kid in Brooklyn who didn't have a single relative, role model, or friend who was a hunter or angler to talk to or learn from, the dream of ever getting to go hunting or fishing seemed far-fetched. At that time in my life, only Fred's Sporting Goods Store linked me, if only vicariously, to the great outdoors.

By the time I was a junior in high school, I spent weekends in Central Park, an 843-acre green retreat in the heart of New York City. Not having a vehicle, I walked ten blocks to the train station, located on

8th Avenue and 62nd Street, and got the N train to the 72nd Street station in Manhattan. There, I would spend the day trying to catch a large-mouth bass as big as the ones I saw in outdoor magazines such as *Field & Stream, Outdoor Life,* and *Sports Afield.* While I never caught one nearly as large as the pictures in the magazines, the lakes of Central Park offered up lots of feisty twelve- to fourteen-inch bass to hone my skills on.

I expanded my outdoor adventures when I turned 17 by traveling to rural areas of southern New York in Orange County. To get there, I would sometimes borrow, and I use that term loosely, my dad's car and head upstate for the day. When borrowing dad's car didn't pan out, I would ride the train from Brooklyn to Manhattan, and then buy a bus ticket at the Port Authority. For the next two hours, including all the local stops, the bus headed north on Route 17. My stop was Tuxedo, New York. There I would spend the entire day fishing the more remote and pristine waters of the Ramapo River, which was full of large smallmouth bass and trout. If time allowed and I could hitch a ride, I would also fish the streams and creeks of Sterling Forest for native brookies and other trout.

During the fall of my senior year of high school, I finally got my chance to go hunting. But it required some extraordinary efforts for a boy from Brooklyn. I actually had to rent a shotgun from Fred's Sporting Goods Store. Again, most times I had to take the train to New York City and the bus to Tuxedo, New York—yes, with the gun and ammo in a gun case. No one ever gave it a second look or thought. Once I got off the bus and, if I couldn't hitch a ride, hiked a few miles to a likely looking area within the 16,000 acres of woodlands in Sterling Forest. I vividly recall my excitement as I hunted for squirrels, grouse, or any other small game that was cooperative enough to place itself in front of the shiny, silver front bead of my 12-gauge rental shotgun.

It wasn't until my first college semester at the New York Institute of Technology in Manhattan that I finally bought a car—a slick black 1957 Chevy convertible with a white top. The Chevy gave me the freedom to leave school a couple of afternoons a week and speed along Route 9N to the Bear Mountain Inn at Harriman State Park. There I would fish for bass in Hessian Lake. Having my own vehicle also gave me the opportunity to enjoy weekend fishing and hunting excursions and vacations. I traveled far and wide throughout upstate New York. The trunk of my Chevy looked like a sporting goods store. It was jam-packed, albeit neatly—I'm a Virgo—with spin and fly rods, tackle boxes, fishing vests, waders, and walking sticks. During hunting season it was packed with boots, hunting clothes, gear, ammo, and my rifle, a Marlin .336 Gold Trigger Lever-Action .30-30. My father, may he rest in peace, bought the rifle for me at a department store in Brooklyn after a prolonged argument with my overprotective mother who didn't want a gun in our house. Dad bought it at E.J. Korvette's—the Wal-Mart of its time. When the sales clerk handed me the rifle, I forgot about girls—at least on weekends.

For several years, my .30-30 and I hunted deer from the southern tip of Orange County to the most northern zones of the Adirondack Mountains. One season, I got a shot at a nice buck but cleanly missed. To make matters worse, I couldn't work the rifle's lever action quickly enough to chamber a second round before the deer got away. That night I bought a Winchester 1964 Model 70 Bolt-Action Rifle chambered in .270 and equipped with a new 3-9x40 wide-angle Redfield scope, purchased at Fred's Sporting Goods Store. That rifle and I would remain inseparable over the next twenty years, and together we accumulated

Photo Credit: Fiduccia Ent.

Jack O'Connor (1902–1978) was the shooting editor for Outdoor Life *for thirty-one years. O'Connor was well-known among hunters for his passion for the .270 Winchester. His knowledge of hunting and shooting was extensive, and he had a firm opinion on everything, especially the Winchester .270—which was the reason why I bought Ol' Betsy.*

a variety of big game. Her name, of course, was Ol' Betsy. Not a very original or imaginative name, but it worked for me then and it works for me now. I haven't hunted with her in a very long time, but each time I pick her up I begin the conversation with, "Well Ol' Betsy, how are you doing?"

In 1970, I booked my first out-of-state outdoor adventure, a trout fishing trip in Crawford, Colorado at the Bar-X-Bar Ranch. From that time on, I made detailed plans to take regular hunting and fishing trips to Colorado and other states closer to home in the Northeast. More and more I found the call of the wild irresistible. However, it was on this particular Colorado fishing trip that I realized my day job was interfering with my love of the outdoors.

In 1973 I moved to Crawford, Colorado and worked in the hospitality industry. When time allowed, Ol' Betsy and I hunted for deer, elk, and other big game. I also fished for trout in the many streams and rivers whenever I could. While my friends at work would gather to party and watch the Super Bowl each year, I would make some excuse that I couldn't be there. Instead, I would go out to jump shoot waterfowl along the banks of the Smith Fork or Gunnison Rivers with my hunting dog, a Weimaraner named Daisy. My time in Colorado helped me accumulate a lot of hunting and fishing experience.

In 1977, I relocated to New York. My new job as the general manager of a hotel and restaurant was demanding and I had limited time to hunt and fish. This was the first time I gave serious thought to how I could make a living in

This is the first bull elk I killed, circa 1976 on Saddle Mountain in Crawford, CO.

Photo Credit: Fiduccia Ent.

the outdoor industry. I thought that if I did, I would be able to live and work wherever I chose and have more time to enjoy the outdoors. The trick was, as it is for many of you, to figure out how to do that.

Not long after that revelation, I read an article in *Field & Stream* titled, "How to Make Your Living in the Outdoors." The article discussed how to become a guide out West. It touted how working as a guide would provide experience and credibility for anyone wanting to make a living in the outdoors as an outfitter. There was an accompanying ad on how to become a licensed guide in, of all places, New York. I thought that sounded like a solid first step, so I applied and received my New York State Guide's License. Over the next couple years I booked only three deer hunting clients. Not great for earning a living, but I had to start someplace. Thankfully, I didn't leave my day job to be a full-time guide at that time. So there's that to be said for working a "real" job.

By the late seventies, I had my New York State Guide's license. I offered my guiding services to potential guided clients in both New York and Colorado for waterfowl and big game hunts.

Photo Credit: Fiduccia Ent.

In 1979, I met Kate when she interviewed for a job as a desk clerk for the hotel. I hired her, and she started working during her summer vacations and holidays from college. Over the years, I shared a lot of my hunting and fishing stories with Kate. While working at the hotel during one of her winter breaks from Cornell University, I talked to her about a deer tactic called rattling, with which I was having a lot of success. I also mentioned how it was not used by many hunters in the Northeast because it was primarily confined to Texas at that time. When I finished telling her the story, Kate said, "Peter, you know so much about this subject, you should write an article about rattling and submit it to a magazine." I can vividly remember thinking, "Wow, that is a terrific idea." But I didn't know how to get started or even how to submit it to a magazine.

My First Magazine Article

Kate suggested that I start small and send a story to a local newspaper or a small magazine. At the time, *New York Sportsman* was just such a magazine. It was privately owned by the late Paul Keesler, who was the Editor in Chief. I sent him a three page, handwritten article on yellow notepad paper on how to rattle. Two months later, I received a note from Paul. I'm paraphrasing what the note said, but in essence Paul wrote, "I liked your article. I'm willing to pay you thirty dollars to publish it in the *New York Sportsman*." Little did Paul know, I would have paid him fifty dollars to print it. He continued, "If you accept my offer, I suggest you take this advice: Never again send the editor of a magazine a folded-up, handwritten article on yellow note paper. If I didn't like the article so much, I would have filed it in the garbage can. From now on, use a typewriter and double-space your proposals." I took Paul's advice seriously and from that time on did exactly as he suggested when I submitted article proposals.

After reading Paul's note, Kate suggested I go to the library and read a book called the *Writer's Market: Where and How to Sell What You Write*. She assured me it would provide all the details on how to properly send an article to a magazine editor and much more. As usual, Kate was absolutely correct. The 1,000-plus-page annual book contained more than 2,500 writing markets, including outlets to sell to magazines, newspapers, literary agents, book publishers, journals, and more.

More importantly, it provided detailed information on what each magazine's guidelines were for freelance submissions. It included information on what to send, how to send it, who to contact, what type of articles the outlets were currently looking for, when to follow up, and how much and when they will pay. I often tell people *Writer's Market* is the bible on how to get any written work published.

When I checked the book out of the library, the librarian asked me, "Have you been published before?"

"Yes, I have," I said, bursting with pride.

That thirty dollar article launched my writing career. I was fortunate, however, because if I hadn't taken Kate's advice, I would most likely never have submitted an article to the *New York Sportsman*. At least not at that time, but it ended up being the perfect time for me.

My Writing Career Was on Its Way

After my first article in *New York Sportsman,* Kate continued to encourage me to send more articles (which, I learned through the *Writer's Guide*, were correctly called queries—using and learning jargon is important) to other magazines. After researching all the outdoor magazines in *Writer's Market*, I discovered a company called Harris Publications. They owned several outdoor magazines and their listing noted that they accepted freelance manuscripts for consideration. I sent a query to the Editor, Lamar Underwood, for a DIY article on how to build a permanent tree stand.

As the *Writer's Market* suggested, my query included information about my outdoor experience, such as organizations I belonged to (National Rifle Association, Outdoor Writers Association of America, and others), that I was a licensed hunting guide in New York State, and that I had an article published in the *New York Sportsman*. The editor bought the story for $250. Over the next few years, I wrote dozens of articles for Harris Publications and other magazines that paid from $500 to $1,250 each. I was making money writing about hunting tactics and enjoying every second of it. Interestingly, I enjoyed seeing my name in print more than I enjoyed the money I was making from writing the articles.

The Masthead

One of the more impressive things a writer can achieve is to have his or her name listed in a magazine's masthead, as it helps establish credibility.

As I continued to write more articles over the next few years, I eventually proposed an idea to Stanley Harris, the Publisher of Harris Publications, and Virginia Commander, the Associate Publisher. It was a proposal to publish a new magazine entirely about whitetail deer, called *Whitetail Strategies*. They accepted the proposal and successfully launched the magazine nationally. I was very happy and grateful. The magazine listed me as the Consulting Editor on the masthead. It was a paid position and an impressive title. It was the next step in helping me gain more recognition and credibility, and it also fueled my desire to have a full-time career in the outdoor industry.

By 1982, my outdoor writing career had taken off. I wrote articles for several of the biggest outdoor publications. I was also the Consulting Editor and creator of Whitetail Hunting Strategies *for Harris Publications. The magazine articles provided my first national exposure.*

Achieving the Goal

Over the next few years, with the kind help of magazine editors like Jay Cassell, Glenn Sapir, Jack Bauer, Vin Sparano, Rick Sapp and others, I was published in every major outdoor magazine, including *Deer and Deer Hunting, Field & Stream, Outdoor Life, Sports Afield, Petersen's, Bowhunting Journal, Fur, Fish, and Game,* Various Harris Publications, and many others. Without the guidance of these professionals I would never be where I am today. I owe each of them a huge debt of gratitude. The hard work, persistence, dedication, and good timing were paying off. I could hardly believe that I was achieving my long-time ambition of making a full-time living from writing about hunting. This was a goal that I had thought was virtually impossible only a few years earlier. But the fact was, I was earning enough now to seriously consider leaving my current position for full-time writing.

Offers Came My Way

The first was from Jack Bauer, the Publisher of *Deer and Deer Hunting* at the time. Jack offered me the Editor in Chief position. I was flattered and dumbfounded. After long and careful deliberation, however, I had to turn the unbelievably gracious offer down, even though it was a chance of a lifetime. It would have required me to move to Wisconsin. At the time, I just couldn't to do that. I explained my decision to Jack and, fortunately, he understood. I still regret that decision, but, at the time, I had no choice. As it turned out, two other editors took *Deer and Deer Hunting* to high levels of success (Pat Durkin, the former Editor, and Daniel E. Schmidt, the current Editor in Chief).

A few months later, I received a phone call from Mark LaBarbera, a well-known editor, writer, and board member of a professional organization that I belonged to, the Outdoor Writers Association of America. During our conversation, Mark asked me to run for president of the organization. I was flattered and excited, but apprehensive at the same time.

"Me?" I asked.

"Why not you? You're qualified!" Mark replied.

I told Mark that I was grateful for the opportunity but I had to think it over. The position would surely demand a lot of time and attention, which I didn't mind, but I was worried about what I could bring to the table. After a lot of consideration, I graciously declined the offer.

I simply felt I didn't have enough experience as an outdoor communicator to run for president of such a prestigious organization—yet another decision I regret.

Then the NRA contacted me and asked if I would be interested in becoming an A-list speaker on their Great American Hunting Tour, which traveled throughout the country. Some of the nation's most well-respected and knowledgeable celebrities were featured speakers. To boot, it was a paid gig and provided its speakers with exposure and prestige. The tour included speakers such as Chuck Adams, Ted Nugent, Mike Hanback, Jim Zumbo, and yours truly. I could hardly believe my good fortune. I accepted and signed on immediately.

It wasn't long after that when I started getting offers from the promoters who ran large consumer sport shows. They wanted me to be a seminar speaker at their shows. One of the largest and most well-attended consumer outdoor shows was, and still is, the World Fishing and Hunting Expo in Suffern, New York, located just north of New York City. It was owned and operated by Paul Fuller. Paul had other sport shows as well, and I soon became a featured speaker at each of his shows. Three-plus decades later, I'm still a featured speaker at those sport shows, though the shows are now owned by the National Marine Manufacturers Association. The NMMA sport shows are managed by Tod Alberto. Paul Fuller and Tod Alberto are yet other professionals who I am deeply grateful and indebted to for their support and help over the last 30 years. Along with Jay Cassell, and Glenn Sapir, Paul and Tod have my complete gratitude.

Launching the *Woods N' Water* Television Series

By 1986, my standing within the outdoor industry had grown by leaps and bounds. It was at this point that Kate suggested I go to the local cable station, Group W Cable, and propose a hunting and fishing television program. She said they could air this program on their local public access channel. I thought Kate had lost her marbles and told her so.

At that time, cable stations had to entertain programming ideas like this because of a clause in their national charter. The clause said that they had to provide local producers access to local programming. We wrote a twenty-eight-page proposal for the first *Woods N' Water* television series and submitted it to Tom Halsey, the station's Program Manager. We made a list of the twenty-six programs we wanted to produce and provided a brief, detailed synopsis of each episode. Since we were on a local channel, we proposed that each show would include local hunting and fishing

Photo Credit: Fiduccia Ent.

My new found luminary provided me the opportunity to meet and befriend celebrities over the years, including John Denver, Tony Randall, Joe Engel (astronaut), Ted Nugent, Tim Russ (Star Trek), and several sports stars, such as Bo Jackson, Bobby Thigpen, Jimmy Key, Wade Boggs, and Tim Silvia.

activities. We also projected that it would be financially self-sustaining because we would sell advertising to local businesses.

The general manager and the program director of Group W Cable Company, owned by Time Warner, responded positively to the proposal and asked us to meet with them to discuss it further. During the meeting, we talked about all aspects of producing the show, including ownership, the cable company's responsibilities for equipment and manpower, advertising possibilities, and more.

At the time, a local thirty-second commercial spot on Group W Cable sold for ten dollars. In 1985, cable companies were in their infancy. I was sure I could sell our program for much more than ten dollars per spot and mentioned that to both men. Once they stopped laughing, they made me an offer and basically said, "If you can sell the show for half that amount we have a deal." Within four weeks, I had the show sold for fifty dollars per spot, three hundred fifty per week. Over the next eighteen months, *Woods N' Water* became an overwhelming success and went from a local program to being aired in three states, New York, New Jersey, and Connecticut. We were written up in outdoor magazines, several newspapers, including *The New York Times*, *Daily News*, and *Times Herald Record*, and were even highlighted on the front cover of Time Warner's *TV Guide* magazine.

Photo Credit: Fiduccia Ent.

Soon after Group W Cable launched the television show to a dozen states east of Missouri, I received an offer to do an outdoor radio show (Woods N' Water). I hosted the program for about eighteen months before the work required to produce and air the weekly radio program put a tremendous strain on our time.

Here is where anyone who wants to launch an outdoor television show really has to pay attention. Although the show was prospering, everything wasn't coming up roses. For more than a year, I hosted the program and sold the advertising, and the cable station didn't pay me one red cent. They kept emphasizing that airing our show was providing me a "huge amount of exposure and the opportunity to make a name for myself." It made good business sense to me, at least for a while.

Because the program was not a full-time endeavor, I had to make a decision if it was financially beneficial for me to continue to work without receiving financial compensation. After thinking long and hard about it, I decided it was. For the next six months, I continued to live off my savings and the funds I could generate by writing articles and speaking engagements at outdoor shows. It didn't take long before money became tight. Although I understood I had to pay my dues, I also knew that it was time for the cable company to ante up a salary if they wanted to continue to air *Woods N' Water*.

In 1985, I proposed to Kate and she miraculously accepted. At the time, she was working as an Operations Manager at Morgan Guaranty Bank in Manhattan. As a graduate of Cornell, she was making a terrific salary. We were both assured by the fact that her salary would help us withstand our financial situation until I could negotiate with the cable company for a salary.

I went to the general manager of the Time Warner Cable Company and told him I could sell *Woods N' Water* to prominent outdoor companies within the industry for $3,500 per advertiser for thirteen weeks—a

Endorsement deals were the next logical progression in my career. Here is an ad I was in for the Coleman Company, which owned Ranging Rangefinders, Western Knives, Crosman Airguns, and other outdoor companies. I began to think a higher entity was watching over me.

Peter J. Fiduccia takes to the woods with the 50/2

"I trust the 50/2 to give me the right distance so I can put my arrow right on the mark."

Bowhunting rangefinders

full quarter on television. This is not an exaggeration—he actually laughed until tears came down his face. The program director, Tom Halsey, took what I said much more seriously, however. Finally the general manager agreed if I could secure two sponsors for the amount I suggested to him, he would pay me $350 per week plus a 20 percent commission on each of the sponsorships I sold. If I didn't sell the advertising, however, I wouldn't get a salary. I politely asked him to draw up a contract. He did and I signed it.

I picked up a few sporting magazines and starting calling outdoor companies to ask if they wanted to sponsor a television program about hunting and fishing. My plan was to contact New York–based companies because they would recognize Group W Cable and might have even seen *Woods N' Water* on television. The first call I made was to Pete Rickard, Inc. Larry Rickard was the owner at the time and, after a long conversation, he agreed to buy thirteen weeks. I had to assure him in writing, however, that we would actually show deer and other big game being shot on camera. Then I contacted another New York–based company called Coleman-Ranging. They owned Coleman, Ranging Products, Coleman-Western knives, Golden Eagle Archery, and Crosman Air Guns. After promising them that the program would include actual impact shots of game being taken on camera, each of their companies bought thirteen weeks of advertising on the program.

Next on the list was Remington Arms. Getting this company to advertise was a more difficult task. I was going to make a sales presentation to a group of outdoor manufacturers who were seasoned professionals. I was scared and apprehensive. Kate suggested we develop a presentation folder that detailed everything we thought they would like to know about the program and me. Our work paid off. We walked out with signed contracts for thirteen weeks for each of Remington's companies, including Remington Firearms, Remington Ammunition, Remington Clothing, and Remington Knives.

I couldn't believe that I had sold the show out in less than one month. I felt blessed and lucky. While I like to think it was my salesmanship that sold the program, it wasn't that alone. At that time, *Woods N' Water* was a television oddity and one of the first outdoor programs, other than the *American Sportsman* on ABC and a few others, that actually showed animals being taken on television. I was fortunate to be in the right place at the right time. There wasn't much competition to worry about. In retrospect, it was an easy sell for that reason alone.

I had sold sponsorships to ten professional outdoor companies. I walked into the office of the general manager holding the signed contracts

PAGE 14   THE GROUP W CABLE COURIER   *L/O programming*   JUNE, 1985

Expand successful L/O program to six systems

WARWICK, NY - Although everyone would like to think he can spot a winner at a glance, the truth is that no one here dreamed **Peter Fiduccia's** idea for an outdoor show was the beginning of a local phenomenon.

"It didn't take long, though," says Program Manager **Tom Halsey**, "before we realized we had a real hit on our hands."

Education and entertainment are the twin principles behind the "Woods n'Waters Outdoor Show," the public access program hosted and produced by sportsman Fiduccia. Video Tech **Kevin Nelson** is director, editor, cameraman and sound engineer; and Halsey, who is also Warwick's Ad Sales Manager, completes the team.

Cablecast at 6:30 p.m. on Mondays, and repeated on Thursdays, the half-hour taped program, followed by a 30-minute live Q&A segment, is devoted to hiking, hunting, fishing and many other outdoor activities.

What began as unsponsored L / O production for public access now carries three and a half minutes of national advertising, with two and a half minutes of local avails.

"It's perfect for advertisers of related products, who really have very few outlets for promotion," says Halsey. "We provide them with a highly targeted audience."

The show has developed a huge following, as evidenced by fan mail, phone calls and turn out of some 250 people for a special showing at the local high school of a film on field-dressing a deer.

Fiduccia, a licensed New York State guide and Hunter Safety instructor, is originally from the Bay Ridge section of Brooklyn. He lived and worked in Colorado for a number of years, serving as a guide and managing a restaurant, before moving to Warwick in 1974.

In addition to hosting "Woods n' Waters," he writes for such outdoor publications as *Fur-Fish-Game, Deer Hunting Annual, Archery World,* and *New York Sportsman.*

Kevin Nelson is an Air Force veteran who graduated from Ramapo College of New Jersey with a BA in communications. He interned at Warwick and stayed on as a jack-of-all-trades in the studio.

Despite his mere 27 years of age, Kevin's experience is vast. "I picked up a camera when I was 12," he explains, "and I've never put it down."

Halsey has been Ad Sales Manager for two years and recently assumed the additional responsibilities of Program Manager. His is a radio and management background, as an Account Exec for two Beacon, NY radio stations and as Sales Manager and General Manager for Waldbaum's Supermarkets.

Tom says his biggest contribution to the show is administrative. "Kevin and Pete are the creative ones. I try to support them with coordination and with local sales efforts."

Peter is the national sales Account Exec.

The program has a surprisingly wide range. Noted outdoor photographer Leonard Lee Rue III was a guest for several segments on nature photography, for instance, and the team recently traveled to Altamar, NY for a tour of the salmon and trout fish hatchery there.

With a van to transport cameras and sound equipment, Peter and Kevin are limited only by their imaginations and the road conditions in taping on-location.

On May 6, "The Woods n'Waters Outdoor Show" went syndicated, and is now seen throughout the North Coastal District. The whole team is excited about its future, and doing whatever they can in the way of tune-in promos, suggestions for local sponsor tie-ins etc. to assure its success in other systems.

They have no reason to expect anything less than success. Viewers now report that they come home early to watch it, schedule dinner around it, and some even claim to have bought VCR's just to tape it.

Everyone's favorite story about the show's broad appeal, though, is the report from a friend who claims that she came home to find her 96 year old grandmother watching the segment on field-dressing a deer.

ON THE BANKS OF THE WAWAYANDA - Here is the team that produces the successful "Woods and Waters," photographed along the banks of the Wawayanda Creek which flows right behind the studio. Left to right, Tom Halsey, Pete Fiduccia, Steve Houk and Kevin Nelson.

Soon after selling national sponsors, Group W Cable saw the financial potential of Woods N' Water. Group W Cable ran this article nationally, promoting that the show was available for any Group W Cable system that wanted to air it.

in my hand. The total revenue generated was $35,000—a lot of money back then. The general manager was flabbergasted. I'll never forget what he said, "Well, it looks like I'll be paying you $350 a week and a lot of commissions, too." I took a deep breath and reminded him that he had agreed to do that if I sold two contracts. I sold ten. I asked him to double the salary. He refused. I sucked it up, bit my lower lip, and agreed to the offer. We went on the air in three states that fall.

During our fall run, the sponsors received countless calls and letters from viewers of our show. While the show continued to air on Group W Cable, I proposed an idea to each sponsor. If *Woods N' Water* could air nationally, would they be willing to pay $7,000 per quarter? To my amazement, each sponsor agreed without hesitation. I walked into the general manager's office yet again and asked if he would consider airing the show nationally. I told him I could double the revenue if he did. In the end, it wasn't about money—he just didn't think Time Warner would agree to air a hunting show nationally. Today, the airing of hunting shows is no longer an issue with even traditional non-hunting networks like the Discovery Channel, History Channel, A&E, and others.

In 1987, I amicably parted ways with Group W Cable and Kate and I had to make a decision about *Woods N' Water*. Should we take it on our own or should we let it come to an end? We discussed it and soon came to the realization that to launch it successfully, Kate would have to leave her job. This was a scary thought.

We would have to invest our own money to buy all the video and editing equipment. It would also require the financial sacrifice of Kate's loss of salary. I mention this to help you understand that launching a television program requires a considerable financial investment and risk. I don't recommend launching a show without first having advertising firmly and contractually in place. Today it is less expensive than when we bought all our equipment because television equipment is more affordable. But it still takes a sizeable investment that can range between $50,000 and $100,000, depending on the cost of airtime, quality of the camera, audio, lighting, editing, and other production equipment needed.

After many long discussions, Kate left Morgan Guaranty and we marched forward with our idea to go out on our own. We eventually aired *Woods N' Water* on a new national network called the Tempo Network, which was the first cable station to air all hunting and fishing programs nationwide. After the first season on Tempo, *Woods N' Water* was a big success. We garnered dozens of awards for

The first national awards for Woods N' Water *came from the Tempo Network. From that time to the present, the program and my articles have garnered dozens of awards some from The Outdoor Writers Association of America, the NYS Outdoor Writers Association, Telly, CAPE, and SIVA awards— and Kate even received the prestigious George Foster Peabody Award for her work at ABC News.*

Photo Credit: Fiduccia Ent.

producing our program. Advertisers were plentiful and competition was still low. But that would soon change.

Within a few years, there were dozens of other outdoor shows being launched, one of which was *Buckmasters*, hosted by a relatively unknown hunter, Jackie Bushman. Other hunting shows popped up like gophers out of holes. It was the genesis of producers competing for sponsors.

Within a few years, the Tempo Network failed financially. We scrambled to find other cable outlets and were fortunate to sign contracts for our show on a variety of networks. Subsequently, *Woods N' Water* aired on the Madison Square Garden Network, New England Sports Network, Cable Television of NJ, Outdoor Life Network, The Nashville Network, and The Outdoor Channel (and our rates rose to $19,750 per sponsor per quarter). With each passing year, more and more outdoor shows flooded the market. Potential sponsors were being inundated with advertising proposals. Securing sponsors became difficult for all but the longest-running shows and most prominent producers.

We continued to air our show on the Outdoor Channel for several years. As the outdoor networks were having financial success, the airtime rates were starting to double and triple. To stay financially viable, producers had to raise their advertising rates considerably. Our rates rose to $39,995 per sponsor per quarter and with ten sponsors we still couldn't afford to remain on the network. It became more and more difficult to secure advertisers, especially for new producers.

Over the past few years, we have aired on the Sportsman Channel and Wild TV in Canada. Along the way, we also produced a three-pilot nature series called *Wildlife of North America* for a relatively new network in the late 1980s, called The Discovery Channel.

So there you have it: from a locally launched cable show seen only in my hometown of Warwick, New York, to a regional show watched in three states, to a nationally televised program in just a few short years. More than thirty years later, *Woods N' Water* is still a popular outdoor program, even though there are hundreds of hunting and fishing shows now airing on more than ten networks nationwide and throughout Canada. Today, the program has access to over a million households and reaches about 1.7 million viewers per week. Woods N' Water is also seen 24/7 on YouTube, Roku, and other video on demand (VOD) outlets.

Along the way, we turned our hobby into our business by keeping many irons in the fire, as they say. I have authored fifteen books, was the

Photo Credit: Fiduccia Ent.

For twenty-nine years, Kate and I have appeared as featured guest speakers at sports shows. This is The World Fishing & Outdoor Expo in New York, our favorite show. I owe a huge thank you to Paul Fuller (the former owner and now director for the current owner, the American Sport Fishing Association) for helping launch my outdoor career.

Editor in Chief for the Outdoorsman's Edge and On the Rise Book Clubs, and have written countless magazine articles. I write two monthly outdoor newspaper columns, have produced many hunting DVDs (or VHS videos not too long ago), launched a deer scent called Love Potion No. 9, have my own line of deer calling products, continue to give seminars at sport shows, and produce not only *Woods N' Water,* but also two other outdoor programs.

In addition, Kate has authored several wild game cookbooks, won a Peabody Award in broadcasting during her time with ABC News, launched a line of wild game cooking sauces, and has written articles for outdoor magazines.

But even all of that isn't necessarily enough to make a full-time living from the outdoors. We also started a book publishing company and published more than forty-five titles written by some of the most prestigious names in the industry, including Chuck Adams, Ted Nugent, Dr. Wayne

Since the mid-1980s, we have produced dozens of how-to videos. The first were VHS and sold for $79.95 each. Today, our DVDs sell for $9.95. The drastic difference in prices gives you an idea of how intense the competition is today to make a living in the outdoor industry.

Van Zwoll, Greg Miller, Hal Blood, John Trout, Jr., Steve Bartylla, Kathy Etling, Judd Cooney, and others.

Oh, I almost forgot. During all of this, in the early 1990s, we also opened a fine-dining Italian restaurant and sold it four years later.

I mention all of this not to brag, but to demonstrate what it takes to earn a full-time living in the outdoor industry. If we had only one or even a few of the mentioned businesses, we would not generate enough income. To produce enough money to be full-time outdoor communicators, we have learned it takes a lot of irons in the fire, which doesn't come without risk. To get where we are today, we invested our life savings on

Cover art courtesy of Skyhorse Publishing

Prior to writing Whitetail Tactics, *I wrote* Shooter's Bible Guide to Planting Food Plots, *which was also published by Skyhorse Publishing. Kate and I have proudly written several books for this publisher over the years.*

several occasions. Anyone who isn't willing to pay their dues to make a living in the outdoors industry and take a financial risk to launch their career will succeed only if they work for a well-established outdoor company, magazine, their own outdoor product company, or organization.

I want to note that when we started our outdoor careers, it was a lot easier than it is today because there was much less competition. Without question, anyone trying to make a full-time living in the outdoor industry today by launching a television show or becoming a full-time outdoor writer will find it difficult. It takes a lot of hard work, money, more work, and more money. It is worth repeating that the competition to obtain advertising dollars is far more complicated than when I got started. Advertisers who sponsor outdoor television hosts tend to go with well-known and proven names within the industry. They choose hosts with reliable reputations and big followings.

There are still other factors to consider. Today, almost every manufacturer in the industry produces a television show. The same holds true for most, if not all, magazines and organizations. To make things more difficult, they often cosponsor each other's shows. This accounts for why outdoor television advertising revenue shrinks dramatically every year. Lastly, there are television producers who hold full-time jobs outside the outdoor industry. They are often satisfied to trade exposure for nothing more than free product. Some also negotiate with outfitters for free hunts and do not provide the television exposure they promised. These two factors only further deplete advertising revenue.

If you are not deterred yet, then you may have the type of I-won't-take-no-for-an-answer drive to make a living in the outdoor industry. If you do, it pays to have a thick skin. You'll have to be prepared to accept the fact that you will get a lot of rejections from editors who turn down your queries and sponsors who are not interested in buying airtime on your show.

As I said before, I was lucky—very lucky. I was in the right place at the right time. To remain viable today, I have to be creative when selling advertising to my sponsors. I can't compete successfully against magazines, outdoor companies, or outdoor organizations that use corporate funds to produce their shows. To stay competitive, Kate and I have to stay on our toes, be flexible, and resourceful.

If I wanted to launch a television show today, I would think about it long and hard before making the positive decision we made many years ago. Even getting an article in a magazine is more difficult because most magazine articles are now written by staff writers. However, I want to make it clear—what I just said should not put you off if you really want to try to make a full-time living and career as an outdoor communicator. If you have a dream and a burning desire to make your living in the outdoor industry, you will find the will and way to make it happen. Remember, always write or talk about a subject you know, and start by launching a television show locally or sending an article query to a small magazine or local newspaper instead of trying to start at the top.

This story would not be possible or complete, nor would it be worth telling without acknowledging the people who were kind enough to extend their guidance, support, professionalism, and a helping hand to me.

I would like to extend my heartfelt thanks and gratitude to Virginia Commander, Tom Halsey, Stanley Harris, the late Paul Keesler, Jerry Kenny, Ken Moran, Ted Rose, Leonard Lee Rue III, Glenn Sapir, Rick Sapp, Vin Sparano, Lamar Underwood, and particularly to Paul Fuller and Jay Cassell for providing me with their three decades of unwavering support.

If you have a burning desire to host an outdoor television program, feel free to contact me and I will provide you with free advice and leads on how to get started (peter@fiduccia.com).

Photo Credit: Ted Rose